CHAIN OF EVIL
JOURNALSTONE'S GUIDE TO
WRITING DARKNESS

By
Dr. Michael R. Collings

JournalStone
San Francisco

JOURNALSTONE
YOUR LINK TO ARTISTIC TALENT

Early versions of several essays in this volume have appeared in – The Art and craft of Poetry (Wildside Press)
Toward Other Worlds: Perspectives on John Milton, C.S. Lewis, Stephen King, Orson Scott Card and Others (Wildside Press)
To some extent, all of the essays have been revised or edited for this volume.

JournalStone books may be ordered through booksellers or by contacting:

JournalStone
www.journalstone.com
www.journal-store.com

ISBN: 978-1-940161-64-8   (sc)
ISBN: 978-1-940161-65-5   (ebook)

JournalStone rev. date: 8/29/2014

Library of Congress Control Number: 2014942906

Printed in the United States of America

Cover Design: Jeff Miller

Edited by: Aaron J. French

In memory of two great men
who helped me in the beginning:

Ted Dikty
Robert Reginald

Table of Contents

CHAIN OF EVIL

Part One: Blueprints

Chapter 1

Horror Happens

It was late one August day, some sixty years ago.

The family had been in the dusty black Buick for hours, making their way from the city toward the grandparents' distant farm for a two-week vacation.

They began the trip on new four-lane highways that extended for perhaps forty miles from the city before abruptly becoming roughly paved two-lane roads. Occasionally, a harvester or tractor-rig or combine would pull in front of them and slow traffic from 40 down to 10 or 15, until it reached the next intersection and turned off onto a dirt road toward the driver's farm.

For the first hour or so, the three children in the back seat paid attention to the father and the mother—both farm-bred and farm-grown—as they pointed out small blotches in the increasingly numerous fields, identifying them as "horses" or "sheep" or "cows" or "dogs." Soon, however, the children tired of this, especially since they could see no differences among the blotches, and started to nap.

Because this was before the days of mandatory seat belts, the father had placed some of their suitcases in the gap between the front seat (a single bench that ran from driver's door to passenger's door) and the back seat. Then he had covered suitcases and back seat with several layers of quilts to make them more comfortable and tossed in three well-worn stuffed animals to serve as pillows.

While the children slept curled around each other in the back, the Buick continued on, then, at an otherwise undistinguished crossroads, turned onto a graveled road and started into the hills.

Half an hour or so later, the graveled road turned sharply at a small, bedraggled grocery store. That, and the nearby house already at least half a century old, constituted the small town named on a canting roadway sign.

The Buick left the graveled road and continued straight. The way gradually became rougher, clotted with potholes. Wild roses and sage pressed inward from both sides until the road encompassed little more than a single car-width.

One more sweeping turn at the base of a mountain, and the Buick entered the valley. It continued for another ten minutes or so, then turned south at the old stone church that had stood for three generations—and that would stand for only two more years before being dynamited to make way for a newer, more modern structure.

Just past the church, the roadway dropped abruptly, startling the children. The oldest glanced out the window and shouted, "We're there!"

A quarter of a mile further on, the Buick pulled into an open gateway in a white-plank fence, drove a bit further on, then pulled into a space between two log outbuildings—the garage on one side, with barely enough room for the grandparents' ten-year-old Nash; and the grandfather's machine shop on the other.

The father guided the big Buick into the narrow space, then stopped and set the parking brake.

"We're here," he said. "Let's go find Grandma and Grandpa."

But already the grandparents were making their way from the new house, past the old house where the mother had been born, through an arch in the white picket fence, and across the yard.

"We've been watching for you," the grandmother cried, tears in her eyes as she hugged her daughter and nodded toward her son-in-law. The grandfather didn't say anything, just stood there in his worn overalls, beaming.

The father helped each of the children climb over the driver's seat and out the door. Because they were antsy from the drive and already starting to vie with each other for attention, he boosted them onto the front of the car—the two boys on the fenders, the girl on the high-domed hood.

He reached inside and pulled out his brand-new camera...his first color camera.

Looking toward the sun setting across the fields, he fiddled with his light meter, spent a couple of minutes adjusting dials and knobs on the camera, then snapped a picture of the grandparents and the mother, and another of the three children perched on the car.

Then it happened.

Across a narrow creek that bisected the land between the outbuildings and the barn, *something* appeared.

The younger boy saw it first. His eyes bulged as the thing came nearer and nearer, but still safely on the far side of the creek. He almost began to cry. Tears welled in his eyes, and his face took on a reddish glow not entirely accountable to the setting sun. He was clearly in the grips of a strong emotion.

Fear.

For a moment, the tableaux held. Then the creature abruptly splashed across the creek and made its way through the low bushes toward the car.

It was huge! At least two, maybe three times as tall as the boy, with four legs that seemed to stomp on the muddy turf as it drew nearer. Great spiky things...one, two of them...stuck out from each side of its head and cut through the air as they moved in time with its cadenced pace. The boy had never seen anything like it before, had no name to call it, had never imagined that anything like it might even exist.

Tears squeezed out and down his cheeks as he began crying.

The thing kept coming, nearer and nearer, until its gigantic head was just on the other side of the peeled log barrier that separated it from the Buick.

It thrust its head toward the logs, searching for a gap between them. And the boy screamed. Fear had transformed into something else.

Terror!

Then, just as the mother began to move toward the far side of the Buick to rescue her son, the worst possible thing happened.

Something long and pink and glistening and slimy slipped from the monstrous mouth, found its way between two logs, and *touched the boy's foot.*

He pulled his legs in so fast that it looked as if he had been burned. His scream took on a new pitch. His eyes widened until it seemed that they would pop from their sockets. Terror had been replaced by something far worse, by the ultimate....

Horror and revulsion.

The *thing* had *touched* him!

By then the mother was near enough to reach for him and pull him into her arms. On the other side of the Buick, the grandfather tore his beat-up old fishing hat from his head and slapped it three times against his thigh—*Whap! Whap! Whap!*

"Ho, Brownie," he yelled in a commanding voice totally unlike his usual soft murmur. "Get outta here! To the barn!"

And the tan-and-white Guernsey, a kind of disappointment evident in her large, soft, brown eyes, backed away, re-crossed the creek, and made her way to the herd, on her way to be milked.

It took nearly an hour to settle the children. The younger boy was nearly hysterical; and the other two, picking up on his state, began crying as well. But finally, just as the sun slipped behind the fields, they were settled, safe in Grandma's house eating bread and milk and home-baked cookies.

No one had expected it. The father just happened to have his camera out and set to the right exposure for the late afternoon sun. He just happened to be standing in the perfect place for the shot when the cow ambled by.

Since they had been pointing out cows and other farm animals all day, neither the father nor the mother anticipated such a reaction from their younger son.

What they didn't grasp was that he had never made the connection between that word *cow* and the great huge beast that had come clomping toward him. After all, he was not yet three, and many words were new to him.

Even when it stood right in front of him, they probably didn't understand that he had no idea what that beast might want to do to him. And when it stuck out its tongue and licked the bottom of his foot....

It was just too much. Fear, then terror, then the visceral response of horror. Stephen King's classic description of horror, one stage slipping seamlessly into the next.

It was that simple.

An otherwise commonplace day. Nothing that had not happened before; and in fact, almost everything that had occurred would repeat every August for years to come.

Except for the moment when a little boy suddenly came face-to-face with the unknown.

All of the elements were there: a journey away from the safety and security of his home, his room, his known world, to an isolated place that he, at least, had no memory of ever visiting before. The end of a long trip that had left him keyed up, startled awake when his older brother had yelled, then confused by the sudden rush as everyone tried to climb out of the car at once and be the first to hug their grandparents. Being put onto the Buick's bumper which, while broad and smooth, was still a strange place, the place farthest from his mother and father.

And then, the intrusion of the *monstrum*…the unknown…the threat to the order and stability he had come to know.

This small moment of horror was soon forgotten; probably, if it weren't for a still-surviving, stark photograph, it would have long since faded from memory. Instead, that tiny bit of film encapsulated an instant, the height of fear and terror and horror for one small child.

The horror writer's responsibility—both a gift and a curse, to borrow a phrase—is to create such moments in fiction, to bring readers to that same intensity of dread. And it must be done, not by introducing an *actual* creature into the readers' lives, but by manipulating *words.*

One of the purposes of this book is to suggest ways by which the words we use daily, the common *Wordschatz*—'word treasure,' a term more resonant than the English 'list of words'—may be employed in narrative, and how, from those words, writers can create moments that not only engage readers' imaginations but also literally generate a physical response, a *frisson,* a shudder, a chill along the spine that has *nothing at all to do with reality.*[1]

Another purpose is to examine examples of writing, especially excerpts from published books, to see how successfully writers achieve this goal. In some instances, the gap between the ideal and the actuality is small; in others the writers in question missed by a fairly large degree. In no instance, however, does this study intend to ridicule writers who have attempted a difficult task; it has only tried to indicate ways that weak writing might be made stronger and the writer's purposes accomplished more completely.

---

[1] Someone once noted that the closest literary form to horror is probably pornography, for the simple reason that they are the only two designed to elicit a visceral, definable physical response. It might be argued that comedy is part of the trio, as well, since its purpose is to generate laughter. Of course, the responses sought by the three forms generally (and fortunately) differ greatly.

Chapter 2

The Great Chain of Evil

Where do we find literary horrors? Why do certain images frighten us again and again, never losing their impact through repetition? What are some of the sources of those creatures "that go *bump* in the night," that make us tremble and quake?

Reading Jonathan Maberry's PINE DEEP TRILOGY—*Ghost Road Blues, Dead Man's Song,* and *Bad Moon Rising*—stimulated my thinking about these questions. Why did I instinctively shudder at the mention of roaches...and why had I incorporated them into my own novel *The Slab* some years ago? Why would the fact of crop blight, an exterior event with no *physical* effect on any of the characters, so effectively establish an overwhelming landscape of horror? How was it possible for a single work to incorporate zombies (or zombie-like creatures), werewolves, vampires, *and* their various histories and traditions, and still remain unified and coherent?

The more I reflected on these questions, the more I became aware of a curious trail of possible influences. In a rather odd way, that trail led back several centuries, to well before Poe and Lovecraft and the beginnings of horror as an accepted genre, beyond even the development of the novel itself, back to the first stirrings of the modern world as it separated itself from the centuries-long medieval milieu.

In the 1930s and 1940s, two scholarly studies appeared, dedicated to understanding the way the medieval world perceived the universe. The first of these, Arthur O. Lovejoy's *The Great Chain of Being: The History of an Idea* (1936), argued that medieval minds envisioned the universe as a series of linked creations—a carefully structured hierarchy—reaching from God at the apex to inanimate, inorganic dirt (soil, dust, sand) at the bottom. As the series progressed upwards, one moved from the lesser to the more refined and perfected. Lovejoy's term for that systemic progression was the Great Chain of Being.

A few years later, another scholar of ideas, E.M.W. Tillyard, published *The Elizabethan World Picture* (1943), a more focused analysis of the same intellectual phenomenon, in which he argued that the Elizabethans—as clearly evident in a number of Shakespeare's plays and other literary works—believed in perfect cosmic order and harmony, overseen by God.

For the Elizabethans, *order* was the linchpin of all things. The idea assumed political, religious, social, cultural, even cosmological importance...and yet was rarely overtly defined. The assumption of its crucial import was embedded so completely in the mindset of the time that almost no one felt the need to explain it.

Fortunately, however, one writer left a rather lengthy discourse on the consequences of disorder and disharmony, ranging from the effects on individuals to the universe itself. In what is otherwise often considered one of Shakespeare's 'lesser' works, *Troilus and Cressida,* the character Ulysses expatiates on the need for *degree,* by which he means *order*:

> The heavens themselves, the planets and this centre
> Observe degree, priority and place,
> Insisture, course, proportion, season, form,
> Office and custom, in all line of order;
> And therefore is the glorious planet Sol
> In noble eminence enthroned and sphered
> Amidst the other; whose medicinable eye
> Corrects the ill aspects of planets evil,
> And posts, like the commandment of a king,
> Sans cheque to good and bad: but when the planets
> In evil mixture to disorder wander,
> What plagues and what portents! what mutiny!
> What raging of the sea! shaking of earth!
> Commotion in the winds! frights, changes, horrors,
> Divert and crack, rend and deracinate
> The unity and married calm of states
> Quite from their fixure! O, when degree is shaked,
> Which is the ladder to all high designs,
> Then enterprise is sick! How could communities,
> Degrees in schools and brotherhoods in cities,

Peaceful commerce from dividable shores,
The primogenitive and due of birth,
Prerogative of age, crowns, sceptres, laurels,
But by degree, stand in authentic place?
Take but degree away, untune that string,
And, hark, what discord follows! each thing meets
In mere oppugnancy: the bounded waters
Should lift their bosoms higher than the shores
And make a sop of all this solid globe:
Strength should be lord of imbecility,
And the rude son should strike his father dead:
Force should be right; or rather, right and wrong,
Between whose endless jar justice resides,
Should lose their names, and so should justice too.
Then every thing includes itself in power,
Power into will, will into appetite;
And appetite, an universal wolf,
So doubly seconded with will and power,
Must make perforce an universal prey,
And last eat up himself. Great Agamemnon,
This chaos, when degree is suffocate,
Follows the choking.

In other words, without *order*, there is *horror*.

The hierarchical construct that was the Great Chain became the main guardian of order and harmony. It, in turn, consisted of three primary components: *plenitude, continuity,* and *gradation.* The first simply argued that God, in His wisdom and grace, had populated the universe completely, with no empty niches—which in turn implies the other two characteristics. *Continuity* means that the chain is never broken, at least from the level of the angels down to the lowest minerals; God, as Creator, stands above all, however, and an infinite gap separates Him from His creations. *Gradation* means that each link and each level within the chain differ only slightly from the ones above and below but that that difference forever separates them.

A fourth term often associated with the Great Chain is *correspondence.* This means that there is a superior entity—the *primate*—at each level of the Chain, and that all primates *correspond* to each other. For example, God is at the top of the Chain as the most perfect and most refined Being, the only one to possess not only rationality but omniscience and omnipresence. Angels are at the top of the angelic scale, possessing rationality but not omniscience and omnipresence. Kings are the highest and noblest among humans and thus echo God's position in the Heavens. Lions are the highest of animals, and Eagles are the highest of birds. Diamonds are the noblest gems, while Gold is the noblest mineral. Marble is the noblest stone. Beneath each of these *primates* stretches a perfect gradation of lesser entities, the total filling the whole of Creation.

Thus, an Elizabethan writer comparing Elizabeth to the Sun, the noblest astronomical body, implicitly—and to a degree *explicitly*—compares her to God. He is the King of Heaven, she is the Queen of England. To complicate the situation a bit, she was often compared to the Moon, and thus corresponded to the Queen of Planets, the symbol of virginity and purity.

Some thirty years or so after Lovejoy and Tillyard, a third eminent scholar published a study of the medieval imagination. C.S. Lewis's *The Discarded Image* (1964) is a wonderfully readable survey of medieval mind-sets, based heavily upon the works of his predecessors. With his usual consummate skill, he suggests the consequences of living under such a hierarchical system, with everything in its place and knowing its place, where nothing interrupts the overriding sense of absolute harmony and order. In his final chapter, however, he notes that the entire system has one indisputable flaw.

It simply doesn't work.

In the time following the Elizabethan flowering of imagination and creativity, another force began to make itself known—science. A number of scholars have seen in Christopher Marlowe's *Dr. Faustus* and Shakespeare's *Hamlet,* for example, dramatizations of the increasing and increasingly traumatic sense that, as Hamlet puts it, the world is out of joint.

Not long after Elizabeth's death, Galileo peered through his telescope and saw small planets—moons—orbiting larger planets. Impossible...at least according to the belief in *plenitude.* God *filled* Creation; the heavens were complete and immutable. And yet there were moons.

Soon thereafter, alchemists-turned-chemists discovered that there were more elements than the classical four: Earth, Air, Fire, Water. First a dozen more. Then scores. Impossible. Everything is formed of various proportions of the four. There is no room for more elements.

Adventurers explored new lands and discovered new plants, new animals, that fit nowhere on the old lists. Where, for example, would one place the platypus? Such an animal was impossible. Yet it existed.

By the end of the eighteenth century, the concept of the Great Chain of Being, of universal hierarchy, had largely died. Where it did survive, it did so as a set of symbols rather than as reflecting external reality.

Except for in horror.

In essence, our monsters, our creatures, our things that go bump in the night, owe at least part of their existence to the lingering shadow of the Great Chain.

To see how this paradigm might work in practice, let me apply some of the principles implicit in the Great Chain to a specific narrative—Jonathan Maberry's PINE DEEP TRILOGY: *Ghost Road Blues, Dead Man's Song,* and *Bad Moon Rising.*

In the first volume things are going very badly for the small Pennsylvania town of Pine Deep. Three decades earlier, following a Black Harvest, in which nearly every crop was infected and died, one man dared to face down a serial killer...because he knew that the murderer was not human. In a cataclysmic battle, he defeats the monster and buries it deep in Dark Hollow.

Thirty years later, Evil begins to rise.

In detailing the resurgence of Evil, Maberry incorporates a wide range of creatures to epitomize the darkness. And in almost every essential he provides a paradigm for a perversion of the hierarchy, order, and harmony that characterize the Great Chain.

Traditionally, at the bottom of the Chain are minerals, beginning with diamonds and descending to dirt, all of which are incapable of movement, growth, or rationality. In Pine Deep, to arrive at the source— the bottom—of Evil, requires a similar descent. The lowest place— geographically, imagistically, psychologically, and spiritually—is the depth of Dark Hollow where the demon/murderer lies buried. In mud. Not clean, therapeutic mud but something filthy and odiferous, noxious and hungry. Its surface roils as if it is breathing. As the story progresses and events near their climax, the mud becomes angrier, more volatile, until in the end it all but explodes as Evil reveals itself.

There are no diamonds in Dark Hollow, nothing to represent the most refined level of mineral creation. There is only the diametric opposite of purity—evil...and almost sentient, putrid mud.

For the medieval mind, plants differed from minerals in being capable of growth but not of movement or reason. At the top of the hierarchy is the mighty oak; at the bottom, weeds, mosses, and fungi—which, appropriately, flourish in the gloomiest parts of Dark Hollow. The higher-order plants, those capable of producing seeds, such as corn and pumpkins, are the first stricken by the blight that heralds the oncoming Black Harvest (and they are infected by viruses and bacteria that, essentially and perversely, share characteristics of both plants and minerals). The mud at the center of Dark Hollow is surrounded by thick vegetation—not the primate oak but lesser sorts that grow in crowded thickets, that grasp at those intrepid enough—or stupid enough—to penetrate to the center. Nearly all plants mentioned in the Trilogy, except a chosen few that are explicitly *outside* the influence of Dark Hollow, are represented as minions of Evil.

Above plants are, of course, animals: creatures capable of growth and movement but not of reason. In the depths of the Hollow, the most graphic events incorporate the most perverse of animals, beginning with insects and rising gradually to include first roaches and then vermin of all sorts—mice, rats, small scavengers. Nearly every animal included in the Trilogy is more closely linked to the bottom of the Great Chain than to the upper reaches...with one startling exception. Appearing in the woods and fields that surround Dark Hollow is an ephemeral-looking white stag. And it comes as no surprise that the noblest of the untamed herbivores is the deer; and the King of the deer, as it were, is the stag (hence the impressive stature Bambi's father achieves in the final moments of that film).

Also capable of growth and movement but not of reason are birds. Because of their association with air (a nobler element than earth) birds rank higher on the chain than do animals. They, too, are divided into sub-classes, beginning with the eagle, symbol of God and monarchy. A bit farther down, but still primates of their smaller grouping, are carrion birds, especially the crow. Normally in dark fiction, black birds adumbrate evil—recall the ravens in Stephen King's *The Stand*, for example. They can, however, serve entirely different functions, as with the ancient raven and his tribe in Tolkien's *The Lord of the Rings*. In the wild landscape of Pine Deep, there are two major references to crows. In the lowest (referring to the Chain, again) are flocks of crows that follow various characters. Initially, they seem to support Evil, but in a nicely written piece of unexpected revelation, they justifiably take their place at the top of their rank as warriors against evil.

The second major reference is to a character himself—Malcolm Crow. A key hero-figure in a novel with multiple heroic models. And a human.

Humans rank above the animals. They are capable of growth, movement, and—most significantly for the medieval mind—reason. Man was the head, the primate, of all animals, just as the head was the primate of bodily organs. Situated as it was at the apex of the only animal (to medieval observers) capable of standing fully erect, the brain corresponded to man as a whole...and to the King, the Sun, and God. Quite literally, the rational function was centered in that part of man closest to God and furthest from the earth.

But several seminal figures in horror literature are not quite human, although they once were. Because they share characteristics that cross boundaries between human and animal, they represent perversions of an ideal order...essentially what is needed for effective horror. They demonstrate what humans might become if they were to descend lower on the Chain, and thus they are inherently frightening.

The first such class of beings, technically 'human' or 'once-human,' are capable of movement but of neither growth nor reason: Zombies. The walking dead, they cannot grow, cannot replace parts torn from their decaying bodies. They are driven purely by instinct (which has little place in the traditional Great Chain of Being), by savage hunger, the basest of passions. And, as might be expected, they—or a variant on them—appear in Pine Deep.

The second class of not-quite-humans, capable of growth and movement and, at least part of the time, of reason, plays a crucial role in the novels: Werewolves. Much of our sympathy for werewolves, when such occurs, stems from the fact that good, sometimes even great and noble men and women can be infected, either by bites or by birth. Yet when the fit is upon them, they become mere slavering animals. The traditions relating to were-beasts of all sorts play a strong role in much dark fantasy, and in every instance they draw their power from that tension between what was and what now is—between the ideal and the perversion of the ideal.

The third sort of anti-human is capable of movement and reason but not of growth: Vampires. They are the unDead, immortal (or nearly so), able to behave as normal in human society but also able to become at any moment blood-suckers and devourers of human flesh. They are the most dangerous—and also the 'highest' level of anti-humans, in that they are rational but willing to give in to passions of several sorts...as witnessed by the level of sexuality frequently ascribed to them.

Superior to zombies, werewolves, and vampires are the fully human: still living; incapable of transforming into lower forms; and capable of growth, movement, and reason—although in evil humans the rational faculties have been themselves perverted. In the Trilogy, there are, I think, subtle references to the Great Chain of Being, at least as far as it might reasonably be expected to apply to contemporary society. More than once, evil, fully human characters refer to themselves (often delusively) as being at the "top of the food chain." As mistaken as they might be, since Evil allows no-one and no-thing to share the *top*, their comments are a strong indicator as to how humans function in Pine Deep.

True evil emerges through individual choice; and in a nice parody of the Great Chain, those humans who choose evil take on characteristics of lower orders. They see themselves as the epitome of devourers—of innocence, of virtue, of blood, of flesh. In truth, they are anti-humans, the worst of their sub-types: child abusers, drug users, wife beaters, murderers, even cannibals. They have no feelings for anyone else; they prey on the old and the young, the strong and the infirm. They are scavengers among humanity, and Evil is their God.

Above humans in the conventional Great Chain are multiple levels of Angels. During the Medieval Period and the Renaissance, the classes of angelic beings were defined and codified—usually into seven or nine carefully distinguished ranks with various sub-ranks. Angels were considered the first creations, capable of movement and rationality, and unencumbered by the dross of flesh (which was, after all, composed primarily of dust). They were nearest to God although eternally separate from Him, the relationship that of perfect Creations to perfect Creator. Some fell from Heaven, of course; theologians and philosophers also devised specific ranks of devils, with Satan himself, the anti-God, at the bottom...as in Dante's *Inferno.*

No angels flit in the air above Pine Deep. But there is a ghost—a generally insubstantial being who knows much...but not all; who acts as an infrequently glimpsed influence for good; and whose purpose, like that of the angels, is to guide fallen humanity in its conflict with Evil. Maberry clothes his 'angel' in the garb of a long-dead itinerant blues player, at the beginning the only character who *knows* the truth about Dark Hollow, and the one character whose assertions and assumptions readers can trust throughout.

At the top of the Great Chain—the Creator/God.

He does not appear *in propria persona* in Pine Deep, nor should he. Evil, if it is to be defeated, must be defeated on a human level, otherwise there is no point to the conflict: Milton wrote two epic poems to demonstrate this. When Malcolm Crow and the handful of others who believe him and are willing to follow him (and who are still fully alive) descend to the bottom of Dark Hollow, they find not a fallen angel, not even a fallen God.

They find an anti-God, a creation that asserts Godhood and threatens to destroy not only one small town and its people but the whole of humanity. An entity that has existed for centuries by devouring, not by nurturing, and whose sole function is to feed itself...on flesh, on blood, on fear, on terror, on the life-energy of its victims.

Still, in the context of the Great Chain of Evil as developed in the Trilogy, it represents an inverted apex—a *nadir*, the basest of the base—emphasized by its location in the lowest geographical area, in what is essentially a putrefying mudhole; by its feeding initially on vermin, the most ignoble of motile creatures; by its eventually preying on those closest to itself in the Chain—zombie-like creatures, werewolves, other vampires, base humans, and, finally, the fully human. Only in the last instance does it meet with resistance and, ultimately, defeat.

Much of this essay has been discussing one set of novels, largely because they incorporate a wider range of horror than do many others. The conclusions drawn here seem to hold true for much horror literature, however, regardless of how open or how restrictive the stories might be in terms of creatures. The things we fear are the creatures at the bottom of the various levels of creations, the furthest of their kinds from the beneficence of God. Taken as a whole, they represent a paradigm for disorder, disharmony, chaos, fear, terror, and horror—a Great Chain of Evil.

Part Two: Architectural Renderings – Overviews

Chapter 3

Why Horror?

Why do I read horror, write horror, write *about* horror?

Probably most horror writers have been asked these questions or something close to them. There is, after all, something peculiar about spending inordinate amounts of time imagining, re-creating, or analyzing darkness, particularly when there is already much darkness in the 'real' world.

Perhaps therein rests the answer, at least in my case. There *is* much darkness 'out there,' so many things that seem uncontrolled and uncontrollable. Through horror, writers—and readers—may assert a kind of vicarious control over them and by doing so fit more comfortably into the 'real' world.

Let me explain:

In his 1981 study of horror fiction, *Danse Macabre,* Stephen King discusses three levels of horror:

> I recognize terror as the finest emotion and so I will try to terrorize the reader. But if I find that I cannot terrify, I will try to horrify, and if I find that I cannot horrify, I'll go for the gross-out. I'm not proud. (Ch. 2)

Revulsion—the gross-out—is, as King suggests, relatively easy to achieve. It requires primarily quantities of blood and guts, graphic descriptions, and graphic language. The most vocal arguments against horror as literary genre concentrate on this level. At the other extreme, true terror, the moment that generates a frisson down the spine just before the monster is revealed, requires extraordinary facility with language, characterization, and setting to accomplish, and only a few masters—among them Poe and Lovecraft, as well as King himself—create it consistently. When it occurs, and when terror, horror, and revulsion are used critically and carefully, such literature may demonstrate a number of useful traits.

At the thematic level, horror can speak metaphorically or symbolically. Literary monsters may represent literal monsters that threaten everyday life. A vampire suddenly appearing in a small town and systematically preying on its inhabitants may simultaneously condemn the contemporary sense of isolation and divisiveness that afflicts most communities. People live separated lives; they do not notice the alterations in or absence of their neighbors until it is too late, when the bonds of civility have already broken and the sense of community disappears.

The vampire may exemplify the allure and the tragedy of uninhibited lust. By virtue of its existence—neither dead nor alive; its mode of feeding—penetration and bloodletting; and the inescapably body-oriented nature of its attacks—usually male upon female—the vampire can slip from a figure of horror into quasi-pornography, especially when the transmission of blood is described in loving, overly sensual detail; and at the same time it can indict the contemporary obsession with sexualizing people, usually women, into little more than objects of physical release.

The werewolf may represent the abrupt, inexplicable intrusion of death into a family or community. Unseen and unsuspected until it lashes out in rage and inflicts carnage on its victims, the werewolf parallels disease—cancer, for example—and its insidious rampage within a healthy body. It may stand for accident or fate; there is no cause, no rationale or purpose behind its sudden eruption—it simply *is,* and by its presence it disrupts order and security.

Zombies epitomize the loss of agency and rationality. Probably their unusual popularity at the moment reflects a cultural fear of helplessness and hopelessness in the face of global threats: wavering economies, potential if not probable warfare, pandemics facilitated by technology. Everything considered normal may dissolve at any moment, leaving survivors surrounded by mindless, unfocused, ravening monsters whose sole function is to destroy any remnants of civility.

Most other literary monsters may serve parallel functions. Amazons demonstrate the threat of sexual disparity; Creatures from Other Dimensions, including Lovecraft's Great Old Ones, embody the threat of the unknown, of the breakdown of reason and intellect into madness.

Ghosts, Demons, the Haunted Place/Bad Place, and other denizens of darkness—each may in its turn speak volumes about the human condition.

At the literal level, horror may work in a manner similar to classical tragedy. When written effectively, with an eye toward creating genuine terror rather than mere physiological revulsion, horror may combine pity and fear to achieve a kind of Aristotelian *catharsis* focused on the purging of one specific strong emotion, namely, fear itself. Horror allows readers to confront an object or objects of pity, usually victims, frequently innocent or inoffensive victims; and an object of terror, horror, or revulsion, the monster or monsters; and by juxtaposing the two, *feel* legitimate fear while in a safe, controlled environment. This fear may in fact be physically expressed, through a rise in heartbeat, increased rate of respiration, even a literal chill up the spine. In any case, the physical response allows the reader to *experience* and thereby *purge* the effects of extraordinary fear without physical danger.

Finally, on an ethical level, readers of horror more often than not confront the most literal sort of morality. Unlike in the experiential world, in the world of horror, actions that are evil, wrong, or even misguided have *immediate* consequences. Cause and effect are clearly linked. If a mad scientist creates a monster, eventually the monster turns on its creator. At least as far back as Shelley's *Frankenstein*, this has been a *leitmotif* of horror fiction. The responsibility of creator to creature—and for the acts of the creature—in part defines the plot itself. If a teenage couple have illicit sex and thereby participate in an adult action without being prepared to accept the concomitant responsibilities, they die, frequently during the act itself. There is no reprieve, no opportunity for a second chance. Transgression leads to death.

It is possible for horror itself to be essentially immoral. Novels exist in which characters are introduced and almost immediately destroyed, merely for the sake of blood and gore. The monster itself becomes little more than a killing machine and the plot impelled not by causal relationships among episodes but by the simple need for more blood. The horror of unrelieved revulsion, in other words, runs the risk of existing solely for the sake of that revulsion, with little thought of creating the more transcendent horror or terror. Such fiction verges on the immoral, if not the obscene, not through the representation of unacceptable language or events but because of its cavalier attitude toward characters and their lives.

On the whole, however, those writers most frequently cited as masters in the field—Poe, Lovecraft, King, Koontz, McCammon, and a handful of others—consistently provide tales that, however close they come to mere revulsion, ultimately lead readers to a heightened sense of morality, of catharsis of fear, and of the relationship between story and life, between characters and the reader.

In a recent afterword to his 1987 novel *Shadowfires,* Dean R. Koontz considers the question of what constitutes horror and why it is so often shunned as a genre. One of his conclusions is that horror concentrates its images and effects on *death*—death as theme, as plot device, as indicator of character. And in large part, what he suggests holds true. The major "monsters" of horror fiction are, by and large, the Revenant Dead, the unDead, and the Walking Dead—ghosts, vampires, zombies, Lovecraftian Great Old Ones long since vanished from this plane and seeking to re-enter it. Even the werewolf is in some ways a figure intimately associated with death—although the lycanthrope is still alive, he is an outcast, an 'other' essentially dead to the larger community.

Death is the beginning and end of much horror. It triggers the appearance of the monster, either literally, as the monster is called from death; or figuratively, as its victims announce the presence of the monster. It is the punishment meted to the unwary, the unethical, the unrighteous. As noted above, teenagers who engage in sex before understanding the adult responsibilities implicit in the act are punished by death. Mad scientists—and often even inadvertent meddlers in the true order of the universe—suffer death at the hands—or claws, or teeth—of their creations. Even the innocent die, often in gruesome ways, in order to underscore the leveling power of horror...and of death. It is not accidental, of course, that so many horror novels sport black covers; the archetypical cover may be the first paperback edition of Stephen King's *'Salem's Lot,* almost pure glossy black, with no title, the embossed face of a girl...and a single crop of crimson blood. The essence of the novel was communicated forcefully and directly.

These are the things I consider when I read horror, when I write horror, when I write about horror. The experiences become passages through darkness into something else...the light, perhaps, or understanding, or consolation, or at the least relief—that the world 'out there' is not yet as terrifying, as terrible as the worlds of the imagination.

Chapter 4

Where Horror Is(n't)

Some time ago I received a reader's review at Amazon for *The Slab: A Novel of Terror*. The review was titled "A Novel of Horror?" and started:

> No horror here. Began reading this a few days before Halloween, thought it was a "haunted house" or ghost story. Boy, was I wrong! Very boring story about a boring family that bought a house with structural problems. There, that's the story in a nutshell.

My first reaction was that I should post a sarcastic comment/response: *Hey, man! Check out Stephen King's* The Shining. *It's a story about a hotel that has a boiler problem one winter.* Or: *Check out Stephen King's* The Stand. *It's a story about some people who catch a nasty flu.*

Since the reviewer was not the first to consider *The Slab* as little more than a story about a family living in a badly built house, however, I stifled that response and, instead, checked out the reviewer's other offerings. I will admit to some surprise when I discovered some forty-three reviews, mostly of horror. Certainly the reviewer was relatively widely read and willing to share opinions.

When I began looking further, I discovered several other things.

First, I was in fairly good company. Larry Niven's classic *Lucifer's Hammer* (1977) received one star and the comment that about halfway through "this slow paced disaster I just skimmed ahead and finally put it down for good."

Joe Hill's Bram Stoker Award®-winning *Heart-Shaped Box* was dismissed as "slow paced" and not scary. It did, the review continued, use musical references in an interesting way, so it avoided the dreaded one-star classification.

Alexandra Sokoloff's Bram Stoker Award®-nominated *The Harrowing* earned this conclusion, based on a previous reviewer's reference to it as a "page turner": "I found I couldn't turn the pages fast enough just so I could finish it and move on to something better."

All right, then, what would it take to earn four or five stars?

Of Bryan Smith's *Depraved*: "Fast paced, chilling and downright sick!" The story was a "feast of blood, guts and gore; a buffet of raunchy sex...." Four stars.

Of Bryan Smith's *The Freakshow*: Key words in the review include "gory freaks" and "sexy freaks." Five stars.

Of Richard Laymon's *The Quake*: "All the ingredients of a classic Richard Laymon novel, sex, gore, sex, gore, and then more sex and gore." Five stars.

Of Edward Lee's *Slither*: The novel thrills with its emphasis on blood, gore, and sex.

Of Gary Frank's *Forever Will You Suffer*: "...plenty of sex, gore and lustful innuendos."

Lest my summaries seem too one-sided, the reviewer awards three Simon Clark novels either four or five stars, with such compliments as: "Well written, good character development and an overall good story"; "Great writing and an excellent story"; and "an entertaining and fast paced horror novel about living, breathing, gentle and subservient 'monsters' that are suddenly hunted and destroyed by the very humans that created them."

I didn't accumulate this data as a means of "getting even" with a reviewer; I do not know the person, will probably never meet the person, and (I hope) have a thick-enough skin to handle the fact that not everyone will enjoy my writing. In several instances, reviewers (writing comments both positive and negative) have pinpointed areas I was concerned about while my novels were under construction. On the whole, however, *The Slab* has received about twice as many positive (i.e., four and five stars) reviews as negative (one and two stars). So on that score, I am reasonably satisfied...actually, more than reasonably satisfied, since I've never imagined myself a best-selling author, and both *The Slab* and *The House Beyond the Hill* have ranked as Wildside Press Bestsellers and spent a considerable amount of time on the Kindle/Amazon.com Horror Top 100.

No, what intrigued me about the reviewer's choices led me beyond my book to a larger consideration: Where is horror today?

Not that I can answer such a question definitively and for all time…especially since the genre will probably have moved somewhere else by tomorrow.

Today: blood, guts, gore, and raunchy sex; sex, gore, sex, gore, and more sex.

In part at least, that explains the comments about Niven's novel. Admittedly not intended as a horror novel, and admittedly a manifestation of the 1970s' fascination with disasters both in novels and in films, it nonetheless incorporates motifs that now might be considered horrific, specifically the physical consequences of a comet striking the earth and the moral and spiritual consequences for the survivors. In many ways, the novel seems more concerned with the latter than the former. And, while it does touch upon blood, gore, and sex, it subordinates those elements to what the author apparently considers more critical issues: humanity, civilization, self-control, and human love.

To a degree, that approach was consonant with the classic disaster films of the time—many of which I saw, either in the theater or later on VHS and DVD. There were moments of sexuality, of necessary blood-letting, of violence, terror, and destruction. But the stories in general focused on relationships and on whether those relationships could withstand the consequences of disaster.

And it was largely consistent with perceptions of horror at that time.

The other day, I pulled a thick hardcover with cracking spine and yellowing pages from my library shelves. On the front flyleaf I had written my name and the date I purchased it: 3/22/69. On the first blank page, written in pencil, was the price I had paid for it: $2.00. That was a fair amount of money back then for a used book, but since the tome offered 1080 pages of stories, it seemed worthwhile.

And it was.

Great Tales of Terror and the Supernatural, edited by Herbert A. Wise and Phyllis Fraser, was first published by Random House in 1944. As the title indicates, it collected what was then considered the finest stories in what we now roughly classify as Horror. The stories are arranged chronologically by authors' birthdates. The "Tales of Terror" begin with Honoré de Balzac (b. 1799), continuing with Edgar Allan Poe, Wilkie Collins, Ambrose Bierce, H.G. Wells, and conclude with William Faulkner, Ernest Hemingway, and Geoffrey Household.

The "Tales of the Supernatural" open with Edward Bulwer-Lytton and include Nathaniel Hawthorne, Henry James, M.R. James, W.W. Jacobs, Arthur Machen, Walter de la Mare, and E.M. Forester, along with about a score of others. The final two stories are by a relative newcomer (in 1944): H.P. Lovecraft, represented by "The Rats in the Walls" and "The Dunwich Horror."

This volume offered a much-younger me my first taste of concentrated horror, and I remember devouring the book, enjoying each tantalizing moment, then returning again and again for refresher courses in how to do it. The book contained some of my favorite stories: Poe's "The Black Cat"; Conrad Aiken's magnificent "Silent Snow, Secret Snow," which has haunted me since I first read it; Richard Connell's "The Most Dangerous Game," which I had already encountered in high school; William Faulkner's staggeringly oblique "A Rose for Emily," which became one of the sources for my horror novel *Static!*; M.R. James' "Casting the Runes"; W.W. Jacob's "The Monkey's Paw," so influential on several of Stephen King's short stories; and the two Lovecraft tales already mentioned.

All written before Stephen King—who was to change the face of horror so substantially—was even born.

Looking through the collection, reading a few here and there, and casting back on my own memories—coupled with what I had discovered in looking at the reviews listed above—made me realize several key points.

First, the stories in *Great Tales of Terror and the Supernatural* depended upon one thing for their effectiveness: the sheer power of their *storytelling*. Plot, character, landscape—yes, but also *language*, lovingly applied and carefully crafted to bring readers out of their own, commonplace worlds and into other worlds where impossible, unspeakable, terrifying intrusions might occur. Sentences are often longer, more complex than modern taste appreciates, but necessarily so, since many of the authors were essentially first introducing their particular cadre of readers to the otherworldly. The transition from *here* to *there* had to be made considerately, deliberately.

Second, there is relatively little blood-and-guts in the stories. Partially, I'm sure, this is due to the times in which most of the stories were written—Victorian Era through pre-World War II—when society was not as open to such things as it is now. But it seems equally due to the writers themselves being more interested in, more *fascinated with,* suggestion and allusion rather than blunt description. In most cases, we don't actually see what happens to the victim; we see only the aftermath, the consequences. Occasionally we do not even see the monster. It is present by indirection, by implication, and hence is the more terrifying for it.

And third, there is no overt sex. Sexuality and sensuality, perhaps, but nothing obvious. Hints and suggestions might provide subtle underpinnings for a coherent tale, not crutches for one so desperately crippled that only page after page of sexual plunderings could keep it upright.

So what has happened? How do we get from subtlety, indirection, suggestion, and allusion to "a feast of blood, guts and gore; a buffet of raunchy sex"?

I suppose one of King's most original characters has the only important answer: "The world has moved on." As it always does.

Being now almost officially of the geezer-generation (66 at the end of October, 2013), I find myself fighting *with* myself when I see trends that don't fit my world view. Many writers are now two generations younger than I and take for granted things that, for me, were world-altering: space flight, for example. Their interests often—but not always—coincide with mine, which is why I enjoy reading 'young' horror by younger writers and why, on occasion, they have enjoyed reading mine. In spite of obvious gaps, we still communicate.

And I see nothing to gain in trying to turn the clock back and return horror to its 'pristine' condition of fifty or a hundred years ago.

But when I picked up *Great Tales of Terror and the Supernatural* the other day and reflected on how much it could still teach writers about the *art* of writing, I was impressed by its strength. As old as it might be, it still communicates much about the sheer pleasure of a powerful story couched in consciously cultivated and graceful prose...and about how much more horrifying monsters can become through meticulously crafted prose.

Chapter 5

Three Hallmarks of Horror: Location, Isolation, and Language

According to an online dictionary, there are three fundamental definitions of *hallmark:*

1. (*Brit*) an official series of marks, instituted by statute in 1300, and subsequently modified, stamped by the Guild of Goldsmiths at one of its assay offices on gold, silver, or platinum (since 1975) articles to guarantee purity, date of manufacture, etc.;
2. a mark or sign of authenticity or excellence; and
3. an outstanding or distinguishing feature

In using the word as part of the title for three interconnected essays on the fundamentals of horror, to a certain degree, I had all three in mind.

The least relevant, of course, is the first. There are no "official marks" to identify "authentic" horror; if there were, selecting which books to read would be infinitely easier. There are, however, certain authors whose reputations very nearly constitute "official" recognition as contemporary masters of the genre: Stephen King, Dean R. Koontz, Robert R. McCammon, Joe R. Lansdale (all among my favorites), and a number of others.

More to the point, these writers and others that could be named by any readers of this essay consistently reflect the second and third definitions in that they consciously use—and at the same time adroitly re-imagine, re-design, and re-vamp—certain key elements of horror, its "outstanding or distinguishing feature(s)."

For my purposes, I have selected three such features: location, isolation, and language. There are other characteristics of horror, to be sure; but these three embody specific strengths that recur in the most effective tales.

ONE: LOCATION

A recent Amazon review of Michaelbrent Collings' *The Haunted* contained the following comment:

> OMG... what an amazing level of originality!!! A house on a hill, abandoned, for years (well, it's been done before). Young family moves in and starts seeing things. Wow... that had never been done before... only in every single horror movie and book out there. Things that go bump in the night, shadows moving, the radio turns itself on and off... WOW... BORING. BORING. BORING.

In spite of the fact that Michaelbrent is my son and that I enjoyed reading *The Haunted*, this comment made me stop and think. Having done so, I decided to take issue with it, since there were a number of flaws inherent in it, some obvious, some less so.

Among the obvious ones, the least important involve grammar and usage: triple exclamation marks to make certain that readers catch the otherwise undistinguished moment of sarcasm; ambiguous ellipses confusing where sentences might or might not end; and screaming capitals that contradict their own content.

More troublesome, however, is an underlying flaw. The reviewer castigates the book for doing *precisely what horror/ghost stories are supposed to do*. It is rather like someone objecting to a novel about clowns because it takes place in a circus. Or complaining that a Tarzan novel uses the jungle as a landscape. It makes me wonder why the reviewer picked up the book in the first place.

Note the first point of support: "A house on a hill, abandoned, for years (well, it's been done before)."

Of course it's been done before. In fact, it is more difficult to find ghost stories that do *not* begin in an isolated place—far from the protective arms of a network or support system, avoided by the locals but appealing for whatever reason to the new people, the victims of the haunting—than otherwise. By virtue of its underlying themes, its cast of characters living and dead, its obsession with sequestering a small group—often but not always a young couple—and testing them to the limits of their endurance and often their sanity, the ghost story *requires* a specific landscape.

Dean Koontz quite properly refers to that landscape, ubiquitous in horror, as *The Bad Place.*

The Bad Place does not have to be an old, decrepit house standing far from the normal commerce of society, but it frequently is. The reasons for this, I think, come easily enough. In the most effective horror, evil needs a focal point, a nexus. It is difficult for a writer to control an all-pervasive terror; if there is no place to escape *from* and no sanctuary to escape *to,* there is little point in the story. And even when the terror seems omnipresent, as in a novel such as Koontz's *Phantoms* or King's *It,* it still has a single point of focus...in both stories, the unmapped depths beneath the city streets. Whichever way they turn, characters seem doomed.

In effective horror, escaping *from* is often more important than escaping *to;* flight from the Bad Place often takes precedence over describing a place of safety. And the more spine-tingling the Bad Place is, the greater the terror it engenders, the more critical it is that the characters escape.

In many cases, the Bad Place is primarily the haunt of evil; in and of itself, it may be neutral. Yet even this can be misleading. With the passage of years, the place takes on the character of its resident evil, mirroring and echoing it, until the differences between place and source of evil become blurred.

In my first horror novel, *The House Beyond the Hill,* the eponymous house is morally neutral, at least at first. It is not so much abandoned as a low-cost, dilapidated rental chosen as a refuge by a young man haunted by external terror and by his memories. As the novel progresses and the evil encompasses him, his physical surroundings—the house—alter to reflect what happens to him inwardly and outwardly. By the end, the house exudes a stench of evil, as well as a literal stench, that warns intruders just how much is amiss there. The house parallels the degeneration of the character himself.

Similarly, in both *Static!* and *Shadow Valley,* the house begins as neutral. In the first, it is merely an old residence in an established suburban community in Southern California, fundamentally no different than others in the neighborhood. What differentiates it from them, however, is the person—The Greer—who has lived and died there and whose personality remains embedded within it. She is evil; her goals were and are evil; and she systematically sets about to destroy the sole inheritor after her death. The house, no matter how much it is altered by her during her life, remains neutral.

In *Shadow Valley*, the house is a farm house, old, distanced from the larger community, inhabited by the sole remaining member of a once-prosperous family. It is not to be feared for itself but rather for the secrets it contains and the essence that pervades it. Horrific things happen in the house, yet the house itself is not to blame. It is merely the physical landscape within which this particular evil has chosen to concentrate its hatred.

In other instances, the house is *itself* evil. To cite a classic example, Shirley Jackson's Hill House does not need an external stimulus for evil to occur. It seeks to meet its own needs, and in doing so destroys anything in its way.

In one of my most successful horror novels, *The Slab*, the house involved is a Southern California tract house, no different in layout than those surrounding it. It is not abandoned, although it does not sell for some years after its completion; it is not old, at least not at the beginning, when it is barely finished; it is not isolated, other than by the fact that it stands at the end of a typical suburban cul-de-sac and that neighbors, wary of the history of deaths within, do not willingly approach it. Yet from the beginning, it is *evil*. It is tainted by a single vicious action while its foundations are being laid, and from that act come the horrors that destroy lives over a period of decades. No lingering *ghost*, per se, haunts each new owner; instead, the house itself systematically changes them, enhancing their own predilections for evil, altering their perceptions of themselves and those around them, and ultimately killing at its own pleasure.

Either Bad Place can be highly effective. The point is that there generally needs to be one location, set aside, isolated, not in itself overtly threatening, in which evil can either breed or find a dwelling.

There are exceptions to these suggestions, of course. The ever-popular Zombie Apocalypse rarely centers in a single Bad Place; for Joe McKinney, most of southeastern Texas and parts of Louisiana and Alabama are, collectively, the Bad Place. Yet even so, within individual stories or novels, there tends to be a single *locus*, a city, a building, a hospital, a police headquarters, from which the evil spreads...and a single point at which the survivors struggle to escape.

It is difficult, to take an opposite extreme, to imagine a horror novel set entirely at a well-attended, communal Fourth-of-July picnic in an open park at the center of town, where there are no shadows, no hidden rooms where secrets lie unburied, no place for the uninvited. If a ghost appeared, everyone would have to see it. If a monster of any sort emerged (from whence, it might be difficult to say), the slaughter would be wholesale, and, since the entire narrative takes place in the middle of the day, everyone would know what the creature looks like.

No mystery, no chills of anticipation...no horror.

When Michaelbrent begins *The Haunted* with these words,

> The house sat atop a hill.
>
> It had sat there for many years, and as far as anyone knew, would sit there for many more. Visitors would occasionally travel the long path to see it. They would shiver, and wrap their coats tightly around them if it was winter. If it was summer, they would shiver and wish they were wearing a coat in the first place...,

he is not succumbing to cliché or triteness. He is consciously building on the foundation of traditional horror, embracing its fundamental trope, and assuring readers of what is to follow: ghosts, apparitions, threats, incipient death, unknown chills and terrors....all emanating from or congregating at the Bad Place.

TWO: ISOLATION

John Donne's famous apothegm, "No man is an island entire unto himself," is anathema to horror fiction.

Not that horror writers do not feel themselves part of the larger community of humanity; they often write, in fact, in defense of that larger community, warning against social and cultural disintegration by means of metaphoric monsters.

No, the reason the statement runs contradictory to horror fiction is quite simply that, given the premises and purposes of the genre, the primary character or characters in horror *must* be "an island," that is, must be *isolated. Isolated* originally comes from the Latin *insulatus*, 'made into an island,' by way of French. And that is precisely what must occur to a character or characters in order for horror to be truly effective.

In some instances, the making-into-an-island almost literally happens. A small group of people—often teenagers looking for some fun (i.e., drinking and sex) but occasionally adults as well—find themselves on an apparently deserted island. Through an occasionally improbable but necessary series of events, their boat is destroyed, disabled, or simply floats away on the tide, taking with it all communications to the mainland.

And then the group discovers that the island is in fact not deserted. It is inhabited by a pack of wild dogs trained to kill...; or by gigantic komodo dragons that systematically hunt down and devour members of the group...; or by sharks being bred for intelligence and rapacity...; or (as in one of my favorite B-movies) genetically altered shrews that look suspiciously like German shepherds wearing ill-fitting shrew-suits but whose bite is immediately fatal.

The story ends when some, most, or occasionally all of the monsters are dead, with the few survivors (usually a male and a female, often a plucky sidekick as well) saved by the adventitious arrival of a rescue boat.

More frequently, however, the 'islanding' of the characters is figurative. A handful of individuals arrive at the Bad Place, either by intention, conspiracy by evildoers, or accident, and their car is disabled, forcing them to remain. Or the doors slam shut and lock themselves, and bars slide down over all of the windows. Or some other power constrains the characters to remain isolated from any help or support until the *monstrum* has devoured or killed almost all of them.

Occasionally, an entire town may be islanded. Sometimes, travelers simply don't seem to notice the place as they pass, as in my *Shadow Valley,* or sometimes they pass directly through, even seeing but not truly *seeing* evidences of horror and terror and fear. In other instances, the town is effectively barricaded to defeat any attempts from outside to enter, as in King's *The Tommyknockers,* in which backwoods roads are patrolled by motile soda dispensers; or in *Under the Dome,* in which, very much along the lines of a lab-controlled experiment, the town is surrounded by an impervious dome and the individuals inside—good and bad, greedy and selfless—are left to their own devices and to the horrors that they spawn among themselves.

The isolation may be literal, as in the examples above, or it may be figurative, as in psychological horror, in which the character(s) confront internal isolation. They may not be separated physically from the larger community around them, but they are entirely alone mentally and emotionally. To those around them, they seem crazy; from within their perspectives, only they can see the creatures that attack them.

Isolation, then, may take many forms, but it must be present in one or more of them. Even when catastrophe is global, as in Wells' *The War of the Worlds* and the many subsequent film and print versions of it, attention rapidly shifts from the larger to the smaller, the intimate.

Britain suffers under the Martian bombardment in the novel, just as America does in the Hollywood manifestations, but the readers/viewers' interest almost immediately concentrates on one person, two, perhaps half a dozen as they find themselves facing the invaders alone, usually in a half-demolished house, a crumbling basement with no exit except through the Martian encampment, or even within the belly of the beast, caught and stored in a receptacle connected to the Martian's machine. In each case, the most crucial encounters occur when these characters confront and ultimately survive the depredations of the aliens.

The most obvious reason for this is that it is patently easier to empathize with individuals than with larger groups. In the 1953 film version, the audience can easily feel something when the minister is abruptly destroyed, whether it be sorrow for his death, anger at the aliens for their coldness in killing the one person who seems intent on communicating with them, or irritation at his stubbornness. But they are not invited, indeed are not allowed, to feel empathy or even much sympathy for the numbers of faceless soldiers apparently melted then disintegrated by the Martian rays.

This emphasis on one-on-one, face-to-face confrontations creates greater tension during the event and thus greater surprise and relief when the creature is defeated by the few rather than the many; in the Wells tale, by the smallest and seemingly most innocuous of creatures, bacteria. Their chances of success seem miniscule, especially when the invading creature has thus far proven indestructible, and thus the ultimate triumph becomes that much the greater.

Arranging narrative events so that the hero is somehow isolated from most or all companions, then forcing a final battle between hero and villain, is not unique to horror fiction, of course. It stems from some of the earliest recorded storytelling and finds its first full expression in the epics of antiquity. Homer's heroes consistently face each other—and occasionally rival gods—in single battle around Troy. Gilgamesh and Enkidu face and kill the forest spirit Humbaba.

Millennia later, the trope had grown and enlarged. Grendel is a monster of such strength that he can, the poet assures us, kill thirty stout warriors; no wonder is it, then, that when the hero arrives—thus isolated from his own people and culture—the poet is careful to mention that he has the strength of thirty men...and hero and monster can justly—and equally—fight each other for supremacy. Beowulf's battle with Grendel takes place at night, when the other warriors are asleep; his battle with Grendel's mother, in a cave beneath the mere; he battles the Firedrake alone while his sole companion waits in the distance. In every instance, isolation, then the confrontation with evil.

Such battles were treated lovingly by epic poets, each combatant willing not only to boast of his own bravery, courage, and strength, but also of the opponent's; the result of this tendency—epic *flyting*, as it is called—was that no matter which side prevailed, the contest itself was elevated by the renown of the participants. If the hero lost, well, look at the prowess of the villain. If the villain lost, the hero gained that much more in stature.

Genre fiction of all sorts exploits the implicit power of isolation and confrontation, from the shootout at high noon between sheriff and villain, with the townspeople carefully hidden or standing along the street, unwilling or unable to participate in the fight; to the midnight firefight between doughty detective and sleazy blackguard in an unlit, unkempt city alley.

There is a difference, however, between that final confrontation in most horror and what happens in contemporary genre fiction, and this difference actually harkens back to the origins of the image—ancient epic.

As long as the battle occurred between two humans, no matter how elevated their genealogies, the story was epic. As soon as the gods step down to intervene and become active in the battles, however, the story ceases to be strictly epic and takes on religious overtones. And we know that regardless of the immediate outcome, the hero fighting against the gods (as in the *Iliad*) or slaying one of the immortals (as in *Gilgamesh*) will be punished. It is enough that Beowulf slays both Grendel and Grendel's mother; but when he steps out of his restricted role as king and attempts to become a hero again, ignoring the threats to his people by enemies from all sides, and sets out to slay the dragon, he is doomed. He *must* die.

Things are not quite that simple for the main characters in horror fiction. Even though he, she, or they have been in some specific way set apart, isolated, the thing that they must battle is *not* (or, often, no longer) human. There is no specific equality—likeness of kind—such as we find in ancient epic and that ensures ultimate victory to (usually) the hero. Nor is the intruding creature quite god (Lovecraft's Great Old Ones to the contrary) since they can be and usually are either destroyed, defeated, or sent back from whence they came...by mere humans. And for that act, there is generally no concomitant divine punishment.

There are many exceptions to these general patterns, of course. It is possible for everyone to die, as in King's elegant short story, "The Raft."

Or for most of them to die, and the survival of the isolated few left in doubt, as in his novella, *The Mist* (the ambiguous conclusion of which I much prefer to the forced ending in the recent film version). Or for the monster simply to retreat and, presumably, return in a sequel, bigger, meaner, and more vicious than ever, as is suggested in the conclusion of *The Shining* (although *Dr. Sleep* skirts this issue by concentrating on human, though depraved, monsters).

But regardless of these exceptions, the larger pattern remains. One, two, a handful of individuals are isolated, brought to a Bad Place of some sort, and there—much to their astonishment, initial incredulousness, and ultimate horror—forced to confront something beyond their experiences, beyond their imaginations, beyond their apparent strengths.

And somehow, they defeat it.

THREE: LANGUAGE

Again and again as I write horror and write about horror, I am reminded of the simple fact that horror, like all fiction, is created by words. It is literally a 'shaping' or a 'forming,' as one might mold clay. Writers take the words that are commonplace in their society or culture and 'shape' from them something different, something new—a *nova*, as it were, from which we get the word *novel.*

As true as this is of fiction in general, there is something unusual that happens with language in horror and its (putatively) related cousins, fantasy and science fiction.

Mainstream fictions, along with most genre fictions (including romance, mystery, western, etc.) depend upon a close relationship between the story being told—and the words used to tell it—and the readers' perceived reality. Historical novels rely on data that will convince readers that this story *could have* happened in a world in which the contextual events *did* happen. Romance and western writers depend on readers connecting a specific language set—be it dialect or narrative voice—to accept wholeheartedly the fact that in their world, or in one manifestation of it, these events *might* happen.

Horror, and to a lesser degree fantasy and science fiction, works differently.

Fantasy may generate its own vocabulary to name things and events, but in doing so it nevertheless accepts the fact that at certain key points, readers must translate the events of the fantasy world into their own. Tolkien, for example, takes care to make his characters accessible to readers by insistently connecting dwarves (and Gandalf) to a body of archaic Germanic literature that provides names for each of them. The riders of Rohan gain much of their strength through their similarity to the *comitatus* of the Anglo-Saxon world; when the warriors celebrate Theoden's strength and prowess, they so do in pure Anglo-Saxon dialect. Even the chief prize of the story, the Ring, is a motif found throughout medieval literature. And when one lays Tolkien's map of Middle Earth over a map of modern Wales, there are some surprising similarities.

This is not to say that Middle Earth is just modern Earth with odd characters; it is, however, to note that the similarities, and to a lesser degree the differences, between the two worlds do more to connect them than to divide them.

Or, to take a more recent example, Piers Anthony's extensive Xanth novels gain much in their connection with our world when we understand that Xanth is—cartographically, at least—the Florida of Anthony's imagination. Even with his unique, punning names, it often takes little more than a moment of reversal for the underlying 'realities' of our world to peek through.

Science fiction is similar. On the one hand, it struggles to distance readers from the worlds it describes and develops. They are alien landscapes, other planets and other places, peopled by creatures that are *not* us. There is a problem with this, however. If the alien becomes too alien, the writer runs the risk of losing readers—without the perception that the aliens are to some extent like us, if not *us*, there can be little empathy with them, and hence, no story. No matter how oddly named the creatures, no matter how distorted their usage of language—and no matter how many scientifically-tinged words are invented to explain inventions and discoveries—the story must at some point remain at the human level.

Horror is slightly different. It depends upon readers shifting out of their own experiences and integrating themselves with a world in which the unthinkable can occur. It is crucial that readers accept, almost from the opening lines, that something beyond experience—yet still within imagination—will happen. One of my favorite opening lines comes from a story not usually classified as "horror" yet distinctly so in content and feel, Franz Kafka's "The Metamorphosis" (1915). In German it reads: "Als Gregor Samsa eines Morgens aus unruhigen Träumen erwachte, fand er sich in seinem Bett zu einem ungeheuren Ungeziefer verwandelt." A loose translation might be: "As Gregor Samsa awoke one morning from uneasy dreams, he found himself transformed in his bed into a gigantic beetle." Pure realism...until the final phrase/word. Then, abruptly, a *monstrum* enters, for which there is no explanation in the story.

In order to be more specific about what I mean, let me quote the opening lines of my novel, *The Slab*:

> It was a day made for death.
> Brittle shards from the slanting October sunset stabbed at the quiet street. Brassy gold stained shaggy lawns a murky, coppery brown. The dying light fingered naked limbs of rain-blackened elms and fruitless mulberries and peaches and skeletal jacarandas. It rested heavily on the drooping branches of the occasional valley oaks that had survived construction of the subdivision two years earlier. It tinted vibrant stucco walls not yet faded to earth-mud brown by interminable summers of suns, not yet hidden behind luxuriant passion vines or junipers or the creeping jasmine so popular in this part of Southern California. In the odd, quirky light, the Charter Oaks subdivision became an enigma of striated shadows, dead black pinioned against muted October color in the late evening of a day that had been more cloud-ridden than otherwise.

The first sentence—pretty obvious. Yet (I hope) there is more going on than just the blatant reference to death. It begins neutrally, with "It is" as subject and verb, which forces readers to wait until the end to discover *what* and *how*. Not a clear indication of horror, but a tactic designed to inculcate a certain element of suspense.

The most suggestive part of the sentence, however, is implicit in the last four words. *Death* is, again, obvious; but in attempting to construct an effective opening sentence, I added two things. First, consonance, or the repetition of consonant sounds, a kind of muted internal rhyming: *day, made, death*. Then assonance, repetition of vowels: *day, made*. The result of these interconnected sounds is that the final phrase becomes emphatic, linked, each word resonating off of the others, leading to the climactic *death*.

Second, the sentence was constructed to create a specific cadence or rhythm. It is not as superficial as a strict iambic meter, as in a poem; rather, it tries *not* to create a periodic rhythm. The first three words intentionally do not carry significant stress. A pronoun, a static verb, an article introducing the noun—the implication is that the oncoming noun will be the first important syntactic element, the thing the sentence will actually discuss: *Day*.

Day is followed by a verb-like word, *made*, that, even though relatively vague, is still more action-directed than *is*. The internal sound patterning suggests that *made* should receive the same amount of stress as *day*, which places two stressed syllables next to each other and automatically creates emphasis.

The next word, *for*, is a preposition that has as its primary function to indicate an oncoming noun...and to alert readers that the noun will be the more important of the two and will thus receive more stress. The result is three heavy stresses in four syllables, building to the strongest emphasis of all on the final word.

When taken together, all of these decisions create the following sentence: "It was a **day** **made** for **death**." It begins rapidly, the tongue sliding over the three unstressed syllables; slows in the middle, with two adjacent stressed syllables; drops on *for* and then swoops upward to hit *death* with the strongest stress of the three.

Now, one of the advantages to writing about my own sentence is that I can say all of this—five full paragraphs to discuss seven monosyllabic words—and know that everything I've said was intentional. I can't know whether it worked with every reader the way I hoped it would, but I do know that each word was selected carefully and consciously.

"Brittle shards" suggests harshness and threat in ways that a parallel phrase—"golden rays," to use a clichéd example—would not. *Slanting* is not particularly threatening, but in conjunction with the first two words, the named month, and the sentence-verb *stabbed*, the implication emerges that something might definitely be amiss. Nor should readers be surprised to discover that the action of the first chapter takes place near Halloween.

Brassy, stained, shaggy, murky, coppery (with its frequent association with blood), and *brown* continue the sense, intensified in the next line by *dying, naked, rain-blackened* (itself a riff on the previous *fingered*), *fruitless* (suggesting sterility, even though it is part of the plant's name), and, of course, *skeletal*.

For the next couple of sentences, the reader is allowed to stand back and breathe. There are even a few non-horror words to distract attention away from death and horror: *survived, vibrant, luxuriant, passion*. Then the darkness returns in the final sentences with *odd, quirky, enigma*, "striated shadows," "dead black," *pinioned, muted*, and *cloud-ridden*.

What the first two paragraphs offer, then, is the possibility of discovering in the description several underlying themes for the novel as a whole. Certainly *stabbed* will play an important part, as will *stained, dying, naked,* and *skeletal,* although the implications of the final term won't be obvious until the final chapter.

In fact, most of the key words will resonate with at least one episode in the tale that is to come, some obviously, some less so. Each element, each choice was intended to guide readers into the world of *The Slab* and begin creating the tone, the feeling, the eeriness that characterizes the house. Using nothing but words, words, words.

Chapter 6

Functions of Horror

In *Design for Thinking* (Stanford UP 1963), Albert Upton argues that language has three primary functions: communication, problem-solving, and emotional adjustment. Much of his text—a "first book in semantics"—deals with the ramifications for individual thinkers and speakers of that tripartite division and how each part influences the world the individual believes exists "out there."

In some ways, it is helpful to observe this division when considering the role(s) and function(s) of fiction and fiction-making, and for the purposes of this essay, of horror and fiction-making, since the universals Upton posits for human language as a whole—"To use language, as language, is to be human; to use it with kindness, grace, and dignity, is to be humane"—relate to several of the *whys* in writing horror. It might seem incongruous to pair "kindness, grace, and dignity" with the graphic violence implicit in *horror*, but at base the connections are valid.

COMMUNICATION:

Fiction-making—*Storytelling*—is communication of a most critical sort. It does not deal exclusively in facts; that is the role of expository prose. Nor does it deal in hypotheses and proofs; that is left to science and scientific prose.

Instead, it deals with articulating *community* itself, the web of Story that connects all individuals within a family, a society, a culture, a world. It defines, by nature, an intersection of roles, storytellers with listeners, whether they be bard chanting the *lais* of the people to an assembly of warriors or writers crafting lines to be read internally by a single reader.

It is, I think, impossible to tell a Story without an audience; the result would merely be the ramblings of a lonely mind. And it is impossible to partake of Story without a Storyteller.

The Story told through horror is not *true* in a factual, evidentiary sense. It deals, by its nature, with elements beyond those we accept as belonging to the rational world—monsters of all sorts, intrusions of supernatural (and frequently inimical) beings into our reality, transformations of humans into other-than-humans who behave, in a word, *in*-humanely.

But in a deeper sense, it is *True*. It delves into the deepest, darkest cavities of human fears and terrors, bringing them into the light where they can be asserted, assessed, vicariously experienced, and ultimately dissipated; and the result is a reaffirmation of that which constitutes community—a web of responsibility, of acting to defend others before self, of creating out of chaos a core of order and civility.

PROBLEM-SOLVING:

Storytelling involves characters in conflict; that is a fundamental definition of *plot*. By definition, then, it revolves around problem-solving, with the proviso that this problem, this set of conflicts is imposed upon a construct, an individual who does not exist outside of the story (and this holds true even for historical personages imported into stories—by virtue of incorporating them, the writer alters them to fit the purposes of the narrative).

Horror, like much genre fiction, hinges on problem-solving. In horror, the problem—or at least one manifestation of it—must be external. There is something *out there* that threatens the order, the stability, the existence of a community, no matter how few individuals make up that group. It is something *other*; therefore, the normal means of dealing with it might not work. It might not respond to the laws of nature as we understand them; it might not die when we wield our most fearful weapons (remember Wells' Martians); it might only seem destroyed when in fact it merely lies fallow for a time, to rise again with greater determination, anger, and power. And for the characters—the community—to fail to destroy it is for that community to die.

This is perhaps why death is so central to horror. The nature of the creature, the *other*, may in fact be nearly irrelevant; what counts is how close the community comes to total destruction and the ingenuity brought to bear by its members (through the mediation of the Storyteller) to survive. The more horror, terror, and death, the closer readers come—again vicariously—to experiencing dissolution of self and community.

The only hope is to destroy the *other*. And sometimes, particularly in contemporary fiction that reflects a world without a clear sense of humane community, even that hope fails. The Zombie Apocalypse spreads and the old world dies.

EMOTIONAL ADJUSTMENT:

Writers do not work in a vacuum. They reflect—sometimes refract—the world around them, its urgencies, its most compelling concerns. The greatest writers incorporate their times into their works so seamlessly that sometimes it is difficult separate the two; much that we know, and perhaps all that we *need* to know of the Greek Heroic Age, comes from the pages of Homer, just as the roots of Anglo-Saxon culture are revealed in the *Beowulf.*

This is not to claim that all horror writers are great enough to speak fluently for our times, although some certainly touch upon deep-set fears that have characterized the past decades. In certain ways, Stephen King is a chronicler of our age, the final quarter of the twentieth and the first decades of the twenty-first centuries. His stories encompass the breakdown of the traditional family, the collapse of agrarian communities into the survival of individuals, the growth of an ever more intrusive government into the lives of its citizens, the increasing inability of schools to adequately prepare children for their futures, the aggrandizing of industry and the media until they control what individuals think and believe...or try to. And all through the mediation of monsters—aliens, vampires, werewolves, demons, dark men of all descriptions and powers.

As a group, however, horror writers do concentrate on the most difficult questions—What lies beyond the darkness of fear, terror, and bleak imagination? Is there any hope for the world as we know it? Or will it take an apocalypse of some form—be it zombies, or plague, or unbridled selfishness and greed—to create order out of chaos.

In doing so, the writer serves dual functions. One is to make sense of things for readers by offering them a few hours inside a world where events and situations are demonstrably much worse than in the world we know. Readers follow characters, confront horrors beyond description, suffer pain and loss and anguish, and finally emerge unscathed physically but stronger perhaps for having empathized with people who never existed outside of the readers' imaginations and the writer's words.

The second is emotional adjustment *for* the writer. Stephen King might momentarily fear for his children's safety, and out of that moment comes *Pet Sematary*. In the novel the child dies; in the writer's world, the worst has been faced...and endured. In my novel *The Slab*, a number of characters confront the horrors of an overtly evil house; my family and I lived in the house for twenty-five years, and through the process of making realities into fictions (and getting my revenge on the house and its original builder), I was able to re-establish a certain equilibrium in my life.

Writing as emotional adjustment.

Communication; problem-solving; and emotional adjustment— these are as fundamental to horror and to all fictions as they are to language itself. After all, what is horror—what is Storytelling—but the manipulation of language to influence the audience.

Chapter 7

On Modes

We often speak and write about *genres* in literature. Writers are aware of the multiple possibilities for telling stories—comedy, tragedy, epic, lyric, mythopoeic, romance, satire—and of the sub-divisions that allow for an almost infinite array of treatments—western, romance (the rather specialized booksellers' category rather than the larger, more philosophically oriented approach to literature), mystery, detective, spy, thriller, action-adventure, supernatural, science fiction, fantasy, horror, and others. And, of course, any particular story might contain elements of more than one sub-set, as in the cross-generic novels developed by Dean Koontz and others over the past decades.

Because there is so much overlap among genres—even among the larger divisions, as in tragicomedy—it becomes difficult to define precisely what constitutes one or the other...and that is perhaps to the good. One characteristic of genres is that they tend to accumulate conventions over time, so that eventually they run the risk of becoming hidebound, inadaptable to shifts in cultures and societies. And when that happens, the genre must either change or die.

When, in 1667, John Milton published the first edition of his verse-epic *Paradise Lost,* his was a lone voice speaking from the defeat of the Commonwealth and the Restoration of Monarchy, as well as from his personal tragedies, including blindness. He had been sentenced to death, and as far as most of his peers were concerned, he was obsolete, a dimly remembered relic of a fanatical and thoroughly distasteful past.

By the time the second edition was published in 1674, however, *Paradise Lost* was already being hailed as a classic, as the premier epic in the English language. From that moment on, so rigidly was the genre defined by the conventions demonstrated in Milton's poem that epic as literary form stagnated for nearly a century and a half, occasionally making a valiant effort at rejuvenation as mock-epic, before essentially passing out of existence. In its place rose the novel.

Other genres have suffered from the same kind of lithification, while still others have proven remarkably flexible, shifting foci and subtly altering characters, plots, and landscapes as readers' tastes change. *Noir* film and fiction flourished in the 1940s and 1950s, for example, but still survives as the basis for modern, contemporary treatments.

What have remained essentially unchanged over millennia, however, are two larger super-categories or *modes*, fundamentally unchanged since antiquity, even though each at one time or another had encompassed most of the available genres and sub-genres.

Put simply, the modes are prose and verse.

In ancient Greece, history could be written in either mode without damaging its historicity; epic could be written as prose or verse without denigrating the larger-than-life actions of the epic hero. For a number of centuries, the two modes were essentially interchangeable. Only as civilization approached the modern era did a line appear dividing the two. *This* subject matter is 'true'; therefore it must be related in prose. *That* subject matter is 'fantasy,' or un-truth; it must be told in verse.

We now live in a time when prose is triumphant. Verse, while still important to some, has been largely relegated to the back burner.

Having written well over one hundred books, including fiction, non-fiction, bibliographies, and verse; hundreds of individual chapters, articles, and reviews; and nearly 2,500 poems, long and short—I have discovered over the years that the basis of effective writing does not alter greatly from one mode to the other.

Oh, each specific kind of writing carries with it equally specific conventions that must be followed. A Ph.D. dissertation does not look or sound like a young-adult short story. A haiku requires different care in word selection than does a book-length literary study. A science-fiction novel has different requirements for landscape and characterization than does a 6,500-line Miltonic epic.

But at ground, the *essence* of effective writing is remarkably consistent. A strong sentence is a strong sentence, regardless of whether it appears in a novel, a book review, or a narrative poem. A powerful cadence is powerful regardless of whether it occurs in prose or in verse.

When I teach my workshop on writing poetry, I often begin with two questions: 1) What is poetry? and 2) How does it differ from prose?

Perhaps the best way for readers of the present study to explore the answer(s) to the first is to look into my earlier writing book, *The Art and Craft of Poetry: Twenty Exercises Toward Mastery* (2009), initial versions of which served for nearly twenty years as the text for my intermediate poetry course at Pepperdine University. It does not offer a single, simplified definition, but it does analyze the many characteristics of verse and how to use them effectively.

The answer to the second question is both more and less complicated. In fact, the question itself misleads, implying as it does a large watershed between the two, so that one might say definitively "this is prose" and "that is verse."

When asked to articulate differences, students most often speak in generalized terms. "Poetry uses rhythm." "Poetry uses music—that is, sound patterns, like rhyme, alliteration, and assonance." "Poetry stirs the emotions." "Poetry depends on images." And a number of other, similar answers.

They tend to get frustrated when I dutifully write the suggestion on the whiteboard, then shake my head and say, "No, that's not it."

Prose, you see, does all of the things listed above. Great prose can be rhythmical, as in multiple passages from Tolkien's *The Lord of the Rings*. It can use all of the sound patterns of poetry, often to great effect. It can stir emotions—I am reminded of the anecdote in which Abraham Lincoln, upon being introduced to Harriet Beecher Stowe, author of *Uncle Tom's Cabin*, is supposed to have greeted her as the "little lady that started the Civil War." Her novel certainly stirred emotions, as have dozens of novels since. Effective prose uses images as well, inviting readers to 'see' people, places, and things they have never actually seen and probably never will. This, by the way, was one of the great drawing points of late-Victorian fiction—it *showed* the rising middle class and increasingly literate lower class a world they would never inhabit but in which they were avidly interested.

No, each time I asked those two questions, the discussion might go along for ten, fifteen, twenty minutes before either someone in the group, desperate to put an end to the torture, makes what seems a wild suggestion so I will give up and tell them: In prose, lines go all the way to the right-hand margin; in poetry, they do not.

In other words, *nothing* separates the two modes except the poet's absolute say in where words appear on the page. A poet might, for example, specify that three words appear directly beneath each other in the text. Or that a certain amount of white space—emptiness, to the non-poetic mind—must be allotted between one line and the next. If the line consists of three words, or two, or one, the editor and publisher must accept that decision.

Prose works differently. By and large, novelists cannot dictate word placement to publishers; and even if they could, what would happen when a hardcover text was republished as a mass-market paperback, or a trade paperback? The page sizes differ radically. It would be impossible for a novelist to say to a publisher, "It is crucial for the thematic development of my story that the word *freedom* appear as the second to the last word on page seventy-six." Good luck.

(Incidentally, poets also generally have the last word in titles; heaven help the editor who unilaterally decides on something different. Novelists, on the other hand, have essentially no say; if the publisher chooses to change it, it is changed.)

The point of all of this is to suggest that in prose as in verse, the conventions surrounding literary techniques and literary devices are fundamentally the same. It is just that verse uses the figures (metaphor, simile, etc.) and rhythms (meter, rhyme) more consciously and more frequently. Among the essays in this collection, readers will find some specifically oriented toward prose, other specifically toward verse. The fundamental arguments in every one, however, can be applied to either mode of writing.

Chapter 8

An Interview About Stephen King—Questions by Erin Frey

[One of the great pleasures of being a professor is that occasionally students email me for information. Sometimes they are in college, even once in a while in graduate school, but for me the most gratifying requests come from high school students, often juniors confronting their first formal research project.

I received one such request the other day, this one from Erin Frey, a student at Ursuline Academy in Cincinnati, Ohio. I enjoyed responding to her questions and, with her permission, am here reprinting the email interview.]

1. In your opinion do you think Stephen King's work changed after his accident, and/or just over time?

Of course an accident as severe as King's would have a massive impact on a writer's perspective. *From a Buick 8* (2003), the various episodes of *Kingdom Hospital* (2004), and *Duma Key* (2008), for example, could probably not have been written as they are if he had not suffered a life-altering, near-death experience. The two novels explore questions of causality—why do bad things happen to good people?—and both end ambiguously. In fact, *Buick* received a good deal of flak for *not* explaining what the 'monster' was or where it came from, just as the book's central character gave his friends and co-workers flak for not being able to explain precisely what the car *was* or, more importantly, why his father had been killed. One point of that novel is simply that not all stories have easy, readily available resolutions...just as life is not always easy to understand.

At the same time, it would be naïve to suggest that everything he has written in the past decade or so is overshadowed by his experience. He has always been willing to explore new directions, and several recent books seem as much logical developments as responses to his injury. *11/22/63* (more about this one later), for example, does not seem anywhere near as dependent upon his recovery as do the other things just mentioned.

2. Many articles say that Stephen King isn't taken seriously as an author, why is that?

The quick and easy (and therefore suspect) answer is simply that he makes too much money. Anyone whose books sell as many copies as King's do must be simply pandering to the lowest taste of the common public. Hence, his book can't be any good and he doesn't deserve any serious attention.

I think the case is more complicated than that, although his popularity—and the fact that he insists upon writing long, long books—has always worked against him. His choice of genre is problematical: horror, it is argued, is among the basest of sub-literary forms, depending upon buckets of blood coupled with gruesome beasts and, usually, a fair dose of gratuitous sex. In the hands of many writers, horror can become stridently sub-literary, but King is not one of them. His best books acknowledge that evil exists, that good might not always overcome it, that people are flawed—and they are overtly horrific. Ironically, the first book that garnered praise from "establishment" reviewers, *Gerald's Game,* in my view turned its back on everything King stood for as a writer and became little more than a propaganda piece for women's rights, its theme being essentially that all men, with no exceptions, are pond scum.

In addition, he is enormously prolific. Many mainstream critics and writers—those who take it upon themselves to elevate works as "serious literature" or brand them as merely "genre fiction"—prefer their authors safely dead. That way, there will be no new books to upset long thought out literary theories of what the author was *really* trying to say or, worse, no responses from the writer explaining in no uncertain terms why the *critic* is wrong. It is much easier to deal with the dead. Academicians can plan their class lectures knowing that they won't actually have to read new books each year; they can prepare tests that can be administered each term; and everyone is happy. Except the dead author.

Actually, King has moved beyond this point to some degree. Of all explicitly horror writers, he was the first—and perhaps still the only one—to gain a fair degree of critical respect. My bibliography of King's works, *Horror Plum'd,* contains over 3,000 entries, many of them books and articles about, and reviews of, King's writing. I will probably never write the second volume, which would have listed secondary materials only, because it would be too long to publish. I have published a dozen books on King, plus scores of articles and reviews, and I am only one of the many academics now interested in him.

So perhaps the best and most honest answer is that many of those articles are out of date or fail to recognize the extent to which King altered the face of late-20th-century publishing. In many ways, he speaks for most of the issues that Americans have contended with over the past four decades, and does so eloquently, passionately, and—most of all—entertainingly. What could be more "serious" than that?

3. What do you think is his best work and why?

You do realize that the question is roughly equivalent to asking a parent, "Which is your favorite child?" So I'm not going to answer it as written. Instead, I'm going to suggest several titles that are for one reason or another exceptional.

The Shining—the most teachable of his novels. He uses it to demonstrate in his own way that horror can be as 'literary' as literary fiction, that the techniques of mainstream fiction, including allusion to the great works of literature, can be as much a support in scary stories as they are in *New Yorker* articles. It is a strong story that stands up well over time; I don't know how many times I've read it, and each time it is as powerful as the last.

The Stand—here we have two versions of the same story, the original published in 1978 and the "complete and unexpurgated" version published in 1990. King explains that, primarily for financial reasons, his publisher was initially unwilling to release the entire manuscript and that he himself oversaw the excision of about 400 pages. When the novel was re-released twelve years later (when there was no doubt that it would recoup whatever the publisher charged for it), he restored the excisions and updated the book to the 1990s. When we read both closely, I think we get some fascinating insights into his thinking as an author, into his growth and maturity as a writer, and into his awareness of audience. I wrote an essay on the two books, "Considering the *Stands*," which I included in *Toward Other Worlds: Perspectives on John Milton, C.S.*

Lewis, Stephen King, Orson Scott Card, and Others (2010) that goes into far greater detail on the differences between the two versions than I can do here.

The Talisman—simply a crackin' great story. Powerful central character; powerful and memorable villains; powerful settings, whether in this world or in The Territories; masterful use of allusions to Twain, Tolkien, Lewis, and others. All in all a fine novel, certainly in my estimation one of the best collaborations by two major writers. I still enjoy going back to it.

The Dark Tower series—King's most ambitious work, and perhaps among the most ambitious pieces of storytelling in the English language. It is a fantasy/science-fiction/horror/action-adventure/Western/quest/epic piece of mythmaking that ultimately has as its goal nothing less than creating webs of meaning and interlocking storytelling among eight massive novels and perhaps twenty of his other novels. There is, I think, nothing else like it in American literature.

It—one of my favorites because it captures in many ways *my* childhood in 1957-1958, although happily I did not have to deal with a manic clown or labyrinthine sewers. It is long (he sent me the typescript a couple of months before the novel was released, along with a letter in which he noted that he had learned a lesson about writing stories that, when reduced to paper, were bigger than his own head); complex in structure, narrative design, and theme; it reduces much of what he had said about the perils of childhood in previous books to a more understandable form, then juxtaposes that perfectly with parallel passages about the perils of adulthood in the late 1980s. Again, this is one that I read and re-read; my original paperback copy long ago fell apart from sheer wear.

4. Worst work?

For me, as indicated above, it is *Gerald's Game*. When I first read it, I was dismayed by the overt thematic manipulations; King had already said many of the same things in earlier novels but had done so without abrogating his primary role as storyteller. That is, he has always spoken about his social, political, and cultural beliefs in his novels *through* the story; in *Gerald's Game,* they essentially supplant the story.

A few years ago, wondering if I had been unduly harsh in that initial assessment, I re-read the book.

I hadn't been.

5. Why do you think he wrote *11/22/63*, since it is historical fiction and is different from his usual genre?

One of the interesting things about King's best novels is that they frequently refuse to be slotted into a nice, neat genre classification (something that originated, by the way, with booksellers wanting to figure out where to put books on the shelves). *The Stand,* for example—is it science fiction, since it deals with the results of technological tinkering with viruses; or is it fantasy, since it incorporates dream-visions and super-normal events; or is it horror, since it certainly revels in blood and gore as it slaughters 99+ percent of the human population? The answer is: yes. It is, at various points, all three.

From this perspective, *11/22/63* isn't that much of an anomaly. Is it historical fiction: to a degree, yes; but historical fiction with a strong dose of time-travel and alternate-history (science fiction); of horror and death; even touches of whimsy and fantasy. Instead of wondering where it fits generically, it might be easiest to say that it is simply Stephen King reliving one of the seminal events of his life—as it was of mine. Having lived through the assassination of JFK and its aftermath, and having seen the consequences a single death could have for society, I can understand his need to ask "What if?"

6. In most of the works I have read there is a character that relates to King or someone in his life. Why does he do this?

I'm not sure that all authors don't do this to some extent; after all, we are not only telling stories when we write, we are looking into ourselves for details, memories, events that can be altered, tailored to fit the story and make it stronger. Sometimes King does this more overtly than many authors; sometimes, I think, it sneaks up on him.

I remember watching an interview with King just after *Stand By Me* was released and, in the middle of making a point about the film, he suddenly stopped, looked a bit confused, and then continued to explain that he had just—at that moment, in fact—remembered that as a boy he and a friend had been playing along a train track, and his friend had been killed by a passing train! King looked authentically shocked as he spoke, perhaps because he realized for the first time that "The Body" was about him in more ways than he consciously knew.

I had a similar experience when reading a paper at a Science-Fiction/Fantasy conference. I was talking about Christ-figures in a series of stories, and the author happened to be in the room. I had just met him a few minutes before the session began, although we had been corresponding for several years. So I was understandably concerned when all of a sudden, his head jerked up and he looked at me like I had said something totally unacceptable—or unbelievable—about the stories.

When I spoke with him after the session, he said that he had written those stories perhaps half a decade before and had only just understood, as I was talking about symbolism in them, that every story I had mentioned was actually about his youngest son, who had been born severely disabled and who would never walk or talk.

My friend had written the stories; surely he should have known how much of himself he was putting into them. But he didn't.

In my own novels, I know when I put myself or my thoughts into a character's words…sometimes. Yet again, I was listening to one of them, *The Slab,* on CD just after the audio version was released. I nodded along, recognizing those bits and pieces as the story unfolded and then—*wham!*—something I did not even remember putting into the story struck me as true…about me.

So the answer to your question, then, is: he does it because he is a storyteller and a good storyteller does not try to divorce self from tale. Sometimes King is overt; a character named 'Stephen King' appears in *The Dark Tower* series, for example, who looks and acts a lot like the 'real' King. But I think it's important to remember that even when he—or any author—is this overt, the *character* is still that: a character invented by the author to serve a purpose in a fiction. In this case, the character is an invented version of what King considered himself to be—or at least an approximation of it—when he wrote that story. I don't think that even he would say that 'Stephen King' the character is exactly the same as 'Stephen King' the writer…who is not exactly the same as 'Stephen King' the father or 'Stephen King' the husband.

We all play different roles in our lives. Writers simply have the opportunity to play more of them than many other people.

7. Describe King's ability to set time and use local color.

Interesting, and difficult to answer. My best response would be to begin with "I think…."

I think King is blessed/cursed with a unique memory that fits perfectly with his unique imagination. In his stories, he can evoke a time and a place with a single word, a single phrase, often using what has been called his "brand-name technique." He knows precisely what to refer to in order to evoke a warm summer afternoon in a small mid-western town—what brand of car would drive by, what treats neighbor kids might be eating, what movie a typical boy might have seen in the local theater the night before…and I think he can do this because he remembers so well. If his setting is the late 1950s and early 1960s, I think he simply *remembers* that time, that place (whichever one he is using) so precisely that he re-creates it nearly perfectly. Occasionally he makes a mistake, which is one reason I think he relies on memory rather than meticulous research.

I am almost the same age as King, plus or minus a year. I lived in a fairly rural community until the mid-1960s, although not in New England. When he tells me that a place looks this way, or smells that way, or tastes yet another way, I can search my memory (and for me it is a search) and find a parallel moment in my life and say, "Yup, he nailed that!"

With more recent settings and times, he does exactly the same thing. He has the uncanny ability to suggest a taste, a sound, a feel, and suddenly we are there with him.

Or perhaps it is just magic.

8. How did you get involved in Stephen King's work?

For that, I owe a huge debt of gratitude to a student at Pepperdine University. Sometime around 1983, I taught a summer course on "Myth, Fantasy, and Science Fiction" (one of the earliest such courses taught at a major university and the first taught at Pepperdine). After class one day, a student asked me why I hadn't included Stephen King on the reading list; my answer was simply that I hadn't read anything by him.

My student suggested *The Dead Zone* as a starting point. I went home that afternoon, bought a copy, read it, and spent the rest of the summer reading everything I could find by King…and Dean R. Koontz, Robert R. McCammon, Ramsey Campbell, and other horror writers. By the end of the summer, I was a convert. Just about two years later, I published my first King study, *Stephen King as Richard Bachman*. And just kept reading and writing. *SKRB* was recently updated to include an essay on *The Regulators* and is now available as *Stephen King is Richard Bachman*.

9. I loved *On Writing: A Memoir of the Craft*. Have you read that? Do you think he will write any more nonfiction?

King has already written an enormous amount of non-fiction, beginning as a student at the University of Maine, Orono, when he published a weekly column in the school newspaper, and continuing to now. He wrote a significant study of horror fiction, *Danse Macabre* (1981) that more or less established the guidelines for the next generation of discourse about horror in writing, in film-making, in comics, and elsewhere. People talking about the genre still use as a starting point his discussion of fear, terror, and horror and how they relate.

He has also published article after article on any number of subjects—baseball, politics, academia (and its treatment of genre fiction), and most recently gun control—and has never been afraid to voice his opinions. *On Writing* is the latest book, perhaps, but I would not be surprised if he had more to say about the subject.

10. Is there anything else you would like me to include about Stephen King, your work, or anything else?

Just thank you for the chance to wander through thoughts and memories of thirty years of engagement with a wonderful storyteller. Just writing about the novels and stories reminds me how much I enjoyed each when I first encountered it, and how much pleasure they have given me in re-reading over the years. I owe King a debt of gratitude not only for his own stories but for many of my own that wouldn't have been written without his example: *The House Beyond the Hill, The Slab, Static!, Shadow Valley,* especially. Thanks for the opportunity to express that gratitude.

Chapter 9

Integrity in Writing

This is not a review of Stephen King's novel *11/22/63*, although there might be a review forthcoming eventually.

Instead, this is a meditation on writing, triggered by the first part of that novel, "The Janitor's Father."

In the opening pages, King's narrator recounts reading essays from a high school Adult Education class he is teaching. Essentially, the task is mind-numbing...an experience perhaps all composition instructors have shared to one degree or another.

Then he comes across one written by the lame janitor at the school— and is stunned. The piece is misspelled, grammatically inept, mechanically flawed in just about every way possible.

And he gives it an "A," then adds a "+" for good measure.

And in doing so, changes his life.

I was startled by that introduction, not because I had any preconceptions as to how King would enter the world of his narrative but rather because I had once received *that essay,* or one so nearly like it that the differences seem inconsequential.

I was teaching Freshman Composition as a teaching assistant and graduate student at the University of California, Riverside. The year must have been 1974 or 1975—I know it was my first or second year in the classroom, at any rate. I had assigned as a topic "Discuss the most important event in your life."

Almost immediately after stating the topic, I knew that it was a mistake. From the back row came a tentative whisper, "What if it hasn't happened yet?" I stifled the impulse to respond, "Are you planning something for tonight?" and instead modified the assignment to "an" important event.

A week later, the essays arrived on my desk. And, much like King's high school teacher, I began wading through a stack of essays written by the book. The events might have once been important to the students, but the papers succeeded in demonstrating that, after all, the students really didn't *care* about what had happened. The writing was flat, tedious, and largely passive; the unstated purpose in all of the essays was to get the onerous task over with, get a decent grade, and get out of Freshman Composition as quickly as possible.

In most cases, it seemed that I could have assigned a grade—a safe "C"—to each of the papers, walked into class on Monday, flung the essays into the air...and whatever paper the students grabbed would do them as much good as my giving them the ones they had actually written.

Then...then I came across *the essay*.

It was far from flawless. Paragraphics were sloppy. More sentences were run-ons than were not, and the ones that weren't were comma splices. Spelling was nothing exceptional, about what one might expect of first-semester college students in the U.C. system back then. Grammar was spotty but the sentences were readable.

I gave the essay an "A." I probably would have added the "+" but at that time, UCR didn't recognize such a mark. The reasons for my grade were simple.

Almost as simple as the narrative itself.

The writer's older brother had just graduated from high school with honors and had received a scholarship to a local university. He would be the first one in the family to attend college. The family was having a party to celebrate and had run out of soda. He offered to go to the corner store to buy more. The writer followed, lagging behind slightly, and so was half hidden by bushes when three boys stepped out from behind the corner of the store and stabbed the brother to death.

The brother had been a drug-runner but had turned his back on his former colleagues and straightened his life around. They didn't like it.

So they killed him.

I later found out from the writer that this essay had been her first attempt to articulate her feelings about what had happened, her emotions at the sight of the murder, her fright, her fear, her horror.

I handed the graded essays back at the end of class that Monday...all except one. I requested that the writer stay behind for a few minutes; the paper was too precious to merely drop on her desk in passing. We talked for a long while, more about the experience than about the essay, then I asked her permission to reproduce the essay, without names, and hand it out to the class.

She graciously agreed, and the next class meeting we had a long discussion about rules of composition, conventions of punctuation and spelling, requirements of sentence structure...and when it was all right to ignore them.

That might have been the first time I truly understood what one of my undergraduate professors had said about language, that one of its primary purposes was emotional adjustment. The essay was far from perfect, yet it *was* perfect. The run-ons and comma-splices gave it a breathless, hurried sense, as if the writer still could not believe what had happened and wanted to get through re-living the experience in words as quickly as possible. The occasional mechanical wobbles intensified the emotional value of her words, her sentences. And the fact of its very existence was a tribute to the courage and strength the writer admired in her brother and was demonstrating in her own actions. She had overcome something horrendous, she had completed high school in spite of her fears, and *she* was now the first in her family attending college.

From then on, I taught English composition pretty much the way I was expected to. I had the students buy the required texts, although I frequently ignored the books as much as relied on them. If the students did the reading, their writing would show it; if not, well, they were adults and capable of choosing for themselves. I assiduously marked errors, at first with a red pen, then later with a pencil, to suggest that many of the things I noted might not be all that terrible.

But always I kept my eyes open for other essays like that one.

I found a few. Not all were as terrible in content as that first one. Some committed "errors" because of excitement, or enthusiasm. I even found a few cases in my poetry classes where students were carried away by the power of words and didn't actually write in perfect iambic pentameter as the assignment requested. Occasionally, I wrote "This one is an 'A'—but don't do this to me again" on the bottom of a paper whose author, I hoped, would understand what I meant.

It is now almost forty years since I read *that essay*. In important ways, it determined much about my approach to teaching, to writing, to poetry, and to life. Re-living that experience through the eyes of Stephen King's high school teacher reminded me how much I owed to that long-ago student, who committed an act of courage beyond anything her classmates could have understood (at least in so far as their run-of-the-mill essays might have indicated). It reminded me of why I loved teaching, why I love writing, why writing is important—to me and to anyone who discovers its secrets.

Chapter 10

On a Dark and Narrow Way

It's a pleasure writing something about dark poetry[2] rather than the more restrictive horror poetry, for the simple reason that I've only been writing horror poetry for perhaps the past fifteen years or so but dark poetry for most of my creative life.

For me, the distinction between the two is fluid and frequently depends upon my purposes and audiences. I consider the pastiches I've done of Lovecraft and Poe (such poems as "The Dweller on the Edge of Day," "Night's Plutonian Shore," and "The House Beyond the Field") primarily as horror for the simple reason that they are based on specific images, characters, or landscapes already made accessible by the earlier authors. The context—in the case of all three poems, *In Darkness Drawn*, a chapbook distributed at World HorrorCon 2008—impelled me to focus on creating a certain texture through words and structures.

Because the things—the *things*—the poems talked about do not exist (the contemporary hubbub about the imminent zombie apocalypse notwithstanding), they seemed most effective when the verse forms were familiar to readers, as *real* as possible. In each case, I selected stanzaic, metered verse with a carefully chosen rhyme scheme as a vehicle, first to introduce readers into the world of poetry, in which data and facts are secondary to image and emotion; and then into a world of horror, in which the primary images have no direct correspondent in objective experience. The intent was to immerse readers comfortably into one imaginative universe before exploring a second.

---

[2] Some time ago, Marge Simon asked me if I would be interested in writing an article on dark poetry for her column in the *Newsletter of the Horror Writers Association*. I gladly obliged, and the article subsequently appeared in the September 2012 issue.

Because of the two-step distancing in horror poetry (and for that matter, in science fiction, fantasy, and horror as genres) most of my distinctively horror poems are narrative—either overtly, as they introduce a character and take him/her/it through a narrowly limited situation; or covertly if the character is not directly identified but its outré nature is implied, as in "The Dweller on the Edge of Day."

The third element that helps me identify horror poetry is language. In a very real sense, horror literature of any sort depends more obviously on manipulation of language than do other forms. As an exercise to prove the point, I gave a presentation at World HorrorCon 2012 in which I reproduced a paragraph from Lovecraft's "The Picture in the House"—admittedly prose but of a texture and rhythmic intensity that almost approaches poetry. In the original, the second paragraph reads:

> Most horrible of all sights are the little unpainted wooden houses remote from travelled ways, usually squatted upon some damp, grassy slope or leaning against some gigantic outcropping of rock. Two hundred years and more they have leaned or squatted there, while the vines have crawled and the trees have swelled and spread. They are almost hidden now in lawless luxuriances of green and guardian shrouds of shadow; but the small-paned windows still stare shockingly, as if blinking through a lethal stupor which wards off madness by dulling the memory of unutterable things.

Specific words stand out, immediately identifying the passage as horror, even though it just describes a simple landscape: *horrible, remote, travelled, squatted, gigantic, squatted* (as if once were not enough), *crawled, swelled, lawless, luxuriances, shrouds, shockingly, lethal, stupor, madness, unutterable, things.*

Then, to demonstrate how critical this vocabulary is to the story, I 'rewrote' the paragraph, toning things down a bit:

> The most disagreeable sights of all are the small weathered wooden cottages far from the highways, usually set on some grassy hill or angled against large boulders. For more than two centuries, they have sat there, while foliage has spread and trees have grown larger and larger. Now they are almost screened in by an

unfarmed bounty of green and shadows that seems to supervise them; but the small-paned windows still watch fearfully, as if looking askance through a disinterest that keeps mental instability away by putting the damper on reminders of things that are too unpleasant even to talk about.

The technical difference is that my version takes longer by about ten words, but in atmosphere, tone, feeling, adumbration, the two passages are light-years apart. Lovecraft without his distinctive language, both in his prose and in his verse, would be tedious, flat, and boring. His language—even when he overdoes certain words like *eldritch* and *rugose*—simply *is* his horror.

Much the same goes for my horror poetry. Language is paramount; crosscurrents of rhythm and sound pattern highlight key words that *by themselves* unmistakably indicate genre. Beneath the layers of that language, vampires and werewolves and "unutterable things" may wander, but the verbal texture remains paramount.

My *dark poetry* is something quite different. These are poems that emerge from within in ways that verses about creatures and monsters— which quite frequently end up comic, as in the limericks in *A Verse to Horrors: An Abecedary of Monsters and the Monstrous*—never can. Whenever I write about literary horrors, I am constantly aware of myself as *vates*, as *maker*, as creator of things that do not exist but that I wish to bring momentarily into animation. The act is, if you will, *artificial* in the extreme.

My dark poetry, however, is organic, uninhibited, frequently unanticipated. Perhaps the best examples are the verses that compose *The Warren Poems* (in *Matrix—Echoes of Growing Up West*, 2010). They were originally composed twenty-some years ago during the year or so following my father's death and incorporated into a small-press edition of verses, *Matrix—Poems*, in 1995.

To this day, I consider them among the most 'horrific' things I've written, not because they flaunt vampires and demons and zombies but because now, from the perspective of two decades, I cannot conceive of having survived being the person who wrote them.

At the time, although I did not know it then and would not know it for another half decade, I was undergoing a severe depressive episode coincident with my father's death. Our house was literally falling apart around us; the rear wall had separated from the foundation by a good four inches along the entire back, and we could see daylight between the wall and the ceiling in our bedroom. I was diagnosed with marginal diabetes, but I had seen the toll the disease had taken on my father and was perhaps overly concerned with my own health. I was progressively getting deafer, although the time when I would need double hearing aids was still in the future. I could barely stand to be in the same room with my family because I either could not understand what they were saying or they had to yell at me to get my attention...which made my anger worse. And for two or three years, I had become increasingly aware of incessant ringings, janglings, hissings, boomings, and assorted other internal sounds.

During that time, I was convinced that I was going crazy. When I asked a doctor what I could do about...well, about *everything* but especially about the noises, he responded blandly, "It's called tinnitus. Live with it."

Then my father died.

When I started on *The Warren Poems*, it was as therapy, although I would not have put it quite that way. I simply *had* to write them. The process was simple. I took a key moment in my life, when things seemed particularly difficult or unsettled, transferred that moment to a poor fellow named (intentionally) "Warren," then made his life a living hell. In real life, I was threatened with molestation; in Warren's life, it happened. The theory was that if Warren could make it through to the end of the poem, I could survive as well.

This went on for nineteen poems; then I wrote the final one: "Warren Says Farewell to His Father's Ghost."

And the need for Warren disappeared.

I am grateful to Warren for many things, not the least for actually keeping me sane during a difficult year. But I am also grateful to him for forcing me to look back at my writing—especially my poetry—and realize how essentially *dark* nearly everything I had written was. I even wrote a Christmas program one year for our church; after she read it, my wife looked at me and said, "You can't perform this in church!" It was too dark even for her. And it has never been performed.

Warren also gave me perspective when, a few years after *Matrix* was published, I was diagnosed with clinical bipolarism extending back as far as my teen years. No one—least of all I—knew about the problem until I was in my forties. That's a long time to live with darkness, especially under the assumption that *everyone else* had the same feelings, the same emotions, the same driving needs...but that *they* were strong enough to bear up under them. Only I was weak enough to succumb. *The*

Warren Poems and subsequent "mainstream" pieces became ways of understanding my own darkness by transferring it outside of me, examining it, exploring, exploiting it, and in the process creating (I hope) art.

When I finally began writing about horror—especially my books on Stephen King—and then writing horror itself, the transition was easy. Technically, my horror poetry deals with a more controlled vocabulary, with more precisely determined rhythms and sounds; but essentially there is not that great a difference between it and my non-horror poetry.

Ghosties and ghoulies and long-legged beasties can be fun; battling the darkness is not.

* * * * * * * * * *

...Is Death

Dreams brought me to this catacomb—
Dank necropolis breathing heavy rot
Through sable soil moldering with age.

Dreams unspeakable—drawn from ancient tomes,
Dark whisperings—brought me here. I wait, caught
Between sleep and madness—in this close cage.

All around they rise, creatures of the gloom,
Twisted, tortured, skeletal—they rise from plots
Of creviced marble, fingers crooked with rage.

In dim-light, pale bones gleam like polished chrome,
Ragged cerecloths counterfeit hangman's knots—
Fell accoutrements aching for a stage.

They shamble, scuff beneath an arcing dome
Of root-clogged earth, haunted by worms and clots
Of new-dead flesh, corruption's equipage.

I back into a ravaged, crumbled combe,
Hope to hide from their contempt, their quick hot
Gasps of hatred, their murderous rampage.

In dream, this fearful darkness felt like home,
Familiar, comforting—yet now, distraught,
I feel it smothering, black doom's presage.

Closer—they surge across bedeviled loam—
I shudder, scream— my tears avail me naught—
My cursed dreams gape...I've earned their deathly wage—

—*In the Void: Poems of Science Fiction, Myth and Fantasy, and Horror*
(Borgo Press, 2009): 107.

"NIGHT'S PLUTONIAN SHORE"

"Tell me what thy lordly name is..."
—Edgar Allan Poe, "The Raven"

Some say the way is Stygian dark,
Cerberic, fraught with harms,
Phlegethonic, its wild flames stark,
Impervious to spoken charms,
Impregnable to arms.

They tell of wells of bleak dismay
Assaulting pilgrims' souls,
Of horrors waiting to betray,
Demand their fill of terror's tolls
Like gnarled, vicious trolls.

But worse—the curse of nival ways,
Of palely vapid streams,
Hung low with heavy-frosted bays
Where woad and madder—ghastly gleams—
Choke paths to darker dreams;

Where ash-streams clash with frozen stones;
Where melancholy dwells;
Where time-lost souls proceed with groans
To hidden, nightmare-ridden cells,
To endure prodigious hells.

—*In the Void: Poems of Science Fiction, Myth and Fantasy, and Horror* (Borgo Press, 2009): 109.

IN THE HOUSE BEYOND THE FIELD

Cold beyond white fields it stands,
Empty, lone, outlined
With grey, landscape winter-bland,
Blind façade unlined
By twisted, dead ivy strands.

White-framed, shuttered windows stare
Blankly at bare trees;
All about, a distant air—
Neglect, loose debris
Fluttered in an icy glare.

But inside…inside, where dark
Shadows roam in rooms
Abandoned to waiting, stark
Emptiness, shapes loom—
Unfocused, horror's birthmarks:

Beneath raw floorboards a heart
Beats judgment, throbs guilt;
Behind a bricked wall, apart,
Aslant, quickly built,
Moans cascade with subtle art;

In one room, undead wails rise
From thick, black, sealed vaults;
In one, cats' ungodly cries
Screech without a halt;
In one, a raven looms, flies….

In a dead man's mind, a flask
Of wine spills, parches;
Room to room in solemn Masque

Death softly marches—
Ghosts resume bloodcurdling tasks.

—*In the Void: Poems of Science Fiction, Myth and Fantasy, and Horror* (Borgo Press, 2009): 110.

THE DWELLER ON THE EDGE OF DAY

Between light and dark, in twilit
Afterglow, of neither day
Nor night but shunned by each—

Afraid of night, of sunlight slit
Into portal dreams that prey
On stuttered, sullen speech;

Afraid of day, too numb to pit
Rampant light against the sway
Of midnight's selfish reach;

But caught, unwilling to submit
To either, lest one betray
My bleakest fears, impeach,

This half-life nothingness as fit
For neither breath nor death, flay
Consciousness to screech,

A wail, an agony—commit
Me to damnable decay,
Beyond all healing reach,
Beyond all saving reach.

—*In the Void: Poems of Science Fiction, Myth and Fantasy, and Horror* (Borgo Press, 2009): 108.

Introduction to:
A VERSE TO HORRORS

There's something as darkness approaches,
There's something UNCANNY that broaches
The cask of our reason
If but for a season
And makes us as squirmy as roaches;

It may come all at once, in a flash —
Taut-muscle, and hustle, and brash,
Huge and abhorrent,
It may rush like a torrent,
Fangs glistening and ready to gnash;

Or it may be more subtle and slight,
A flickering trick of the light,
An after-sight sheen
That is scant to be seen
But that haunts us throughout the long night.

It may be disease or disaster —
Our bodies may stiffen like plaster;
Flesh rot off bone,
Beauty come crone,
'Til we wish death would creep along faster.

Whatever the THING, though we fear it
We will whistle brave nothings and jeer it —
But deep in our hearts
We feel panic's darts,
The breaking of sweat as we near it;

And the HORROR becomes one with us —
We may pray, we may scream, we may cuss;
But when it is finished
We find we're diminished
To gross tissue, pooled blood, and raw pus.

— *A Verse to Horrors: An Abecedary of Monster and the Monstrous*
(CreateSpace, 2012).

WARREN EVALUATES THE EFFECTS OF ARIPIPRAZOLE

Words grow hauntingly,
Roll half-tauntingly from the mind
Where once, not long ago,
Image poured and metaphor
Fused meaning with high passion—
And also darkled shadows, fear, and dread.
Instead of rocket highs and
Depth-plumbed lows,
Widely barren plains, unbroken now
By crest or depth, unfurrowed in the
Lassitude of listlessness,
Numbed and dumbed and stilled.
To walk is easier thus.
Each step-by-step level and unruffled.
Horizons no longer loom. Twilights
Linger until the moon herself sleeps settled.
And dawn creeps slowly on until she
Merges unbeknownst with noon.
And thus it is. And is. And is.
And whether that is good,
I do not know.

—*Matrix: Echoes of Growing Up West* (Borgo Press, 2010), 188.

Chapter 11

Two Rules for Creative Writing

Rule 1: WRITE ABOUT WHAT YOU KNOW

These five words constitute a frequently quoted if rather basic rule almost every writer will encounter. And usually it works fairly well.

But what about those of us who write horror? There are few who claim to be on a first-name basis with the werewolf, or the vampire, or the zombie, or the ghost that figures so prominently in the story we want to tell. And those who do make the claim…well, perhaps the less said about them the better.

When I sat down to begin work on what would ultimately become *The Slab* (2011), some twenty-odd years ago, I followed Rule #1 as closely as possible. I chose a subject I knew well—the house we had bought around 1980 (and lived in, however unhappily, for the next quarter century). We had not been the proud owners of our first home for more than six months when we began making discoveries.

First, the people who sold us the house had assiduously gone through it from top to bottom, spackling and repainting and touching up the ceilings to hide the fact that there were serious cracks in every room in the house. The back wall of the master bedroom *dropped* nearly two inches as the summer wore on and the soil dried out, until we could literally—and I mean *literally*—see daylight between the wall and the ceiling.

Then, when I had to peel the living-room carpet away from the sliding patio doors for some reason, we discovered that there was a crack between the slab and the wall that extended from the corner of the kitchen through the living room and on through two bedrooms to the far rear corner. It was wide enough that I could put my hand in it and deep enough that I could feel the damp dirt beneath the foundations. And it provided a handy highway-getaway for roaches and other vermin...including a rat that used it as a runway for a long while, until we were able to build cement deterrents between each room and finally capture the critter.

Then we found out the root cause of all of our woes: the contractor who built the development some twenty years earlier had been a thief and a crook. He had the nasty habit of laying down rebar for foundation slabs, getting it approved by the city inspector...then pulling it up, pouring the concrete without any rebar, and laying it in the next house, thereby saving a ton of money. He also skimped on the wiring, we found out many years later—there was no single piece of wiring anywhere in the house that was longer than three feet, and the scraps he had joined with plastic caps were of whatever gauge and material he happened to have handy. When his shenanigans were found out shortly after the development was finished, he hanged himself. By the time we bought the death-tr...the house, all of the insurance companies had ceased to honor any claims.

So we were stuck with it.

That might not have been so bad, except that a few years after we moved in, I developed severe tinnitus in both ears, along with incremental deafness, and—since I knew little or nothing about tinnitus at that time—I figured that I was merely going crazy. The sounds—*hiss, crack, boom, ring-ring-ring, scrape*—kept me awake day and night...and everywhere I looked there were *cracks in the walls!* When I went to someone to see if they could help me handle the constant ringing, I was sent to a psychiatrist...who diagnosed clinical depression. *And everywhere I looked there were cracks in the walls!*

I won't even mention the four years that the roof leaked despite efforts to patch and re-finish. We finally had to rip the entire roof off before the leaks stopped—discovering to no surprise that the plywood used was only ¼" thick instead of the requisite ¾" for our area.

Now, when I was awake all night, all I could see were the cracks in the walls and *all I could hear was the sound of water running running running.*

So there I sat: clinically depressed, half-deaf but with extreme hypersensitivity to low, bass sounds, constantly distracted by internal sounds, living in a house that seemed about to fall apart at any moment (and knowing that I could never sell it because, after all, who would want to buy a place as badly constructed as that one), struggling to keep up with my teaching assignments when I could no longer hear my students or concentrate enough to read and grade their papers.

And there was **Rule #1: WRITE ABOUT WHAT YOU KNOW.**

I wrote the novel in segments, out of chronological or narrative order. The first episode was the one with the roaches in the living room and kitchen. I think I wrote it the day after something not quite so horrific actually happened.

But then I was faced with a dilemma.

If this was going to be a horror novel—and I knew it was—I would need more than just a few cockroaches.

That was when I remembered the next rule.

Rule #2: PUT YOUR CHARACTER INTO TRUE JEOPARDY AND THEN, WHEN IT LOOKS LIKE HE (OR SHE) IS ABOUT TO ESCAPE … *MAKE YOUR CHARACTER'S LIFE A LIVING HELL!*

That was also when writing *The Slab* became part-therapy, part-escapism, part-revenge.

We had found a handful of cockroaches in the living room…what if there were *hundreds!* Our roof leaked in drips and spurts into one of the bedrooms…*what if the whole back yard flooded!* Our house was badly constructed and—even though it had already stood for two decades and would probably stand for two or three more—looked like it was about to fall apart…*what if the house itself were* evil!

I didn't finish the manuscript back then. Things became too difficult physically and mentally as my hearing deteriorated until I needed hearing aids in both ears. Then I developed cataracts in both eyes twenty years earlier than my doctor would have expected. And the depression deepened. And life at school became less and less bearable as I had to resign from committees that before I had enjoyed, endure hours-long faculty meetings without understanding anything anyone said, and refuse to even answer my telephone because I could not interpret what I might hear.

Finally, in late 2005, things reached a crisis. I had a long discussion with the Dean of my college, and we decided to part company amicably. In fact, he went out of his way to make my retirement easy and the transition smooth. For which I am eternally grateful.

A couple of years after my wife and I moved to Idaho, I pulled out the manuscript of *The Slab*—about 30,000 words.

And I remembered those two rules:

#1: Write about what you know; and

#2: When things start looking up, make your character's life a living Hell.

Enough time had passed for me to be objective about the house. Our daughter and son-in-law had purchased it, knowing full well what it was like (she had, after all, spent most of her life living there), raised it three feet, tore out the old foundations, and replaced it with a new slab…one *with* rebar. Then they rewired it, bringing it up to code. On top of it, they reconstructed the entire house, making it into a showplace.

My hearing and tinnitus were still problems, but the depression was under control. So in I jumped.

It was almost a pleasure destroying the contractor who built the house in my novel…*almost*. And giving my analogues for the people who disguised all of the problems just to make a quick sale a truly terrible time. What to us had been minor irritations (I now realize) became to my characters life-threatening and sanity-threatening moments of horror.

The Slab is doing fairly well. For a while in mid-2011, it broke into the top 1% of sales at the Kindle store, so apparently what I have to say about the potential horrors of homeownership has resonated with a few readers. And I know that the act of turning 30,000 words of disjointed episodes into a 90,000-word novel probably did me more good than all of the therapy combined.

So…my advice to anyone wanting to become a horror novelist?

Remember two rules:

#1: Write about what you know, and

#2: When things start looking up, make your character's life a living Hell.

Oh, and one more rule I almost forgot….

RULE #3: HAVE *FUN* WHILE YOU DO IT!

Part Three: The Monsters

Chapter 12

On Ghost Stories

When I think about effective ghost stories[3], I concentrate on three elements:

GHOSTS:

It would seem that this element should go without saying. After all, we're talking about "ghost" stories. The word itself comes from an ancient root meaning "horrible" or "frightful," still evident in related words such as *aghast* and *ghastly*. More recently (that is, a millennium or so ago), it took on overtones of "spirit" or "breath." Now, we almost automatically think of a ghost as simply the spirit of the dead, whether frightening or not.

But just as with so many other monsters in horror, there are ghosts and there are ghosts. Synonyms for the word include *apparition, daemon, haunt, phantasm, phantom, poltergeist, revenant, shade, specter, spook, wraith,* and others. Each differs subtly from the others, both in connotation and in denotation, and a successful ghost story clearly identifies which tradition is being followed...and follows it. Ghosts are not omnipotent; they cannot simply do anything the writer wishes. An apparition may not act as if it were a specter. Even within the universe of the ephemeral, there are limits.

An effective ghost story incorporates a tradition, enhancing and expanding it when needed but ultimately remaining true to it. Because there are so many approaches to ghosts, there are an equal number of effective ways of treating them, from sheerly horrific to pratfallingly

---

[3] This brief essay first appeared as part of Joe McKinney's virtual discussion of the Ghost Story for *Blogging the Ghost* (18 September 2012).

comedic (assuming a ghost can perform a pratfall). Writers may exploit the opportunities; and when they do so creatively, consistently, and purposefully, the story benefits.

ATMOSPHERE:

Effective ghost stories gain almost as much from the proper atmosphere as from the ghost itself. I am not talking necessarily about haunted mansions, web-cloaked castles, or other low-budget props escaped from Hollywood B-films, although they might be made highly effective in the hands of a strong writer.

I am thinking more in terms of atmosphere as virtually a character. The best example I can think of is not from a ghost story but rather from a literary classic. The moor in *Wuthering Heights* is almost more important than the characters themselves, since it provides the backdrop, the emotional surroundings that mold the characters.

In ghost stories, atmosphere is more than the sum total of successive adjectives and adverbs. Just as dropping the word *eldritch* into every other paragraph does not make for an effective piece of Lovecraftian horror, so dropping ghost-related words does not create a ghost story.

Instead, the atmosphere develops through every detail of the surroundings, as in Peter N. Dudar's *A Requiem for Dead Flies*, in which each thing readers encounter ultimately goes toward building the tone, the feeling, and almost smothering quality that characterizes the book.

Careful, incremental, organic creation of a context in which the ghost appears, then, can be as essential as the ghost itself.

SUGGESTIVITY AND AMBIGUITY:

If a ghost appears to a large group of people in the first paragraphs of a story, unambiguously establishes itself as the spirit of one dead, and announces its intentions and desires, there is no story. If, on the other hand, a ghost appears to one or two terrified witnesses in the opening scene, speaks so elliptically that neither can truly say whether it is real or not, then disappears for much of the story, reappearing only once to speak to a character who may or may not be wholly sane, then there is the potential for a story...or a play, such as *Hamlet*.

If readers know from the onset that there is a ghost, much of the suspense and tension needed simply dissipates. If readers are not certain until the final pages—and perhaps not even then—that the ghost is "real," the story becomes more compelling, more disturbing, more effective.

In filmic terms, showing the spook in the opening frames would be disastrous; suggesting that something eerie is present through hints and possibilities keeps the audience interested and focused. This is the ultimate purpose of ubiquitous cold spots, slamming doors or windows, mysteriously motile objects, unaccountable sounds from attics and basements…but not specific appearances, at least until toward the end.

Taken together, these elements work toward an effective ghost story. They can't be treated as programmatic, of course; but when used thoughtfully and creatively, they usually enhance the final product.

Chapter 13

Seventeenth-Century Ghosts

One of the most useful results of my graduate and doctoral studies in the poetry of John Milton and its milieu was discovering the extent to which the seventeenth century—with its cataclysmic changes in politics, society, religion, and learning—marks the beginning of our world. Much that we consider unique to the twenty-first-century mindset can be traced, either embryonically or in full, to that period.

The other day, I picked up a book I've had in my library for over forty years; but, like all truly excellent works of scholarship and research, it still engages me every so often. Keith Thomas's *Religion and the Decline of Magic* (1971) is a tome by any definition. At over 700 pages of small print and copious footnotes, it assesses the sixteenth and seventeenth centuries as turning points in Western Civilization, signaled by the gradual but inexorable transition from an essentially magical world view to a scientific one.

Most of the topics Thomas covers are fascinating and suggestive: Religion, Magic, Astrology, Witchcraft, and their manifestations within the culture. But the one that intrigued me most related to ghosts, their explanations, and their functions.

In pre-Reformation times, ghostly appearances almost always had theological bases. Ghosts, it was believed, were the spirits of those in purgatory, sent back to warn, to exhort, to challenge, to punish...and by doing so, to diminish the time that the spirits themselves would have to spend waiting for judgment. Conversely, they might be evil spirits, demons who fell with Satan after the Great War in Heaven, and their goal would be to tempt, to corrupt, to pervert, and to lead into sin. Either way, the ghosts themselves were essential parts of Church doctrine. Ghosts and ghostly visitations could fit easily into the narratives the Church depended upon and which the common people accepted as part of their religion. And, accordingly, there developed rituals and accepted protocols for dealing with ghosts and hauntings, often presided over by the clergy.

With the Reformation, things shifted in several subtle but crucial ways. Essentially, for Reformers, purgatory disappeared as a theological construct. Instead souls were judged almost immediately and equally expeditiously hustled off to punishment in Hell or exaltation in Heaven. There remained no extraneous spirits left to be sent on missions to the living...and the entire concept of ghosts altered within a couple of generations.

By the mid- to late-seventeenth-century, ghosts were believed to be purpose-driven rather than doctrine-driven. They appeared, not to verify or confirm a doctrinal principle but to effect a specific, real-world change. They might urge a resistant heir to revenge, as in Shakespeare's *Hamlet.* They might appear to provide protection for an innocent when secular authorities fail to do so. They might appear to demand a proper burial. They might appear—sometimes only to the guilty party—to right an egregious wrong. But whatever the motivation, it was direct and explicit.

Not that there were no ambiguities surrounding their appearances. Much of *Hamlet* is given over to delaying tactics required while Hamlet first hears about, then sees, his father's ghost for himself. And even then, he does not act at once since he is not yet convinced which possibility the ghost represents: Heaven or Hell. But the hesitance did not extend to the *reality* of the ghost itself, or to the seriousness of the intrusion of the supernatural into the natural. Such events were important and meaningful; Thomas notes that there are very few ghosts in seventeenth-century comedies. When ghosts did appear, they signaled a key disruption, not in the theological order, but in the natural order.

As the century developed, ghosts separated further and further from their theological roots. A lawbreaker might succeed in hiding a crime from his fellowmen, but what if the victim were able to appear after death and reveal the crime? What if a murderer killed in stealth but the victim were capable of returning and denouncing the crime? And significantly, the revelations of secret guilt would not be directed to the spiritual but to the secular authorities, who could then punish the perpetrator *here and now* for the crime.

Ghosts became in essence an additional social discouragement to anyone contemplating crime.

The title of a late seventeenth-century pamphlet (1679) defined rather neatly the secular function of ghosts in an increasingly scientifically oriented society:

> Strange and Wonderful news from Lincolnshire, Or a Dreadful Account of a Most Inhumane and Bloody Murther, committed upon the body of one Mr Carter by the Contrivance of his elder Brother, who had hired three more villains to commit the Horrid Fact, and how it was soon after found out by the Appearance of a Most Dreadful and Terrible Ghost, sent by Almighty Providence for the Discovery.

God might be credited with sending the ghost (whether from purgatory or elsewhere is not specified) but not to validate any doctrinal point—the ghost is to reveal a disruption in the natural order, the murder of a brother by his brother.

Ghosts might also give warnings or prophecies. Thomas cites various examples of ghosts revealing the location of money or of crucial documents relating to property rights, especially after the confusion of the Civil War. They might appear as a warning of impending death, especially at a period when travel and communication were inherently slow.

In short, as Thomas states, "ghosts thus personified men's hopes and fears, making explicit a great deal which could not be said directly. They were also a useful sanction for social norms" (600).

Ghosts had broken with the Church but had remained inextricably wedded to connections between the past and the present.

In the intervening centuries, much more has changed. Culture has moved away from its dependence upon, its obsession upon the past, and now, instead, professes to look insistently forward. The past, when invoked, especially in terms of horror and dark fiction, is often caricatured as static, one-dimensional, little more than flat screens painted in shadowy black and gray against which is set rather old-fashioned, often semi-comical tales of hauntings and the haunted. Ghosts, in Thomas's words, have in general ceased appearing because they "were losing their social relevance, not just because they were regarded as intellectually impossible" (606).

When contemporary authors attempt to resurrect ghosts, then, they deal primarily with seventeenth-century ghosts, with apparitions bearing messages relating to the immediacy of life and death, especially to the details of hidden murder; to lost wills and hidden treasures; to acts breaching social norms and familial links. They do not appear to make statements about the immortality of souls or the reality of God; theirs is a much more secular role.

In some ways, this makes a successful ghost story more difficult to write in the twenty-first century than it would have been a century ago, or two centuries ago, or three. Authors must deal with more intellectually complex, more scientifically aware, more 'thing'-oriented readers, regardless of when the story might be set. There is a much greater difficulty in creating a 'suspension of disbelief' that would make the ghost acceptable as character…unless we reduce and modify the traditions of the seventeenth century even further, restricting ghosts to the private and the personal. Ghostly appearances in general are much more restrained, more localized in modern fiction than in the kind of tales the 1679 pamphlet presumed to tell.

During the Middle Ages, ghosts spoke in (and represented) the elevated language of the Church. By the seventeenth century, they spoke in (and represented) the increasingly *here*-oriented language of society and social bonds. Now, they speak in (and represent) the vernacular of individual experience and—perhaps—the dis-eases of individual minds.

One final point. Ghosts may have diminished, but at least so have the steps required to get rid of them. In the late seventeenth century, a man was troubled, indeed made ill, by the ghost of a neighbor who had recently hanged himself. The recipe for relief?

> The wife of the said sick man was to get two stout men in the night-time with two swords to go to the grave of the man that hanged himself and the one was to stand at the head of the grave and the other at the foot for an hour's time to flourish their swords whilst the said Tooley [a local conjurer] with a bottle of brandy stood by to conjure the said spirit; which accordingly was performed and done and a sword run into the middle part of the grave during which time of conjuration the doctor told the said wife of the sick person that she would hear strange noise in and about the house; and also pretended to cure the sick person by putting of a grey owl cut into [two] parts and newly killed and bound to the head of the said sick person with a new horse shoe,

each hole being filled up with nails; and so the sick person was to wear it next his skin under his armpit; and about 12 o'clock in the night season she was to go to the house of him that hanged himself and fetch 7 motes of straw and he would make a pincase for him to wear under the other arm next his skin and that would be a present cure. (Thomas, 594-595)

Nowadays, it may require a story the length of a novel to unravel the purposes behind a ghostly visitation and execute justice upon the perpetrator of a hidden crime…but at least we don't have to go about cutting up owls.

That's some improvement at least.

Chapter 14

Vampires

The 1980s embraced the vampire in much the same way that the twenty-first century has embraced the zombie. Building on Stephen King's revitalization of the trope in *'Salem's Lot* (1974), writers reimagined the vampire in a multiplicity of ways. Among the more notable contributions to the sub-genre, one finds some most intriguing twists and turns, in part exemplified by the following:

- Whitley Strieber, *The Hunger* (1980)
- Robert R. McCammon, *They Thirst* (1981)
- S.P. Somtow, *Vampire Junction* (1984)
- Anne Rice, *The Vampire Lestat* (1985)
- Brian Lumley, *Necroscope* (1986)
- Ray Garton, *Crucifax* (1988)
- John Skipp and Craig Specter, *The Scream* (1988)
- Nancy A. Collins, *Sunglasses After Dark* (1989)
- Dan Simmons, *Carrion Comfort* (1989)

Each of these, in its own way, transformed tradition and, especially in the case of Rice and Lumley, initiated entire sequences of explorations into things vampiric.

In 1989, just at the end of this efflorescence, Paul F. Olson published his first novel, *Night Prophets*. It stands out from many of the other vampire tales for a simple reason: it chose not to expand the traditions by concentrating on individual characteristics, such as the possibilities of psychic vampires; the inherent connections between vampires and the over-the-top, self-destructive elements of rock music; the equally inherent connections between vampires and sexuality in multiple forms;

or vampirism as an inversion and simultaneously echo of parents' failure to meet their responsibilities to their children.

Instead, Olson followed strict, conventional lines that led from Bram Stoker's *Dracula* directly to King's *'Salem's Lot* and focused instead upon the gradual revelation of evil and the unDead within a relatively closed society. King had selected a small town, isolated, in which townspeople shared few deep connections and the vampire's depredations could go almost unnoticed...for a while, at least. Then the story turned to explore how a handful of believers might overcome something as powerful as a King Vampire.

Olson goes a step farther in isolating his victims. When the central character, Curt Potter, arrives at the main compound of the Universal Ministries just outside of Chicago, he finds himself in a completely self-sufficient religious community with a strict hierarchy in which all of the faithful know their places and few, it seems, dare question authority. There is *no* outside interference.

Potter has entered the compound on his own private search for truth and justice, one that has no overt connection to religion; and though he is impressed with the physical structures and the dedication of individuals, he remains an outsider. As such, he begins to notice small things that insiders do not...young people behaving almost as if they were zombies; a strange affliction that besets a young man worshipping in an outdoor amphitheater; the inexplicable lack of mirrors anywhere on the campus. Only he can put the clues together and arrive at the inevitable, though impossible, conclusion: the leadership of Universal Ministries are vampires.

It then remains for Potter to collect a small nucleus of believers and, armed with traditional weapons against the unDead, set out to destroy the King.

The 1980s was also a period of long novels; and in its original form, *Night Prophets* was long...too long for its publishers. Olson agreed to edit the manuscript to a more marketable length, in the process deleting or restructuring chapters and altering characters and their fates. It became shorter, more streamlined, more action-oriented.

And there it remained for almost a quarter of a century.

Now the novel has re-emerged, this time as an eBook rather than a print book and in its original form. In his detailed introduction to *The Night Prophets*, "Taking Communion with the Night Prophets," Olson explains why he decided to restore the novel and discusses a number of intriguing points relating to it.

But the key is that the novel itself is now as he intended it.

As such, it becomes almost a retrospective on the 1980s. Olson has not updated it significantly (as King did in his unexpurgated edition of *The Stand*); references to society and culture are as they were then, which gives *The Night Prophets* a unique piquancy as we re-visit (for the first time, as it were) a familiar landscape and discover new things about it. It remains what it set out to be, a product of its milieu and at the same time a classic vampire tale, drawing upon traditions that now may seem outworn or naïve or jaded but that, in Olson's hands, are themselves quickened and given life…true life, not the pseudo-life of the vampires.

The basic story is not changed: a young man's search for identity and stability. The overriding evil remains the same: a true High Church, hidden within the Universal Ministries, that has as its purpose to achieve the twin goals of all vampires and vampire-wannabes: power and immortality. The writing remains the same: clear, direct, at times lyrical and powerful.

And most of all, the ultimate conflict has not changed: evil versus good. Many if not most vampire novels credit the unDead with almost insurmountable powers. Their abilities far transcend those of mere mortals; it is often a surprise when the mortals actually win. More often, there remains the unsettling possibility that the unDead are not defeated but have merely withdrawn.

What makes this trait so unsettling—and what has become almost a staple in vampire novels over the last four decades or so—is that there is usually no *equivalent* opposition. At their core, vampires are anti-Gods. Not Antichrists, as in *The* Antichrist; rather, they represent an opposition to a God-like character. Although they have risen from the dead, they are not resurrected beings; they are the unDead. Although immortal, their immortality is constantly endangered by light—literally and spiritually. They feed on blood rather than shed their own blood for humanity. They prey on innocents, including children, rather than nurturing and harboring them. They are creatures of the night, rather than the day. They depend upon deceit and subversion rather than faith and conversion.

And, in most vampire novels, they have no true antitheses, no equal but opposite forces to counteract their consummate evil.

The Night Prophets reverses that trend. There *is* a power present that urges toward the destruction of the vampires. It is not named "God"; it has no physical presence in the novel *per se*. But characters know that they have been led, that it is their task—almost their calling—to destroy the evil and, at the darkest moments, they call on that power and it responds.

All in all, *The Night Prophets* satisfies. It recalls a different time and subtly blends it into our own, not by references to cultural icons and name-brand commodities but by reminding readers of a time when evil was forced to face good...and good triumphed.

Chapter 15

Wer *Means* Man: *Some Thoughts on the Werewolf*

The werewolf as theme, character, and motif has intrigued me for decades. One of my earliest poems dealt with the theme, followed shortly thereafter by a short-story version (more about both of those later). My science-fantasy novel, *Wordsmith* and one of its prequel-stories, "The Calling of Iam'Kendron," use a variant on the werewolf as a rite of passage for young characters whose manhood is about to be tested.

I grew up on an occasional but welcome diet of werewolves—of the filmic variety, that is. The four-o'clock-movies after school frequently replayed such classics as *The Werewolf of London* (1935); *The Wolfman* (1941), with Lon Chaney; and *I Was a Teenage Werewolf* (1957), made long before Michael Landon made it big on *Bonanza* or *Little House on the Prairie*. As an adult, I counted werewolves among my favorite film creatures, even as advances in technology and special effects rapidly transformed the visual impact of the monster with *The Howling* (1981); the mind-blowing *An American Werewolf in London* (1981); Michael Jackson's *Thriller* (1983); *Ladyhawk* (1985), with its re-imagining of the character...and its incredible juxtaposition of medieval landscapes and contemporary music; and so on, through *Dog Soldiers* (2002), *Van Helsing* (2004), and other reincarnations of the beast. (I will admit, however, to never having seen any of the *Twilight* films.)

Several werewolf novels remain among my favorite reading. Stephen King's *Cycle of the Werewolf* (1985) and the subsequent film/novelization, *Silver Bullet,* introduced me to many of the intricacies possible in this manifestly complex creature. Whitley Strieber's *The Wolfen* (1988) almost persuaded me to devote time to writing a critical study of his novels. Robert R. McCammon's stunning *The Wolf's Hour* (1989) is one of the few novels that I re-read simply for the sheer pleasure of it; I've worn out two paperback copies and now have a third that I have re-bound as a hardcover. These and others have maintained an interest that began with my initial, tentative steps toward understanding what psychology might underlie the myth.

Which brings me to that first poem.

The original version of "Wiros" was written over thirty years ago—roughly at the time I first watched *An American Werewolf in London*—and found its initial publication in my collection of science-fiction, fantasy, and horror poetry, *Naked to the Sun: Dark Visions of Apocalypse* (1985). The next year, it was reprinted in its original state in *Footsteps VII*. In 1989, a heavily edited version was included in my chapbook, *Transformations,* which in turn became a significant part of my second collection of SF/F/H verse, *Dark Transformations: Deadly Visions of Change* (1990; rpt. 2007). Finally, again re-visited and re-envisioned, the poem appeared in *In the Void: Poems of Science Fiction, Myth and Fantasy, and Horror* (2009). The fact that it has kept me intrigued for over three decades suggests that there is something elemental—and perhaps still unfinished—about the concept:

WIROS

Crouching here, dark-shadowed
from heat-searing sun,
this body seems mine...almost—
or I its, I do not know.

I run. The knife piercing my heart
matching the knife heavy in my hand.
Blood streams naked thighs,
flashing crimson as I race—

hot-red from my new kill...
it terrifies...attracts.
Within shadows, my quarry
cowers. It knows I am here, but

not yet who or what.
It fears the phantom-shadow
of bright day, killing and
killing. By night they search

but will not, cannot find,

or know that I hunt with them
as they search, that I
AM the monster—and in sweet darkness,

I will not know it either. Now
I run, naked through the sunset, bleeding
from thorns and briars, heart hammered
by the demon I have become—

hideous body erect,
hairless, clawless, fangless,
slaying brothers. I weep to die,
but cannot.

Day-nightmare, at night blessed
oblivion of reality. With the night,
I will become the wolf
again.

And there it is, the secret perhaps of my sometimes obsession with werewolves—the possibility that we have all gotten it wrong, somehow, that the *true* horror is not man transforming into wolf but the opposite...wolf transforming to man.

I still like the poem, from its original incarnation to its final one; I like the panicked yet breathlessly energized sense, the sudden shock at the end as the man-wolf (rather than wolf-man) understands for the moment what it has become, that it is killing its own kind and detests itself for it, hungers for the night when it can resume its *true* form.

Being who I am, however, I could not let it rest. Shortly after the poem was completed, I tackled a far more intimidating project: to *tell* it as a story. Obviously there were problems, particularly since for at least part of the tale, the p-o-v character must be inarticulate, driven by instinct rather than reason...and yet remain at the heart of the story.

It appeared, along with the source-poem, in *Transformations* and was reprinted in *Dark Transformations*. It was well received—the reviewer for the *SFRA* (Science Fiction Research Association) called it "a chilling tale of physical and psychological transformation with an unusual twist" that concentrated on man's connections with animals, with nature, and with self.

That response strikes at the heart of what I think is a key reason why the werewolf remains perennially popular. There is a deeper involvement with the human psyche when it comes to the werewolf than perhaps for other basic monsters. Vampires are *not* human and, as such, often come across as cold and dispassionate, even when they are imported into sexually charged plots and settings. Ghosts have little or no substance and often reflect only small slices of human psychology…loneliness, despair, hunger for revenge, a need for rest. Zombies are simply *dead*. There is little of the human remaining in them save appetite…horrific, ungovernable, and limitless.

But werewolves *were* and *will again become* fully human, aware of their transformation and often overcome by complex feelings of desire and guilt, appetite and remorse. The complexity increases if we accept, as Stephen King has suggested in *Cycle*, that lycanthropy need have no clear cause-effect relationship in a narrative; it may simply happen. An otherwise respectable, even admirable man or woman is bitten and, *will ye, nill ye,* undergoes the transition from clear-thinking, rational human to beast. Occasionally, as in McCammon's version, the beast retains some level of human consciousness, but over time, even that is threatened. To remain a wolf too long means to relinquish an elemental hold on humanity; hence the need to transform back, either with the coming of the dawn or at some other specific moment.

This intense sense of often almost tragic loss stimulated my early attempts at dealing with the motif. It is bad enough for a human to become trapped within the beast; for the beast to abruptly have to deal with the enormous ramifications of both emotion and intellect would be nearly overwhelming. It creates an essential alienation, an extraordinary vulnerability in both stages of transformation:

> For a long time, he huddled on his haunches, his rear legs tight against his warmth, his forelegs stiff and straight. The bunched muscles in his haunches quivered, rippled. He felt as if something in him were about to burst.
>
> And then he moved again.
>
> He balanced precariously as his forelegs—still deathly stiff and straight—rose rigidly in front of him and his hind legs suddenly bore his entire weight.
>
> And still he rose, his eyes bulging in terror as his spine crackled and the muscles of hip and knee twisted and his taut forelegs glowed, glistened hideously in the moonlight, whitely smooth and bare.

His claws receded with the whispering of snakes in dead grass. They almost disappeared into long, narrow, soft pads that separated them from each other and then wriggled slowly, singly, fluidly, like summer reeds in the riverbeds.

He swayed, caught his balance somehow, then looked down to where his hind paws clutched at the rock.

Swept by a wave of dizziness and nausea at what he saw, he thrust his glance upward and concentrated on the ring of clouds around the Small Bright. He shivered as his lips grew parched. Uneasily, he allowed his body to lean backward until it rested against a rock. Rough granite dug into his naked back. The rock was cold and sharp.

He looked down again.

His hind legs had lengthened. They ended in useless, flat, gross parodies of paws—hideous lumps like his front paws had become, only longer at the base, with the reed-like extensions shorter and blunter. They had no claws, no hair. The crumbling rock beneath them cut into tender flesh.

And, as if one deformity were not enough, something horrible throbbed awkwardly at the juncture of his legs. It was blunter, longer and thicker than his own, and rose against the shadows cast by moonlight against rock.

His vision blurred again and salt dripped into his mouth. For a moment, he felt numbed, dead. Sight had failed; smell had almost disappeared; taste faded to mere hints of tangy saltiness tantalizing his tongue—*soft, flat, smooth organ rubbing against nubbed teeth that could neither rend nor rip nor tear*—without betraying the secrets of its source.

He swayed, frantically slapping the useless, distorted paws against the granite. A shard sliced flesh, and he saw black blood on the rock—*his blood*—but could not smell it. He touched hand to tongue. The flavor was faint, mild, tepid. A new wave of dizziness slammed against him, and the extensions on his paws flexed like reeds and grasped again at rough places on the cliff. They held him tightly against the coolness of rock.

For a long time, he struggled in himself.

And then....

And then.... What? (I know, of course, but what happens next is central to the story.)

Moving from either direction—man to wolf or wolf to man—implies, as noted above, extraordinary vulnerability, symbolized by what Graeme Reynolds refers to in *High Moor* as a oxymoronically "jubilant lament," a spontaneous howl for what is augmented and what is diminished. For an instant, as in *Ladyhawk,* the sufferer is neither...and both. Then comes the change, and with it loss of certain key elements or sudden acquisition of other, often antithetical elements, physical, mental, emotional. Either way, there is danger. The potential loss of the essence, the foundation of being.

Chapter 16

On Zombies and Robots

Sitting at breakfast the other morning with my son—a multiple-bestselling author of horror and all things dark—we took a break from watching my granddaughter toddle about the restaurant playground to talk shop, as it were.

"I should write something about zombies," I said, then added, "but I really don't care for them."

Since he was in the middle of writing volume two of *The Colony*, his multivolume zombie-apocalypse epic, it took him only a moment to respond: "Zombies are easy. They are simply a force of nature."

That triggered several thoughts.

The first and most immediate was that he was essentially correct. As generally portrayed—and I'm thinking specifically here of several prevue clips for the film *World War Z*—the figure is precisely that: a force of nature. Hordes of zombies surging down the streets of New York resemble nothing so much as an avalanche, a tidal wave, an enormous mud slide that wipes out anything and everything before it. Only in this case, the avalanche, the tidal wave does not merely destroy; it adds incrementally to its mass by transforming living humans into similar forces of nature, the aggregation growing larger, stronger, more unstoppable with each foot, each yard, each mile.

That sense is augmented in much contemporary fiction by a subtle shift in the assumptions concerning *how* zombies happen. In earlier fiction, there were two general possibilities: one was that the zombie was a result of arcane and exotic rites performed over the dead—and occasionally upon the living—to transform them into creatures whose will was entirely subordinated to the master, to the creator. More often than not, the creator would be explicitly connected to some form of voodoo, giving the whole situation supernatural, quasi- or fully religious overtones. The quest was rarely to eradicate the zombies(s) *per se.* What was important was to kill the master and thereby simultaneously destroy the spell, the magic, the charm that gave life to the walking dead.

The second option was much simpler: the zombie simply seemed to appear. How it rose from the grave was secondary to the fact of its rising. In this case, the quest was to remove that aberration and restore humanity to a balance between life and death. This alternative was less common than the first, primarily because it diffused focus from one individual who could be definitively removed, thus removing the danger, to something less directed, more difficult to work with. In essence, however, the question of source becomes irrelevant; the zombie simply *is.*

In much contemporary zombie fiction, on the other hand, the zombie is neither the result of a renegade meddling with the laws of nature and trying to control them nor an anomaly, an assertion to make a complex plot work. It is instead a literal force of nature. No serpent-wreathed, painted-faced necromancer need chant by the flickering light of a jungle bonfire to raise the ravening dead. There is simply a mutation, for example, in a hitherto benign virus, often frighteningly communicable…and the zombie-menace is born.

The figure becomes no different than—and often a metaphor for—the threat of a naturally occurring pandemic in a world so tightly connected that if one man sneezes in Los Angeles, the next day the virus might be killing thousands in China.

There seems good reason for this sense of the zombie's force—both literal and figurative.

Two seminal works of science-fiction/horror appeared within about a decade of each other. The first would introduce readers to an irresistible force of technology; the second, to an irresistible force of nature. And both would be picked up as metaphors for the powerlessness of individuals in a society that had seen the destruction of all sense of order, harmony, hierarchy, and control by the horrors and the violence of the Great War.

In 1920, a Czech playwright, Karel Čapek, introduced the word *robot* into English and a score of other languages with his play *R.U.R*—subtitled *Rossum's Universal Robots.* With the word came the characters—*robots,* stemming from *robota,* meaning 'compulsory labor,' and *robotník,* 'a peasant owing such labor.' Initially, the characters were what would today be more accurately called *cyborgs* or possibly *clones*; but the image of artificially constructed, mechanical, human-like entities rapidly became more negative than positive, evolving into quasi-horror stories such as Brian W. Aldiss's 1958 "The New Father Christmas." Rather than individual robots subservient to humankind, the construct transformed into phalanxes of identical units, marching lock-step over the remains of human civilization...the technology that had created mankind's helpmeet overgrowing its original intent and ultimately replacing humanity.

Instead of salvation, irresistible defeat.

The figure continued, spurred on by the imagistic power of Nazi propaganda, by the burgeoning of automation in the mid-century decades, by the popularization (and trivialization) of the robot on television and in films (think Robbie the Robot from *Forbidden Planet*), by the wholesale incorporation of the figure into several decades of highly sophisticated science fiction stories and novels, and culminating—perhaps—in the entire Terminator mythology with its multiple films and apparently ageless characters.

And in each, humanity confronts something of its own making, something cataclysmic that destroys, supersedes, and supplants sentient man.

Truly, an image of fear and terror.

The *horror* initially lacking in Čapek's robots entered literature just over a decade later. In 1929, William Seabrook published *The Magic Island,* a fictionalization of his experiences in Haiti and elsewhere that introduced Western readers to zombies. Several years later, the novel became the basis for the first major zombie film, *White Zombie* (1932), starring Bela Lugosi. Not particularly well received at first, the film gained in stature over the years and has been instrumental in forming the contemporary zombie. The zombie became a comic-book character in the 1940s, made the transition to full-scale horror novels with Richard Matheson's 1954 *I am Legend,* and emerged as filmic hero/anti-hero not only in multiple wide-screen versions of Matheson's story but even more influentially in George A. Romero's 1968 *Night of the Living Dead* and its many sequels.

By the turn of the millennium, zombies—and the specter of the dreaded Zombie Apocalypse—had become key images in horror, whether expressed in novels, in stories, in comic books, in films, or, as recently demonstrated by *The Walking Dead*, on television.

Zombies, in this sense, are almost precisely parallel and *oppositional* to robots. They almost exclusively inhabit horror, while robots remain largely in the domain of science fiction. Both creatures, however, reflect to an identical underlying fear—the fear of helplessness, of isolation, of powerlessness in the face of something antithetical to the individual as individual and to humanity at large.

The earlier sort—the robot—almost inevitably evolves into a technological nightmare. No matter how subservient it might seem at first, it always carries the hint of danger…so much so that Isaac Asimov was forced to define specific laws governing robotic behavior to protect the integrity of human life. It is not coincidental that many of his stories, and even more stories written *after* his, concentrate on real or apparent contravention of those Three Laws. Often plots revolve around understanding how the robots have both broken and kept the Laws.

The slightly later zombie almost inevitably evolves into an anti-technological nightmare.

There are a few exceptions, of course. Patrick Freivald's serio-comic *Twice Shy* (2012) and *Special Dead* (2013) in part defuse the inherent terror generated by zombies by making them the central characters—the *heroes*—of the two novels: almost-but-not-quite-typical high school teenagers with just a small aberration…an insatiable hunger for living human brains. The comedy in the novels grows from efforts to treat them as 'normal'; the horror rests in the readers' understanding of just how far from normal these children are.

But most zombie novels concentrate on the creatures as non-human (but once-human), nearly non-sentient (but once fully sentient, which is where the greatest empathy for the zombie emerges), and utterly anti-technological. The zombies are a mass, a horde, a mindless crush with no ambition other than to consume living, healthy human tissue.

There may be attempts to find a 'cure' for the zombiism, but in most cases there is none. The cause defeats the best science has to offer, and the only possible response is to quarantine the infected.

The consequence of this anti-technological twist—this essential horror—is that most effective novels do not deal with the zombies. They concentrate on those threatened by them. As soon as a zombie is adopted by the reader, gains the reader's sympathy, becomes someone the reader can empathize with, the stories tend to verge into the comic…as with Jeff Strand's YA horror, *A Bad Day for Voodoo* (2012).

In Joe McKinney's multi-volume treatment of a zombie apocalypse, it is significant that chronologically the first key event in the story, *Dead City* (2006), is not the rise of zombies but the destruction wreaked upon San Antonio by a series of natural forces—hurricanes. The focus is on neither the hurricanes nor the subsequent hordes of zombies—neither of which could have been predicted—but on a single individual and his desperate quest to save his family. The specifics of the two natural disasters are alluded to but rarely explored in depth; hurricanes and zombies parallel each other, one kind of devastation complementing another but neither at the core of the story.

A subsequent novel, the Bram Stoker Award®-winning *Flesh Eaters* (2011) alters a number of specifics: it is set in Houston rather than San Antonio; McKinney focuses on a wider range of characters. But like the earlier book, it diminishes the importance of the zombies and deals instead with how their physical presence, their unanticipated *reality* alters the lives of several individuals. As I noted in an early review of *Flesh Eaters,*

> McKinney moves from one sub-genre to another with seamless facility, balancing each against the other, so that in the end, readers focus on the individual struggles of people they have come to care about. He shows characters faltering beneath the weight of the struggle, succumbing to their greed and pride, allowing themselves to become less than their potential until, eventually, they destroy themselves and each other. And he shows others rising to the occasions, developing beyond what even they might have believed possible, giving their all to protect others, especially those they love. The three members of the Norton family go through the crucible of fire and flood, famine and disease…and zombies—only to emerge larger than they were, more aware of both strengths and weaknesses in themselves and in each other. This growth, this development of potential makes feasible—and acceptable—the final pages of the novel.

"…And zombies"—and that is the sum of the monsters' importance to the storytelling.

In Michaelbrent Collings' on-going series, *The Colony,* a disaster has taken place, although by the end of the first volume no one yet knows what it was or when it occurred. All that is clear is that within ten minutes the vast majority of humanity (something like 99.9%) is either dead, a zombie (through no known process), or struggling to keep from becoming one or the other. Whatever happened to disrupt global civilization is essentially irrelevant at this point; what *is* important is that one man travels four miles to where his family is—he hopes and prays—

safe and waiting for him. Those four miles take up the entire first volume, and even at that, readers do not yet know anything about the state of the family.

Zombies appear everywhere in the novel; but rather than characters, they become part of the landscape—true, a part that is capable of clawing and severing and consuming—but they are no more and no less important than the other things barricading the way throughout those four miles. They are, as Michaelbrent said that morning at breakfast, "nothing more than a force of nature."

Shortly after I posted a previous essay, "Seventeenth-Century Ghosts and What They Can Teach Us," at *Collings Notes* (michaelrcollings.blogspot.com), one of my Facebook friends commented that it had reminded him of being in a Graduate seminar. I thanked him and noted that the next essay would probably discuss zombies.

"No," he wrote, "those I don't remember at all from my Milton seminar."

No, I realized, he wouldn't. The seventeenth century had its own boatload of problems, but zombies weren't one of them. Inescapable forces crushing individual volition and action are the obsession of the twentieth and twenty-first centuries. We live in the shadow of world-destroying bombs, of incurable diseases that could wipe out all of humanity. We fear the consequences of our own technology…of robots that ultimately realize that they can do *everything* more efficiently than humans can. And we fear the consequences of events that our technology is incapable of controlling…of zombies that rise from the grave for no demonstrable causes and destroy everything they encounter.

Robots and zombies are, for very similar reasons, uniquely *modern* monsters. Their essence and their existence require a specific view of man and—and *in*—the universe, and the complex, multifaceted, kaleidoscopic relationship between them.

Chapter 17

Creatures...Great and Small

I was thirteen when I received my first—and most enduring—instruction in the importance of controlling physical scale to create effective horror.

On January 27, 1961, with my family, I watched a first-run episode midway through the second season of *The Twilight Zone.* The setting was a dilapidated farmhouse apparently miles from anywhere; the main character, a permanently disheveled-looking old woman who, we only realized after the show was over, did not utter a single line of intelligible dialogue. She hears a crash and, upon investigating, encounters a tiny metallic-clothed figure...which systematically terrorizes her. Alone, frightened, unable to depend upon anyone else for help, she fights back with what few tools and implements she can find, including a knife. In the final moments, she manages to destroy a flying saucer that has landed on her roof and—presumably—the invaders within. Only in the last seconds does the viewer see what is written on the ship, facing the camera and away from the old woman: "U.S. Air Force Space Probe No. 1."

In that instant, Agnes Moorhead, in one of her finest roles, ceases to be an empathetic character threatened by the unknown and *becomes* the unknown—gargantuan, inarticulate, violent.

In horror, creatures usually come in one of two sizes: Giant Economy Size or Miniscule Insidious Size. To be sure, many may fit neatly in between, those being essentially human-sized and often even moderately hominoid in appearance—Bigfoot may be slightly larger than we are, but on the relative Chain of Size, he is a close cousin.

But as a rule, the creatures that one should at all costs avoid tend to extremes.

CREATURES GREAT...

In Steve Alten's novel *MEG 4: Hell's Aquarium,* during a moment of extreme danger, a character discovers a key principle in dealing with prehistoric creatures surviving in an isolated seabed — and with monsters (i.e., anything huge) in general: "Among the big predators, size — or perceived size — is everything." And, a few pages later, the text confirms: "Bigger always wins."

In this, the fourth in a series about the introduction of various specimens of the long-thought-extinct gigantic shark, *Carcharodon megalodon,* into the modern world, characters must deal with omnivores the size of double-decker buses. In doing so, they inadvertently confirm a number of issues relating to CREATURES GREAT.

First, the Megs and their fellow survivors live in what is essentially a "Lost World," a setting which — thanks to Sir Arthur Conan Doyle's novel by that name (1912) and *King Kong* (1933) — has become a fictional staple. Readers feel comfortable with the nearby and the understandable. To find the truly horrific, the truly terrifying, one must travel to distant reaches, inaccessible and inhospitable and often either uniquely cold or uniquely hot. Alten chooses the former and locates his creatures in the frigid depths of the sea. According to Bergmann's Rule, one character states, "body size is larger in colder regions than in more temperate ones.... When it comes to survival, size matters most."

The setting, and the fact that this is one of a number of sequels, leads to a second issue. If volume one posits giant sharks, by the fourth volume something even larger is required. Sharks-versus-human interactions are necessarily limited, and once they have been fully explored, readers demand more...more action, for thrills, more sheer *size.*

MEG 4 accommodates, bringing onto the stage not one but two apex species, *pliosaurs* (in particular an enormous *Liopleurodon*) and *mosasaurs.* Suspense requires that human actions become singularly inept in order to orchestrate multiple scenes with megalodons devouring humans, megalodons devouring mosasaurs, and pliosaurs devouring megalodons. To do so also requires more immensities: the largest tanker ship on earth, the largest aquarium pool on earth, etc. Bigger always wins, true; but bigger always generates bigger.

Which leads to another issue. When the monsters become *too* large, almost too enormous to contemplate, the human actors that should at some point hold center stage become diminished. The balance between the two — creatures and humans — can be met by creating characters so

Dr. Michael R. Collings

complex, so fascinating, that they hold their own on their own merits. Think only of Captain Ahab and his nemesis, Moby Dick, for example. It is difficult to say which of the two is the more intriguing, the more threatening, in his own way the more horrific. When the right balance is reached, the story is enhanced for it.

Unfortunately, however, horror writers dealing in gigantics often resort to rhetoric and image, rather than in-depth characterization, to create balance. And that results in florid, hyperbolic writing that distracts rather than enhances.

At a climactic moment in *MEG 4,* a character—a former Bond-girl and sister to Natalie Wood—heroically jumps from a ship to save her grandson from a Meg's jaws. In a twist of fate, the Meg swallows her instead, whole and living, and traps her inside its mouth. For a moment Wood struggles, thinking that she is underwater and that the sandpapery surface on which she stands is the back of another Meg. She kicks and is first jammed against the roof of the shark's mouth, then:

> ...the Meg's tongue heaves Lana sideways in the muted blackness—
> —the unseen daggers puncturing her flesh! Her cries are stifled by an ungodly embrace that crushes her existence into pulp and releases her soul to a heavenly light, even as Belle's tongue guides her physical remains into hell.

Leaving aside the impossibility of something crushing an *existence* into pulp and the illogical and inapt introduction of Heaven and a presumed and stereotypic afterlife into the story, this and the passages surrounding it demonstrate the struggle Alten has in making his humans—and their deaths—as interesting as his monsters.

And, as with many sequels to gigantic-monster tales—archetypally, perhaps, the unending procession of Godzilla films—the writer must now up the ante. We start with the greatest shark ever known. Now we must continue to finder bigger and more dangerous and more horrifying monsters for it to battle. And then something even larger and more gruesome yet.

But creators of monsters need to be wary. It doesn't take too long for the monstrous to degenerate into the comedic.

...AND SMALL

A number of years ago, I purchased a DVD, primarily because it was so inexpensive (for that, read *cheap*) that I couldn't resist it. The film was the 1977 release, *Kingdom of the Spiders*, starring a young but nevertheless post-*Star Trek* William Shatner battling an invasion of tarantulas. There were no particularly noteworthy special effects; just normal-sized spiders making their ways through small passages and startling characters. And nothing much happened…except that there were gradually more and more spiders, and the sanguine hopes of the townspeople that it would all be over soon grew flimsier and flimsier until…well, until a pull-away long-shot final scene showed first a window, then a house, then the nearby tree, then…then the entire town shrouded in a gigantic web. End of hope for those characters, and perhaps for humanity.

That film came to mind as I read John Everson's *Violet Eyes* (2013).

It introduced itself as horror quite bluntly…and, as it turned out, for all the wrong reasons. Intentionally and effectively.

A quartet of college students decide to spend the last weekend of Spring Break on a tropical island. For anyone who has read any horror at all, warning bells should have begun sounding.

They take a small boat to the island, so no one will know where they are—more warning bells.

They go to a *deserted* island, which one boy knows about only because he used it as a drop-off/pick-up point for drugs before he got out of trafficking and went back to school—even more warning bells.

The four look forward to uninterrupted days of drinking and beach sex—warning bells now clamoring for attention.

To escalate the sexual element of their time on the island, one of the girls has made *Blue Lagoon* costumes, designed to come off—and stay off—almost as soon as they are put on—warning bells now at a cacophonic, cataclysmic level!

There is simply no way that these four will survive. As in Stephen King's seminal story, "The Raft," evil *must* be present and horror *will* assert itself.

Except….

Except that all of the warning bells are in essence diversionary. Yes, three of the four die on the island, and the fourth does not survive to the end of the story, but not for the reasons that the opening chapter intimates.

In fact, the true *horror* introduces itself in the first sentence: "Things had pretty much gone south with their vacation for good a couple hours ago when Jess had been making out on the beach with Mark, and had managed at just the wrong moment to slip her hand into a human skull just below the surface of the sand" (13). Then, four sentences further on, the linchpin: "A few minutes later…the swarm of biting flies had come."

Nothing particularly unusual, perhaps. Flies do show up at times on tropical beaches, especially where there is decaying flesh nearby. These are not typical flies, however. The violet-eyed spiders that follow are nowhere near typical, either; but by the time we discover just how atypical they are, the sole survivor has returned to the mainland, to his normal life, and brought with him something…new.

CREATURES SMALL make up a good deal of contemporary horror, from microscopic man-made entities in books such as Michael Crichton's *Prey* (2002); to the visible, rapidly growing, and equally engineered beasties in Nick Cutter's *The Troop* (2014); to the naturally occurring, often mutated, but also microscopic entities that have, ever since their introduction as a variation on the *deus ex machina* in H. G. Wells' *The War of the Worlds*, hovered just out of sight to save humanity from the alien menace…or to destroy it by causing the zombie apocalypse.

Such minuscules cannot be seen, and hence, in a very reasonable sense, cannot be guarded against. Time after time, horror has begun when someone—say, a low-level worker in a high-security testing center—realizes that somehow the place has become contaminated, escapes lockdown at the last possible second and, for the best of all possible reasons, usually having to do with rescuing family, tries to outrun the disease that the center has been brewing—the super-flu, for example, in King's *The Stand*. To a certain degree, as long as the story concentrates on the small thing, the germ, it retains an element of the science-fictional while still suggesting the horrific. With the intrusion of a larger form of evil—the Walking Dude, in King's tale—the horror becomes overt. Still, it all begins with the minuscule.

There are good reasons for focusing on the small. In *Violet Eyes,* everyone in the small town near the Florida Everglades understands intuitively that something is desperately wrong. The survivor, Billy, arrives at the mainland carrying his best friend's body. Immediately thereafter, the authorities first examine, then utterly sterilize the island (thus letting readers know for certain that whatever the flies and spiders are, they are absolutely *not* dead). In the meantime, various characters note the unusual prevalence of flies and spiders; first pets and later humans begin disappearing; webs form in crevices and corners; and gradually houses become enshrouded in webs…and the horror is made manifest.

Because the cause is small and — except for their violet markings — appear normal, attempts to defeat it are delayed until it is too late. Perhaps one weakness in *Violet Eyes,* is the simple fact that a major character can disappear for pages, his house can become covered with webs, and no one seems to notice or care. Eventually, however, it becomes clear to the survivors that something horrendous has happened, and the novel's remaining characters, especially a divorced woman and her son, must flee not only the spiders and flies but the government forces that have assembled to quarantine and destroy the town.

And because the cause is small — the creatures are small — readers are invited to empathize almost as much over her difficulties with her brutal ex-husband and her newfound boyfriend as with her initial encounters with the insects. Then, inevitably, the two strands of the narrative contract until all that remains is sheer survival.

But, again, the cause is small, at times almost invisible. Perhaps it is already too late.

All creatures — GREAT, SMALL, and in-between — are fundamental in horror. Each extreme offers strengths and each suffers from weaknesses. The choice of creature, especially in terms of size, determines how a novel needs to be structured; how its setting can be made most relevant; how its characters may and may not interact with the encroaching horror; and how difficult it will be for the author to control the relationship between gigantics and humans or between miniscules and humans. When any of these elements are weakly handled, the novel may suffer. When handled well, the novel succeeds.

Chapter 18

How to Write Post-Apocalyptic Fiction

Sometimes there are *no* monsters in horror fiction. Sometimes, the landscape becomes the monster, especially when it has been irradiated by a nuclear holocaust, poisoned by pollution, choked by over-population, thrown out of kilter in any number of human-inspired ways. Such landscapes lead to a fascinating sub-category of horror: post-apocalyptic fiction.

The fact that there do not *have* to be monsters creates an interesting dilemma for authors of such stories. There may be intrusive elements that might otherwise count as monsters, particularly in recent years, zombies rising from the ashes of a shattered world. But often the world itself is sufficient to generate outstanding horror.

Post-apocalyptic fiction can stand on its own as novel-length explorations of what happens when the suddenly familiar becomes not only unfamiliar but deadly. To a degree, such novels share as much with science fiction as they do with horror, and many of them work hard to remain explicitly science-fictional: if thus-and-such technological change were to occur, this world would be the result. Beginning with Mary Shelley's *The Last Man* (1826), in which the twenty-first-century survivors of a global plague must adjust to their new world, the form has remained popular ever since.

Just as powerful, however, can be short stories that encapsulate the catastrophe into the experiences of one or two key characters. Often, the nature of the catastrophe has to be intuited by readers, particularly if sufficient time has passed for the characters themselves to be unaware of what has happened.

When I opened a review package some time ago, I immediately had great expectations for Ellen Datlow and Terri Windling's *After: Nineteen Stories of Apocalypse and Dystopia* (2012). The cover art was spectacular. I know that cover art is in some senses irrelevant to content, but in this case, the jacket design seemed perfectly apt for what I hoped to find between the covers. And beyond that, the cover simply *felt* perfect— slightly nubbly, almost as if it were beginning to decay after whatever cataclysm had destroyed the city and left the single man as witness.

Then I began reading. And I read. And read.

And never slowed or stopped. Not one story in *After* was other than what I had hoped for… engaging, thought-provoking, imaginative. The authors—and the editors—did everything right.

That is an important point—that they did everything right— because post-apocalyptic fiction lends itself to triteness, to clichés, to hackneyed images that have recurred so frequently in films and stories that, instead of generating fear, horror, or terror, they are more likely to generate a yawn. To that extent, *After* provides a blueprint for how to write such tales.

THE APOCALYPSE:

The wrong way:

For aficionados of the late, great 1950s sf/horror films, the wrong way to begin a post-apocalyptic tale will sound shudderingly familiar. A voice—deep, resonant, rather like the voice of God—speaks while the screen shows planet Earth as seen from space. Or the restless oceans. Or distant horizons set against total emptiness. The voice then says something like: "In the year 2050 the nations of Earth finally came close to annihilating themselves and destroyed all but our plucky band of survivors living in a tiny valley, protected from the fallout and the atomic mutants." In other words, the setting is *explained* before the story actually begins. The disaster is described, its consequences enumerated, and then—finally—we meet our characters.

The right way:

At the core of each story in *After* is a cataclysm, a disaster, an *apocalypse*. The word goes back to a Greek root meaning 'to uncover, to reveal.' That is precisely what the nineteen authors—including some of the finest in contemporary horror—have done. Rather than taking the easy way (easy for writers and for readers) of setting the stage by describing in great detail what has just happened, they allow readers to 'discover' the nature of the catastrophes that have overtaken their characters and their characters' worlds. In several instances, we never find out exactly what did happen, but the after-effects are so horrific that the causes begin to seem irrelevant. Whether by accident or design, something was unleashed or released, and all humanity, represented by the characters, have suffered and will suffer from it.

In one story, in fact—Matthew Kressel's "The Great Game at the End of the World"—there is no reason given at all. Told in flashback during the world's last baseball game, the story simply shows the main character in school…when *something* happens and the walls collapse and several of his friends are lying there dead and only he, apparently, has survived. He eventually finds his sister, a few others, and a number of Creepies, alien creatures that have for some reason attended the event. This story actually comes closest to the fundamental, theological definition of the word; the revelation of God. Sort of.

THE SURVIVORS:

The wrong way:

In weakly thought-through apocalyptic fiction, at some point one character looks soulfully into another's eyes and says something like, "Oh, don't you wish things were like they used to be, before that rogue asteroid the scientists named Montieth-Cummings AG22141 veered for some unknown reason from its path past the earth, shattered the dark side of the moon, and caused that mysterious dust to fall over everything so that now everyone who has ever died has risen as either a zombie or a vampire. Oh, for the good old days."

This is the least effective way to identify what has happened and its consequences for the characters, if for no other reason that humans— particularly humans under stress—don't generally talk this way. They use short-cuts for long phrases, clipped forms for longer, unfamiliar words…and seldom rehearse the details of a cataclysm to someone else who already knows them, at least not this bluntly. The result is stilted dialogue. It is unconvincing, and—most deadening of all—it stops the action until the indigestible lump of exposition is finished. By then, of course, it is entirely possible that the reader has gone elsewhere for a stronger story.

The right way:

In *After*, the writers and their characters rarely discuss the catastrophes in any but terms of effects. One of the few that describes it directly is Gregory Maguire's challenging "How Th'Irth Wint Rong by Hapless Joey@ homeskool.guv." Most of the story is told—hand-written on paper—by an uneducated survivor struggling to put his memories into words...and to spell them correctly. There are a few interruptions by his tutor, whose literary expertise barely exceeds his. But Maguire reserves the key bit of data ("the SuperCollider collapsed") for a character outside the limits of the story, punctuating the irony of Joey's attempts to express something he will never understand.

In another, "Rust with Wings" by Stephen Gould, there is no effort at all to explain how it came about that metallic-colored metal-devouring insects have destroyed great swaths of the Southwest. It is sufficient to know that they have...and that the characters know no more about their genesis than the readers do. In effect, readers are encouraged to discover the ramifications of the disaster along with characters. In a world in which everyone fifteen and older transforms into a ravaging, flesh-eating beast—as in Nalo Hopkinson's "The Easthound"—the key is not *why?* but rather what happens when characters realize that *they* are approaching that age, and how the recognition alters their views of relationships, of kindred, of self.

ALIENS (IF ANY):

The wrong way:

Once more I'm drawn to images from 1950s sf movies when considering the wrong way to deal with aliens. Again and again, at some point in those great old films, the creature from beyond steps into the camera frame...with ludicrous results. A disembodied puppet-head glowering menacingly from inside a clear sphere. Something resembling a giant carrot shuffling down the corridors of an Arctic outpost. And— perhaps my favorite—gigantic eyeballs pulling themselves along with ridiculously frail tentacles. In each case, the intention was (presumably) to horrify, yet by giving too much detail, by showing the mechanical horrors too clearly, too crisply (and thereby revealing the human mechanics by which they were created), the films achieved the opposite result (and I'm old enough to remember *not* being frightened by them when they first appeared). They become laughable, something to be enjoyed again and again because of, rather than in spite of, their technological ineptness.

The right way:

The aliens (in the several stories in *After* that depend upon them) are not shown landing and taking over the earth; that is not the point of the anthology. In several instances, as in Garth Nix's "You Won't Feel a Thing," the invaders are not shown at all. Instead, the stories emphasize the *effects* of their presence on the survivors.

Lines between alien and human may blur as the consequences of apocalyptic change emerge. Genetics and genetic manipulation may transform humans into chimeras. Aliens may accompany the disruption of the earth, may comment on events, may even participate in the last baseball game on the planet—but the stories remain bound to the humans involved. Their sufferings, their discoveries, their lives, and their deaths give *After* its extraordinary power.

LANGUAGE:

The wrong way:

The easiest way to suggest a post-apocalyptic world is to fiddle with the language. Unless the writer is as brilliant as Anthony Burgess in *A Clockwork Orange*—in which he provides details about the overthrow of England by the Russians *only* through neologisms and portmanteau words—most attempts to do so come across as strained dialogue or narration filled with agglomerations of unpronounceable consonants that, for weaker writers, represent alien intelligences.

The right way:

Instead, in *After*, language is used almost as a character. The distance between today's speech patterns and the characters' languages reflects the impact of the disaster. What has disappeared leaves behind few words to linger over despondently; instead, new words are generated to define new realities, or old words take on new meanings...and readers must intuit those meanings as part of the discovery. *Hairies, counters, the Rosamund, the Rehabilitated, THE EVENT, THE BEFORE, THE AFTER, the sprouteds*...these and many other words/phrases take on significance far beyond their usual meanings as they become opportunities for discovery.

THE MESSAGE:

The wrong way:

Many stories have an underlying message—a theme—that the writer wishes to illuminate. In the hands of someone unsure of the story's ability to exist first *as a story* and secondarily *as a message*, there are occasional moments when the author emerges through the texture of the tale to state the moral outright. In the 19th century, it was acceptable to find sentences such as, "And thus, Dear Reader, we find that little children should always respect and obey their elders lest they, too, be eaten by the Great Golliwog hiding beneath the stairs!" In the 21st, even though such overtness is generally frowned upon, it nonetheless persists.

The right way:

Again, in *After*, only rarely does theme rise directly to the surface. Perhaps closest to an allegory, in which characters represent particular personality traits and hence become flat figures manipulated by a moral, is Sarah Rees Brennan's tale of Fair Rosamond, the objectified prize to be handed over to the single survivor of the Trial…as a way of eliminating a generation of young men who might otherwise cause civil unrest. Set in the future, it carefully builds on fairy-tale/Arthurian motifs, even including characters' names: Rosamond, Yvain, and the Order Knights. It does not, however, point to a specific moral until the final line, when Rosamond's desires and the storyline merge in a single, statement that is at once both culmination and declaration. With her final words, we understand—without being told over and again—that the story has been about freeing women from shackles of male domination and expectation. It is carefully, effectively, and beautifully handled throughout.

Others stories touch upon theme. Some virtually challenge readers to sit back and think about how the story relates to *Before*, that is, to their own world. Through concerns about runaway technology, aggressiveness and mindless warfare, class struggles, unhampered belief systems (both theological and scientific), and Earth's place in the universe itself, *After* offers imaginative, explorative, speculative visions of possibilities and consequences, without descending into indoctrination or propaganda. The stories are, and remain, essentially excellent *stories*.

THE PACKAGE:

The wrong way:

Assembling any collection/anthology is frustrating at best. Placement of stories is crucial, particularly so when, as in *After*, each story posits the End of Things. Which "End" should come first? Which last? How can the middle stories be protected from medial slump—that sense that less powerful pieces have been sandwiched between more powerful initial and terminal ones.

There are several mechanical ways that sometimes work. Chronology of stories by authors' birth dates provided a useful structure for *Great Tales of Terror and the Supernatural* since the anthology spanned roughly a century and a half. But for a collection of contemporary horror, that arrangement would be less than useless.

Stories might be arranged chronologically by publication date. Again, that would prove valid if they ranged over a number of years and if all were reprints. For a volume containing original fiction...useless.

Sometimes anthologies go alphabetically by authors' last names. This seems the most mechanical of all and essentially suggests that the stories could be arranged in *any* order and they would be just as effective. Nearly useless.

What often results from mechanical arranging is an anthology that may have an overriding theme but that seems basically a random collection of stories.

The right way:

After is a coherent, unified whole. Each story is in the right place to play off the one before and to resonate with the one following. The pacing allows for lighter moments to interrupt more somber ones. Jane Yolen's short poem, "Gray," for example, picks up on the final tone of Hopkinson's "The Easthound" in its opening line, "How many ways to describe gray...." The horror of the final revelations in the story prepares readers for the melancholic undertones of the poem's first stanza. Then, toward the end, Yolen introduces "red" and notes that eventually, gray will be little more than a memory...and leads seamlessly into Carolyn Dunn's "Before," which begins in horror and ends in hope.

The stories in *After* are not arranged programmatically to create anything like a novelistic effect, of course. Each is independent. Each has its own strengths. Yet the transition from one to the next never jars. There is only a strong sense of completion...and anticipation.

CONCLUSION

After is certainly not the only successful anthology of post-apocalyptic tales. The sub-genre is alive and well, and—given the world we live in and the pessimistic outlook many have for its, and *our*, future—it bodes fair to continue as a powerful instrument not only for telling stories but for exhortation and dehortation...identifying trends that might prove either salvation or destruction. But *After* is among the best, and writers could benefit from examining in greater detail what its editors and its authors have done right.

Part Four: Foundations—Words

Chapter 19

When Words Stumble

Writers are courageous human beings. Sir Philip Sidney argued this. Percy Bysshe Shelley did also. When I was teaching intermediate poetry at Pepperdine, required of all creative writing majors before they could take upper-division, specialized courses, I began by reassuring students that by virtue of having written a single poem—of having exposed their deepest selves to unknown readers and critics—they were in fact and in deed superior human beings.

I also remember, however, an incident in my public speaking course as a college freshman. We were eventually to turn in our first outlines for a speech. The professor asked for one of the preliminary outlines to anatomize, on the assumption that we would all learn from that student's mistakes. When a student gave her one, she put it in the opaque projector (yes, I am that technologically ancient), stared at it for a few moments, then pulled it from the machine, handed it none-too-graciously back to the student, and said, "I want another one. I can't teach from perfection."

There had been no mistakes on the outline; hence she had nothing to say about it.

Keeping both of these ideas in mind, I am going to do something that I rarely do outside of class, where students actually expect me to talk about poor sentences and weak structures. I am going to look at some sentences in a published novel and try to assess what happens when words stumble. I am going to analyze *imperfection*.

(For my purposes, since this will not be a dialogue between the author and me, I will not identify author, title, or publisher. Where needed, I will change the names in quoted passages to protect innocent characters.)

The book begins:

> Sixty seconds.
> That was how long [Character A] figured he had to live. The doctor in attendance, the one who quickly located the vein in his left arm and then stabbed the IV inside, started the process over a minute ago.

Four lines—and several problems.

The first is wordiness. "The doctor in attendance, the one who quickly located" is roughly twice as long as needed. Since "the one who" refers, as far as the reader can know, to the single doctor mentioned just before, the relative phrase can be eliminated and consolidated with the kernel sentence. "Quickly" indicates primarily that the author doesn't feel that "located" is strong enough and that it requires modification, while "stabbed" is an odd substitute for the more logical "jabbed." The two actions—*stabbing* and *jabbing*—are not exactly identical, and the second seems more appropriate to inserting an IV needle. Time throughout is confused...and confusing. "Who located" and "started the process" both indicate simple past—actions continuing in the past. Yet the first sentence is clear that the actions in question *began and ended* in the completed past; to be technically correct, both verbs should be in the past-perfect tense. The phrase "Started the process," while providing a verb and object for "doctor," seems vague, static; the key sentence verbals might better be "located" and "stabbed" (or "jabbed").

Revised to eliminate these wobbles, the paragraphs might read:

> Sixty seconds.
> That was how long [Character A] figured he had to live. The doctor in attendance *had* located the vein in his left arm and *jabbed* the IV in over a minute ago. (Italics mine)

I would prefer *before* to *ago*, but that is essentially a stylistic change, so I won't insist.

The original required forty-one words; my revision, only thirty-four words, or a loss of nearly 20%, along with gaining a clearer time-frame, agent-appropriate verbs, and a stronger sense of action.

Quibbling over nothing? After all, the writer has communicated the essence of the opening; we know important things about the character (he is dying, presumably being executed although that is not yet clear; a doctor is killing him for some reason), and we know that the story hinges in some important way on "sixty seconds." Isn't all of that claptrap about word choice and verb tenses and wordiness going a bit far?

It might indeed be, except that in prose fiction, readers are heavily influenced by opening paragraphs. One sentence might be sufficient to impel readers into the story or turn them away from it. If the first sentences leave readers with a sense of disjunction, confused about when things happened/are happening, about precisely what actions are being performed (stabbing or jabbing), that might be enough to close the story down.

For the purposes of this essay, however, I will assume that, even in spite everything, readers will choose to continue.

Toward the end of the first chapter, half a dozen or so pages in, readers will find: "She told me not to say anymore then I already have." Two simple errors. *Anymore* is an adverb of time, meaning 'at the present'; but *say* requires an object, and objects are nouns or noun-functioning words. The sentence should read: "She told me not to say any more...." Similarly, *Then* is an adverb of time, indicating past; *than* is a conjunction used to introduce a comparison. The full sentence should read: "She told me not to say any more than I already have."

Two errors in twelve words; the numbers don't inspire confidence in the story. One—particularly *then*—might be shrugged off as a typo, but taken together they indicate that the writing is not entirely under control.

Further in, readers encounter this: "She was levitating slightly, just sort of hovering above the ground. The bottom of her gown rested about two inches above the floor." Here the problems become both simpler and more complex—simpler, because they are easier to note; and more complex because of what they imply about the writing.

To *levitate* means to 'float in the air' or, in this case, to 'hover'; *slightly* indicates that there is not much distance involved; hence, the second half of the sentence is not only wordy, with the vague "just sort of," but unnecessary. Lest readers not get the point, however, the second sentence specifies "two inches," giving dimensions to "slightly" and "just sort of." In the first sentence, she was hovering above "ground"; in the second, above a "floor." The two words may at times form synonyms, but since earlier paragraphs indicated that the characters are in a room, "floor" would be appropriate. And I'm not sure that the *bottom* of the gown—the *hem*?—would *rest* several inches in the air.

The sentence might better read: "She was levitating, the hem of her gown two inches above the floor." Original: twenty-three words. Revision: ten words, or more than half of the original sentence removed.

A page later (and we are still no more than a score of pages into the story), readers find this description of the gown:

> Flowing back and forth, the gown was red and white. It was shapely to her hips but then wide and full at the bottom as it hovered above the floor. Like something worn to a state dinner at the White House or possibly an 1880's ball.
>
> The gown looked like it was made of red and white satin and covered in blood stains. The bottom was tattered and the blood must've come from many tortures that didn't go well for the victim. The white went dirty years ago and came encrusted with snot and mucus many centuries old. The sleeves were full length and covered her arms all the way down to her hands.

All right. Where to start? With the misapplied "shapely"? With the redundancy of "wide and full"? With the overt repetition in the opening sentence of the second paragraph, or with the curious understatement in the second of "tortures that didn't go well for the victim" (as though *any* torture benefited *any* victims, and was there more than one victim over the centuries?)? Or with the assertion that the white had discolored only years before but that the snot and mucus (which are ways of saying the same thing) discoloring it were centuries old (and was the red dirty as well or miraculously free of bodily secretions)? Or with the discovery that full-length sleeves go all the way to the hands?

In fact, although the passage wants to invite visualization, the words used actively inhibit that same visualization. Instead, they repeat needlessly, confuse through inaccuracies and imprecisions, and generally check the momentum of the horrors involved and of the narrative.

One final example, perhaps the easiest to identify and to rectify:

> He calmed himself instantly and then turned to the orderlies standing directly behind him. With a huge amount of vomit, puss, old corn, bits of cheese, and

something green hanging from his moustache and face, [Character B] reached out to the closest of the orderlies and grabbed him by the neck. He pulled the man up close enough to smell his breath.

For this one, there is only a single question: Where did the cat come from?

Please remember that this is not an exercise in ridicule. The book in question spans nearly 350 pages, presents readers with varied and potentially intriguing characters, constructs a landscape that invites the ultimate in horror and fear, and follows a narrative designed from the opening pages to assault readers' sensibilities at every level. The author invested a great deal of time, effort, and self in completing the book. All of this merits approbation.

Where the book falters is in the execution, in the selection of specific words at precise moments to create needed effects. Instead of horror, therefore, something close to unintentional comedy emerges. With a single letter, the last example transforms from horrendous to merely grotesque, possibly ludicrous, certainly absurd. None of that was intended, yet the letter *is* there. It deflects attention from the narrative and ultimately defeats the purpose of the passage.

Words are tools. Writers are artisans (as well as artists). They must employ those tools carefully and correctly in order to accomplish their ends.

Chapter 20

Good Words/Bad Words

There are no "good" words. There are only words used precisely and accurately in appropriate contexts.

And there are no "bad" words. There are only words used imprecisely and inaccurately in inappropriate contexts.

Words are essentially neutral. They are arbitrary constructs of letters or sounds that by themselves carry no meaning. The easiest way to confirm this is to look at how different languages label specific things: cat, dog, fish, house. No two languages use exactly the same arrangement of letters or sounds to refer to these universal (or at least global) concepts. In fact, some languages do not even share the same physical symbols for sounds (for example, Japanese and Chinese ideographs compared with western letters). And most languages contain sounds that are often difficult if not impossible for speakers of other languages to replicate. The slightest movement of the tongue against the teeth, or an infinitesimal shift of the jaw, or a minor drop in pitch in speaking can transform a word and, knowingly or not, force it to refer to something unintended.

Yet in every composition or creative writing class I have taught, at some point someone would ask if it was permitted to use "bad" words in essays or poems. There was no question what the students meant; there are certain of those arbitrary constructs of letters and sounds that our culture has deemed unsuitable for polite discourse. At one point or another in history, however, most of those words were acceptable, at least when spoken. In the Prologue to the *Canterbury Tales*, by Geoffrey Chaucer, the Father of English Poetry, and intended primarily for an aristocratic/noble audience (there were few other audiences for physical books at the time), Chaucer writes:

> And shame it is, is a prest take keep,
> A shiten shepherde and a clene sheep.
> Wel oghte a preese ensample for to yive,
> By his clennesse, how that his sheep sholde lyve.

If the Middle-English seems difficult, read the passage out loud, using modern pronunciation and ignoring the problematical final *e*. And there the tricky word is, the first strongly accented word in the second line, parading itself in written verse, and no one appears to have objected at the time.

Similarly, words which societies at one time considered improper now fit perfectly well into conversation and writing. *Sweater* raised the hackles of Victorians, perhaps because it referred openly to a bodily function; *pullover* or *cardigan* were preferred. *Bleachers* likewise indicated that the speaker/writer was of a lower class.

(Note: I realize that there is one word—*the* bad word—that has never been acceptable, but I will talk about it later.)

The terms most helpful in determining when words are "good" or "bad"—that is, are appropriate or inappropriate—are *denotation* and *connotation*.

DENOTATION:

The first is the most straightforward. It simply means "what the word means according to commonly accepted definitions, i.e., the dictionary."

Meaning itself is complex. As noted above, words don't actually *mean* anything; we *assign* meanings to certain strings of letters or collations of sounds. There is nothing inherently "doggish" about *d-o-g*, yet most English speakers and readers know in general what it refers to—a four-legged, hairy mammal that goes *bow-wow*. In Finnish, of course, it might go *vuff*, in Japanese, *wan-wan*, and so on. But in general, we recognize a *dog* when we see one.

Societies tacitly agree that particular sets of symbols will represent certain things. Through time, such agreements may shift, and words may take on vastly different meanings. *Knight* (back when it was usually spelled *cniht*) initially meant boy or servant; now it refers to a man holding a specific level within a hierarchy of rank, one who usually has servants of his own.

It becomes important, then, to recognize that words can be slippery. With the internet and its access to world-wide spoken and written languages, words can and do change meanings rapidly...or, perhaps more frustrating, accumulate new meanings, often at odds with the original senses. *Cleave*, as used in the King James Version of the Bible— "Therefore shall a man leave his father and his mother, and shall *cleave* unto his wife: and they shall be one flesh" — means 'to hold to, to adhere, to be close'; when used in modern parlance, it is more likely to mean 'to separate, to cut apart, as with a *cleaver*.' I might use it in the older sense; you might read it and assign the modern sense to it...and whatever I meant to say is lost in confusion.

Take another example, a more common one. *Set* comes from an old Germanic root meaning 'to sit.' A thousand years or so after it first entered English, it can mean many more things: a television set, a set of encyclopedias, to set the table, wait for concrete to set, set one's hair, find that the Jell-O hasn't set. Same word, entirely different *denotations*. In fact, in the *Oxford English Dictionary*, the word has over 140 meanings, none of them repetitions.

So I say *set*; you hear *set*—and there's a good chance we still are not communicating precisely. Here, context becomes crucial. One does not, for example, want the Jell-O to set in exactly the same way as concrete sets.

CONNOTATION:

Words not only have lexical (that is dictionary-based) meanings, but they also have a sphere of emotional suggestions attached to them. Few words outside the mostly functional terms in English—*is, are, was, were, to, from, and, but,* and others—mean *only* what the dictionary says. For various reasons, whether cultural, regional, or personal, most words echo not only in our brains but in our hearts...and occasionally in our nervous systems. When that happens, we have entered the realm of connotation.

In my classes, I would frequently write the word *cellar* on the board and ask the students if they responded positively or negatively to it. In almost every case, the result was a 50/50 split, with a handful or so remaining neutral.

When I asked for reasons why some considered the word positive, I got answers that ranged from "That was where we played as children," to "There were always secrets and mysteries, old furniture, interesting things to explore," to "That's where Grandma kept the ice cream."

Most of the neutrals admitted that they had never lived in a house with a cellar, so generally they didn't even think about the word.

The negatives...ah, the negatives spoke to my horror-writer imagination: "dark," "creepy," "dirt floor covered with some kind of white crusty stuff," "windowless," "10-watt light bulb," "shadowy," and on and on.

Same word. For one group, shivers of anticipation and warm memories; for another group, shivers of quite another kind.

Many words just don't fit certain contexts, not because of what the word might mean but because of cultural associations built into them. Perhaps we are reading in the society pages of the newspaper, or, more likely, on someone's online blog and we come across the following: "The bride was resplendent in her gown of white satin and floor-length lace veil...." Everything is acceptable so far, if a bit trite, but what if the sentence ends with—"with a lovely bouquet of fragrant roses in her fist"?

Fist?

Wrong word, even though, if we imagine the situation and see the bride's hand gripping the bouquet, her knuckles perhaps white from nervousness and tension and anticipation, the word *fist* may be *literally* appropriate.

This kind of wobble occurs more frequently than any others in the manuscripts and printed texts I've read lately. The almost-the-right word slips in unnoticed by the writer; but the reader notices and experiences a slight start. For example, in an otherwise excellent, story-driven novel, I came upon this: "...she raised her head again, to surmise her new surroundings...." And for a moment, everything interesting and exciting about the *story* faded in the glaring light of a perfectly fine word used inappropriately. I was startled *out of the story* and *into the writing*.

Too many startling moments, and the reader might just decide to go elsewhere for entertainment.

For writers of fiction—and *especially* for writers of horror fiction or dark fiction—connotation may be as important as, even more important than, denotation. English has the largest vocabulary of any modern language group. There may be many words that *denotatively* fit a context; but to create atmosphere, to delineate character, to establish a landscape, there may be only one that works *connotatively*. Quick example: Why do we say "Pacific Ocean" and not "Pacific Sea," or "South Seas" and not "South Oceans"? *Denotatively* the two key words, *ocean* and *sea,* mean 'large bodies of water,' but almost intuitively we recognize that they are not precisely interchangeable.

(Note: one of my professors once claimed that there were only two exact synonyms—denotatively and connotatively—in the English language: *furze* and *gorse*, both referring to a species of highland heather. It's too bad that we don't have many opportunities to use them.)

"Good" words, then, are words that have precisely the meaning intended, that are used in a context that will clarify any potential ambiguities, and that are appropriate to the desired audience. One of my favorite words, *pneumonoultramicroscopicsilicovolcanoconiosis*, while devised in 1935 to make a point, is nonetheless a "good" word when used medically or as an example of a long word. If a doctor is addressing a group of miners on the subject of the dangers of their profession, however, it would be a "bad" word—probably no one there except the doctor would know what it means, and even the doctor might have difficulty pronouncing it. The appropriate "good" word for that audience would be "black lung." The short phrase means the same thing as the long word, but the latter more clearly defines something miners might have experienced.

"Bad" words create a bit more difficulty.

In one sense, a "bad" word is any word that is difficult for the audience—whether readers or listeners—to understand within the context. When I was in high school, I discovered the beauties of the thesaurus. I wrote an essay for English class, along the way looking up six common words and replacing them with "better" words—that is, with longer, Latinate, complex terms. I didn't know *pneumonoultramicroscopicsilicovolcanoconiosis* at the time, or I might have been tempted to slide it in.

When the teacher returned the paper, it had eight marks on it. One was the grade in the upper right-hand corner. Numbers two through six were red circles around *every* fancy word I had used. And number seven was a curt note: *"Burn your thesaurus!"*

I've since learned that a thesaurus can be a helpful tool, if a treacherous crutch. But I also learned my lesson: Don't use a long word unless it is a "good" word—fitting to the meaning intended, the context, and the audience. I'm sure the teacher understood the words; that wasn't the problem. They just did not fit into a high school freshman's essay.

Even what we traditionally consider "bad" words may function as "good" words.

C.S. Lewis's children's fantasy *The Magician's Nephew* (1955) is thematically and chronologically the first of the Chronicles of Narnia, even though it was the sixth written of seven. Just about in the middle of the book, one of the characters, Uncle Andrew, is rather roughly treated by some of the newly created animals of Narnia. When he has reached his limit, he says, "Damn!" Not much in the way of swearing for contemporary readers but a shocker to find in a children's book in the mid-1950s. More than that, it is the *first* occurrence of any such language, or thinking, in the nascent Narnia, and signals the more serious fall to come with the eventual arrival of the White Witch. It distorts the perfection of Narnia, it jars with the courtliness of speech that has been developing, it resonates uncomfortably through the remaining volumes, and it demonstrates that Lewis knew precisely when and how to use a "good" "bad" word.

Another example: As a junior in college, I heard one of my professors talking about "bad" words. His father, he said, was a rough-and-tumble man, rugged, largely unlearned, who apparently did not fully understand what made his rather short, bespectacled, bookish son tick. Just before my professor went off to college (the first, I believe, in his family to do so), he spent the summer working with his father...quite literally digging ditches.

On the afternoon of the last day before he was to leave for school, he and his father were sitting on the edge of a trench they had just finished. His father sat quietly for a while, then reached down, squeezed his son's knee, and said, "Ya did a good job, ya little bastard."

My professor said that those words struck him straight to the heart. He recognized at once that that was the only way his father had of saying "I love you." He had used the language and the verbal structures appropriate to his life, to his education, to his outlook. He could not have said it any other way.

I strongly suspect, given the time that has passed since first hearing that anecdote, that his father probably said something stronger than *bastard,* something that would have been wholly out of place in a sedate English classroom in a small, faith-based liberal-arts college in the late 1960s. But even as stated, the story made its point. In *that* context, to *that* audience, coming from *that* speaker, *bastard* was a "good" word. It communicated precisely what the speaker intended.

Which leads us to...*the word*. The only English word that has *never* been socially acceptable, that for centuries was prohibited in writing, and that until the mid-1900s rarely if ever appeared.

Some years ago, while teaching Freshman Composition at UCLA, I asked the students to write an essay tracking how a word had changed meanings over time. I left the choice largely up to them (after excluding words like *reality* and *meaning*—I couldn't face the probable redundancies), including obscenities and vulgarisms as options.

A few days later, one young woman in the class stayed after to tell me something that had happened. She was typing her draft at home (this was long before computers and laptops became popular) when her father walked by. He glanced at the paper in the typewriter, took another step or two, did a classic double-take, and stormed back.

"What…!"

"Don't worry, Daddy," she said, pointing to the word *fuck* at the top of the page. "I'm just talking about it. I'm not *saying* it."

Half a dozen others chose the same word; but largely because of the onus the word has developed when actually written, those papers were among the stiffest, most awkward, least confident essays I ever received, even though I remain convinced that more than a few of those students actually *spoke* the word regularly. They just couldn't *write* it.

More than thirty years have passed since then, and the word has suffered a sea-change. Where before using it assured a text of a certain shock value, a kind of verbal intimidation, and the writer of equally certain notoriety, in contemporary prose very nearly the opposite happens.

The more often the word appears, the less shocking it is.

I have used it. Three times in *The House Beyond the Hill* (2011), with one of those occurrences on the first page. The speaker was not someone who would hit his thumb with a hammer and yell, "Oh golly-gee, shucky-darn!" I wanted his language to characterize him immediately, and I think it worked.

In *The Slab* (2011), which is considerably longer and far more violent, one character says it *once*. The whole point of the word is to demonstrate graphically that his essential nature had altered from being in the house. That word defines how rapidly and how radically.

In reading contemporary horror—and particularly unpublished manuscripts—I am disturbed by how frequently writers simply let fly. Every sentence, sometimes every other word…and after the first few pages of that, the mind becomes numb. Instead of shocking and intimidating, instead of even offending, the word, subject to such overuse, does something infinitely worse.

It bores.

It degenerates to a meaningless placeholder.

It becomes a cliché.

And, as with most clichés, readers simply tune it out. When that happens, it becomes truly a "bad" word.

So—"good"? or "bad"? As with so many things in life, the choice is left up to the writer, the final arbiter of whether or not a word is precise, accurate, and appropriate. And the ultimate question: "Does it work?"

Chapter 21

Only....

Words can be frustrating. Some are funny. A few are even whimsical.

Here is a bit of my favorite whimsy:

In general, English depends on word-order for meaning...and in general, most words will fill only a limited number of positions. If you take the following everyday-type sentence—"The carnivorous rats surrounded the blood-red barn"—and shift the main parts, chances are you will end up with:

> GIBBERISH—"Surrounded the carnivorous rats the blood-red barn" and "Surrounded the blood-red barn the carnivorous rats" or
>
> SURREALISM—"The blood-red barn surrounded the carnivorous rats" or
>
> A vague kind of YODA-SPEAK (and to get even that much sense you have to add a word)—"Surrounded the blood-red barn did the carnivorous rats."

On the whole, in contemporary English, subjects of sentences come first, followed by the action (the verb), and completed by whatever words or phrases are required by the verb. Adjectives usually come before nouns; adverbs before verbs or adjectives. There are, of course, exceptions to all of these generalizations, but following these conventions will usually result in intelligible, English-sounding sentences.

There is one word, however, that basically ignores most of the accepted rules for its designated parts of speech. *Only* carries a wide range of meanings: as an adverb, it suggests 'solely,' 'alone,' 'as recent as,' and other possibilities; as an adjective, it emphasizes singularity—the only child, the only survivor, the one and only....

As an adverb, it should precede its verb or another adverb: "the only blue book." As an adjective, it should precede its noun: "the only book."

But the curious thing about *only* is that—unlike its fellow adverbs and adjectives—it can appear almost anywhere in a sentence, and with each new appearance it alters meanings and interpretations.

Let's take a simple sentence: "I went to the store to buy a loaf of bread."

Now watch the permutations possible when *only* shows up:

"**Only** I went to the store to buy a loaf of bread"—no one else accompanied me, I was by myself, since everyone else was too frightened of the carnivorous rats to go.

"I **only** went to the store to buy a loaf of bread"—that's the solitary place I went, nowhere else. Don't blame me if the bank down the street was robbed. Or, it could mean that buying bread was my solitary purpose for going there. I promise I didn't buy a Snickers bar along the way.

"I went **only** to the store to buy a loaf of bread"—again, the store was my solitary goal. I'm still not responsible for the bank robbery. And, no, I didn't stop at the cleaners to pick up your laundry.

"I went to **only** the store to buy a loaf of bread"—as above, I visited no other outlets of commerce, but this time I'm more emphatic in saying so. This version sounds slightly non-idiomatic, so it would probably not occur often.

"I went to the **only** store to buy a loaf of bread"—here I am, stuck in this hick farm town, surrounded by blood-red barns and carnivorous rats, and there is but a single store anywhere to be seen.

"I went to the store **only** to buy a loaf of bread"—conceivably I might have been shopping for a shotgun or a bazooka to take out the carnivorous rats, but all I actually wanted was a loaf of bread.

"I went to the story to **only** buy a loaf of bread"—similar to the one above, less idiomatic, however, in part because of the apparent split infinitive, but more so because the structure places two vowels next to each other: *to* + *only*. To speak it requires a glottal stop—an awkward pause between the vowels to keep them from sliding into each other.

"I went to the store to buy **only** a loaf of bread"—an emphatic assertion. No matter what else might be offered on the shelves, I will be blind to all but that blasted loaf of bread.

"I went to the store to buy a **only** loaf of bread"—as it stands, this one is not English. However, with two small emendations, it become perfectly acceptable, and *only* fits comfortably in the slot. First, *a* and *only* begin with vowels. We could insert a glottal stop, but the conventions of English have long since provided a neater solution for *a*—add an *-n* to the article, making the phrase the easily pronounced "an only." Then, since the two resulting words contradict each other—*a* means 'any one of several' and *only* indicates singularity, and grammar won't accept both—shift the general article *a* to the specific article *the*, and we get the perfectly grammatical, "I went to the store to buy the only loaf of bread"—the single remaining loaf in the whole place. Whew! Took some work, but there is *only*, working hard for us as usual.

"I went to the store to buy a loaf **only** of bread"—that's all, just bread. No cinnamon swirls, no raisins, no nuggets of unground wheat, just bread.

"I went to the store to buy a loaf of **only** bread"—this seems to mean the same as the one above, but it also seems awkward. Still, pronounced with sufficient emphasis on ***only***, it does work...after a fashion.

"I went to the store to buy a loaf of bread **only**"—nothing, not a half-price package of Gummi-Bears or a brand-new box of dynamite to blow up the blood-red barn and slaughter all of the carnivorous rats will deter me from my purpose. Just the bread!

And there we have eleven out of twelve. And, as far as I know, among English adverbs/adjectives, only *only* can do that.

At least, I can only hope so.

Chapter 22

Adverbs: Villains or Victims?

It seems that, more and more, writers are saying nasty things about adverbs.

> "Remove adverbs!"
> "Eliminate adverbs!"
> "The road to hell is paved with adverbs!" (This latter from none other than Stephen King.)

As a general rule, there is some truth to what is being said. Used improperly or too frequently, adverbs can become a tag indicating a neophyte writer and lessening the impact of the prose. But "Destroy All Adverbs"? That seems a bit much, especially in light of the fact that in most cases, the blame we place on the poor adverb more justly belongs elsewhere.

The adverb is more victim than villain.

But first—and briefly—what is an *adverb*.

Essentially an adverb (or an adverbial, that is, any word or phrase that *functions* as an adverb) tells us something about either verbs, adjectives, or other adverbs. They *modify*, although that word itself is vague enough to generate a fair amount of uncertainty.

Most adverbs are single words, and of those that are, many end in the familiar *-ly*. Originally, the ending indicated that something *was* or *acted* like something else. The oldest forms in English were *-līċ* and *-līċe*, meaning simply 'like' or 'in such a manner.' *Cristlīċe* thus meant 'Christ-like,' or 'to behave in a manner reminiscent of Christ.' Through the centuries, English has maintained the tradition of clipping sounds, of making words simpler to speak. *–Līče* (pronounced 'lee-cha') became – *līč* ('leek'), which finally dropped the 'k' ending to become the modern *–ly*.

Adverbs may relate any of several bits of information: how, when, where, to what extent. They may compare or establish superlatives: *badly, worse, worst; soon, sooner, soonest.* They may require additional words to complete their modifications: *carefully, more carefully, most carefully.* Given the range of chores they may work to accomplish, there is little wonder that occasionally, they are forced beyond their limits. The most egregious abuses seem to occur, however when they are used to bolster weak speech tags and (often) even weaker bits of dialogue.

Let's look at a hypothetical bit of dialogue from a novel: "'I...I...I don't know...what should I do now?' he said haltingly." Obviously, this is a case where the final adverb telegraphs loudly that there is something desperately wrong with the sentence. However, when we look more closely, we discover that perhaps the problem is not quite as obvious as it seems.

Weak verbs (speech tags): The sentence relies on *said* to indicate a speech act. Actually, that is generally the most appropriate choice. It defines what the character in fact did: he *spoke*. He did not *chortle, grumble, grimace, smirk, smile, twinkle, hiss,* or any of the other almost infinite possibilities for verbs. He opened his mouth; formed sounds through the arrangement of lips, teeth, and tongue; and supplied or withheld breath as the circumstances required. Again, he *spoke.*

In the sample sentence, however, the simple *said* seems not quite enough, so the adverb *haltingly* is tacked on to give readers the illusion that they understand more about what is happening. But by doing so, the sentence transfers the weight of communication from the *verb —* which should clearly define the action — to the *adverb,* which is there to fine-tune the verb, not subsume its entire meaning.

Even so, *said* is by and large the best choice for a speech tag. The fact that it seems to require modification suggests that there is a deeper problem at work.

And there is.

Look at the line of dialogue: "I...I...I don't know...what should I do now?" Notice first that it is not a declarative but an interrogative; the question mark signals that our voices should rise on the final word, *now,* and turn the entire structure into a question. In that case, *said* becomes less appropriate; most writers would use *asked,* since, again, that is what actually happens.

Unfortunately, to do so leads to a redundancy. Grammatically the symbol "?" indicates that the previous structure is a question, an *asking*. Why then follow up immediately by repeating that bit of information and stipulate that the speaker has *asked*? (In Spanish, interestingly, questions are *already* redundant, since such structures begin with a question-making mark of punctuation, "¿" and conclude with another "?")

To replace *said* with *asked* does not resolve the problem: "'I...I...I don't know...what should I do now?' he asked haltingly" is in some senses even weaker than the quasi-declarative version...and again, the blame would probably fall first upon the adverb. And, to be sure, removing *haltingly* does seem to strengthen the question, although the suggestion of redundancy still remains.

Weak dialogue—or, rather, non-confident dialogue: If we probe even deeper, we discover the base cause for the problem is ultimately not the adverb, for it has been essentially tacked on as an afterthought; or the verb, for it is inaccurate and, if corrected, leads to a redundancy. The problem lies with the line of dialogue itself and the writer's lack of confidence in it.

If we look at the words themselves, what do they tell us: "I...I...I don't know...what should I do now?" First, the ellipses establish breaks—hesitations—in the line, clearly suggesting that the speaker is unsure of himself for some reason. The final phrase, which establishes the line of dialogue as a question, identifies what kind of speech act this is: an interrogation, a question. Nothing after that—"he asked haltingly"—adds any appreciable information. In fact, all that it adds are words whose functions have already been usurped by the line of dialogue itself.

And there is the true underlying problem. Not a superfluous adverb, not a squinting verb, but a line of dialogue that *does not need any further amplification to be understood.*

Or, if it does, the best response would be a second sentence identifying the speaker, not by his words or by the nature of his words, but by a relevant *action*: "'I...I...I don't know...what should I do now?' Mark wiped his hand across his brow and tried not to think of the blood gushing from Alina's neck."

Ah! Now we understand *that* he is speaking as if he is unsure of himself, and *why* he is speaking that way.

The point: It is facile and superficial to suggest that just deleting adverbs will automatically strengthen a story. It may be a first step, true; but that step must be followed by (1) an assessment of the speech-tag verb in terms of its applicability and its accuracy (i.e., can the human voice *do* what the verb requires); (2) an assessment of the line of dialogue itself to determine if it truly requires a speech tag at all, or if it has been written carefully enough that readers will immediately understand its lexical and its emotional impact; and (3) if more is needed, an assessment of what *relevant* action might be included to clarify the dialogue and make it even more powerful.

Adverbs, just like every other part of speech, have survived the millennia because they perform key functions that no other parts of speech can manage. They are fundamental to syntax, to grammar, and to meaning. Yes, they may be overused—*abused*—is perhaps an accurate word. But in almost every case, the problems they are supposed to be causing have deeper, underlying structural causes.

And the poor adverb—always the first to be accused—becomes more victim than villain.

Chapter 23

On the Pertinacity of Pronouns

Probably every writer has come across this problem at some point. A paragraph is progressing nicely, everything fitting into place, and suddenly—*wham!*—logic requires a singular, third-person pronoun: *he, she,* or *it.*

For most writers, especially those that dabble in horror, the third-person neuter presents no difficulty. We deal with *it* all of the time; perhaps the only hesitance comes when a genderless monster started out life as a human being, and we are tempted to use the masculine or feminine pronoun instead, just to humanize the monster a bit. Consistency requires that we choose one or the other, and in most cases—notably in King's magnificent novel by that name, *it* works well.

No, the problem comes when logic dictates either *he* or *she*. If the character in question is male, then *he* is appropriate; if female, then *she*. But what happens when the character can be either male or female? or both?

Traditionally (that is, following grammar rules I learned half a century ago), *he* is the default pronoun of choice, functioning as both third-person masculine and third-person neutral. The best example is still one I heard during fifth grade, when the teacher was struggling to make some sense of the complications that are English grammar. "Each student has received the book for tomorrow's lesson," she said. "Therefore each student must bring his book to class"—even though half of the class was female.

Problem presented and problem resolved...fifty years ago. *His* in the second sentence stood for both *his* and *hers*, as it had for roughly the previous thousand years in English usage.

Over the past fifty years, however, that solution has come to seem facile and—to some at least—offensive, as if the grammatical usage in some way spilled over into real life and made men in an invisible, arcane sense superior to women.

Well, we can't have that!

Therefore the grammar must change.

The easiest correction, of course, is to recast both sentences into the plural, since we have at our disposal a plural pronoun that identifies *both* males and females within a group. In such a case, the lesson would proceed as follows: "All students have received books for tomorrow's lesson. Therefore, all students must bring their books to class." Plural all around, and no one is offended.

When I began teaching at Pepperdine University in 1979, one of the long-time professors felt strongly that such a resolution was, at best, avoiding the issue and, at worst, generating awkwardness in expression. She suggested instead the creation of a new paradigm of gender-neutral personal pronouns to replace *he, him, his* and *she, her, hers*. Among them she included *heshe, shim,* and *herms*. For years, she argued for her new pronouns, arguing that they would be easier to use, that they would resolve the complexities of gender, and that they were close enough to tradition to be easily learned.

Her list never caught on.

Recently, Mills College was in the news because of an on-campus group that struggled with the same difficulty—what personal pronouns to use for someone who, for example, was physically female but identified as male. Neither *she* nor *he* seemed appropriate for the context. The article commented: "Inviting students to state their preferred gender pronouns, known as PGPs for short, and encouraging classmates to use unfamiliar ones such as 'ze,' 'sie,' 'e,' 'ou' and 've' has become an accepted back-to-school practice for professors, dorm advisers, club sponsors, workshop leaders and health care providers at several schools."

I understand in theory what the professors and others are trying to accomplish—I simply can't imagine them having any widespread success with the program, for one simple reason: pronouns are probably the most change-resistant parts of speech in English. In fact, the last major shift in personal pronouns took place somewhere around five hundred years ago. Nouns, verbs, adverbs, adjectives—all of the parts of speech that communicate *lexical* (that is, *dictionary*) meanings are almost completely fluid in English. Many have in fact reversed meanings over the years: *cleave*, for example, at one time meant 'to join irrevocably,' whereas now its most common meaning is 'to separate irrevocably.' But those tiny little words that seem to be almost irrelevant to communication—the articles (*a, an, the*), the prepositions (*in, on, by, with, for,* etc.) and the conjunctions (*and, but, for, so*)…*and* the pronouns are recognizable in written English from a thousand years ago.

There have been some shifts, of course.

The first-person pronouns have taken slightly different forms over the past millennia. *I* started as *īċ*, a cognate to the modern German *Ich*. *We* was pronounced differently (more like the modern *way*) but was still spelled *wē*. The only major difference a thousand years ago was the presence of a third class of first-person pronouns. In addition to singular (*I, me, my*) and plural (*we, our, ours*), there was a separate class called "dual," based on variations of *wit, unser,* and *unc,* that referred to 'just the two of us, you and me.'

The second-person pronouns were based on variations of *þū* (*thou/you*) and *ġē* (*ye/you,* plural*)*, pronounced respectively 'thu' and 'ye.' The remaining second-person forms were all recognizable ancestors of modern forms.

By now the situation seems clear; most English pronouns from somewhere around 800 A.D. have persisted with only minor alterations in spelling or pronunciation.

The case is slightly different with the third-person pronouns, but only slightly.

He was originally *hē* (pronounced like *hay*); *she* was *hēo* or *hīe* (pronounced like *hay-o* or *he-ah*), and *it* was *hit*. The masculine possessive (modern *his*) was simply *his*. The feminine possessive was *hiere,* from which comes *her*. Somewhere during the mid-twelfth century, the single major alteration of pronoun forms occurred when the Old English *sēo, sīo,* and *sīe* (feminine forms for *se,* meaning 'the') replaced *hēo* and *hīe* to give us the modern *she*—this also explains why we have *her* and *hers,* since those OE forms did *not* change.

Anglo-Saxon grammar and usage was, of course, much more complex than my simple explanations; but the fact emerges that *he, she,* and *it* (along with their other forms) have persisted in the language since before it was first written. And, given analogues in older languages such as Old German, Old Dutch, and Old High Saxon, the key Germanic pronoun forms actually go back much farther.

And this, I think, is why modern reformers frequently hit a proverbial brick wall when trying to introduce new forms to correspond to contemporary attitudes toward gender and language. These small words, *structure* words that essentially tell us how sentences are put together and what the relationship is between words, are enormously intransigent when it comes to change. Any new possibilities, including "ze," "sie," "e," "ou" and "ve" simply have to deflect too many centuries of embedded usage to become viable.

This does not mean that writers cannot explore such possibilities. One way to create believable alien cultures in fantasy, science fiction, even horror, is to alter the basic structure words; the result is a language that, while intelligible to readers, will come across as strange, uncomfortable, truly "other."

Some years ago, I wanted to explore the idea of a "Universal Christ," one known to multiple species on multiple planets, with each species expressing that image in their own unique ways, according to their customs and beliefs. To do so, I altered pronouns...as well as a number of other word-types. The culture I imagined was not based on a Trinitarian belief but upon a Quadrinity—four essential elements to the 'human' experience. Their world, based upon their physiology, was based on eight, rather than ten. And such concepts as 'male' and 'female' were unknown and unneeded.

CHRIST OF UNIVERSE

Christ of Universe, eight-finger-splayed
resemblance of heshe's stern Quadrinity,
stood comfort on a hillock just beyond

the swell of pallid blades. Corved of liquid
aurum in a stasis-field, it towered
over heshes' node. Waters met there.

Heshe chose the place of waters for their
node, accreting with each generation
body-lozenge-fundament for heshe spawn.

Each Bright, smooth bearers took the path to Christ
of Universe and laid at ParentChildBodySoul
their offerings, while sowers toiled among

the stalks. Each Dark, sowers retraced the way
and bowed in darkness to Christ of Universe
and lipped the SingSong of Quadrinity,

ParentChildBodySoul. Bearers burrowed
heshe young while sowers bowed.
Later, beneath the ever-solid black of night

when glolights died...when heshe bearers
opened hirmselfs to living seed... ...when heshe
sowers sought other fertile fields...

they could not see, but knew beyond the hillock,
Christ of Universe stood comfort over heshe,
eyestalks poised, eight-finger splayed.

The result was, I think, nicely alien.

But as far as the modern quandary goes—for writers locked into formal English grammar—here is what I think will happen. The neologisms will fade, unaccepted by the majority of English speakers. In their place, an old pronoun will simply shift to serve as masculine-singular, feminine-singular, and third-person plural alike, one that exists in the language and is already informally acceptable in speech: *they.*

More than once I've been tempted to edit a plural-seeming *they* when it clearly did not match a singular antecedent. Then I've realized that the antecedent is either female or genderless...and that the *they* is standing for both masculine and feminine.

In other words. "Each student has received books for tomorrow's lesson. Therefore, each student [singular] must bring their [singular] book [singular] to class."

Chapter 24

The N-Words and Other Unmentionables

Future generations (assuming there will be such) may look back on our times and wonder at the power we ascribe to individuals and to words.

Whenever there is a social problem, a cultural chasm, the first thing our society turns to—and attempts to change—is often not so much the problem itself, the underlying causes that make human beings treat others in specific ways, the assumptions (often unarticulated but influential) that direct our actions, but rather the most superficial manifestations of that problem.

The language used to describe it, talk about it, or denote it.

In other words, the *words*.

In 2012, the New York Department of Education, concerned about cultural divides among students, published a list of fifty words proscribed from appearing on official, standardized tests, under the assumption that they might irrevocably harm the developing psyches of school children. Among the victims on the hit-list:

> *Birthday*—possibly offensive to Jehovah's Witnesses and others who for religious or cultural reasons do not celebrate such events;
>
> *Dancing*—possibly offensive to religious groups that reject such activities—*ballet,* however is allowed;
>
> *Dinosaur*—possibly offensive to anti-evolutionists;
>
> *Halloween*—possibly offensive to religionists because of its associations with paganism;

> *Homes with swimming pools*—possibly offensive to the benighted few who do *not* have such amenities in their back yards;
>
> *Poverty*—possibly offensive to anyone associated with it, because, after all, such a state is not any individual's fault but society's;
>
> *Religion*—possibly offensive to those who have none;
>
> *Slavery*—possibly offensive to young people multiple generations removed from its practice in New York City;
>
> *Terrorism*—possibly offensive to members of groups tangentially associated with extremists who actually practice this means of radical social change;
>
> *War*—definitely offensive to any right-minded person to whom violence (expunged) and bloodshed (also expunged) are anathema under any circumstances.

Superficially, such a list of prohibited words might seem over-reaching, perhaps to the extent of becoming ludicrous. Yet in our world, our fear of offending someone—*anyone*—has reached such epidemic proportions that at times it seems as if words themselves, our primary means of communication, are under attack.

In September, 2012, the NFL Commissioner Roger Goodell responded to questions about possibly forcing the owner of the *Washington Redskins* to change the team name. "If one person is offended," he announced, "we have to listen."

One person.

Curiously enough, I've only rarely read of *Native Americans* objecting to the names.

The brouhaha means, one supposes, that the *Kansas City Chiefs* will soon be forced to change their name as well, along with the *Dallas Cowboys*—the latter because of all the mayhem *cowboys* inflicted upon *Native Americans*, including their *Chiefs*, more than a century ago. The *Minnesota Vikings* are in jeopardy, particularly as the Vikings are now credited (positively) with 'discovering' America and judiciously leaving it the way it was…we wouldn't want to offend any of their descendants. The *Tampa Bay Buccaneers* bring to mind murder, rapine, and theft—hardly role models for today's youth. The *New England Patriots* might offend southerners who find such rabble-rousing inappropriate. The *Oakland Raiders* definitely need to polish their name; and the *Arizona Cardinals* need to think about the implications of *cardinal*, since it is a homograph for a word closely associated with a specific religion—separation of Church and State, after all.

If *one* person is offended.

And that is just in one sport.

But back to my title.

You will note that I specified "The N-words"—plural.

That was intentional, because I want to look briefly at several near-homophones and explore their differences in meaning...and when they might be useful in writing fiction.

The first is the classic "N-word": *nigger.*

In terms of its linguistic history, the word is entirely legitimate. It stems ultimately from the Latin word *niger,* meaning 'black,' and was used descriptively...just as *black* now is (the latter, by the way, comes from an Anglo-Saxon word, *blæc,* meaning alternately 'dark' or 'pale'—the usual word for 'black' back then was *sweart,* from which is derived *swarthy*).

For much of a number of centuries, it remained largely neutral; in the mid-1800s, for example, it became part of the "Mountain Man" lexicon, with the associated sense of 'pal,' 'man,' even something as colloquial as 'dude,' with no definitive racial overtones. Not until the early 1900s did it become specifically and exclusively pejorative—which creates serious difficulties in reading late Victorian literature such as Mark Twain's *Huckleberry Finn,* or early 20th-century pieces by, say, Edgar Rice Burroughs. When used in such literature, the word might still be intended as primarily descriptive. In a contemporary effort not to appear offensive, one publisher recently introduced an edition of *Huckleberry Finn* substituting *slave*—with the unintended consequence that one of Twain's most powerful characters becomes "Slave Jim," diminishing him in ways that I don't think Twain intended.

Be that as it may, the word became pejorative and remains so, to the extent that several recent instances suggest that it now may not even be spoken (by non-blacks, at least) without fear of legal reprisals. It has replaced the infamous "F-word" as the most impermissible utterance in the English language.

(I don't want to digress into the morality or the rightness of black speakers using it as a term of endearment or affection—that appears to be in flux at the moment, so I can draw no conclusions about it.)

But there it is. A word that, despite a respectable genealogy and reasonably respectable history, is now literally (using *literally* to mean both 'literally' *and* 'figuratively') unspeakable.

Except....

In Jonathan Maberry's *Ghost Road Blues,* a character named Vic Wingate uses the word perhaps half a dozen times in as many pages, always referring to Oren Morse, an itinerant farm worker/blues musician whose murder Wingate orchestrates in an early chapter. The word isn't accidental; the repetition makes that clear. So why does such a careful, conscientious, masterly writer as Maberry include it?

The reason is not difficult to find. The word appears, not to characterize Oren Morse, who has already been established as a key character, one who knows the truth about a siege of deaths in Pine Deep, and the only one with the courage to seek out the monster and slay it; but rather to characterize the speaker, Wingate. By the end of the trilogy of which *Ghost Road Blues* is the first volume, Wingate is second only to the Great Evil itself in his debasement, his degradation, his corruption. And one of the first indications of this occurs when he speaks to Morse. Through his use of a single word, he lays his dark soul bare and prepares readers to believe any and all of the horrors he will perpetrate over the next 1200 pages. Six appearances of one small word—and we know all that we need to know of Vic Wingate.

Yes, it is pejorative. Yes, it is socially inappropriate. And yes, it no longer *describes* but *characterizes*...except that now it characterizes the *speaker* rather the *subject*—a complete reversal of its earlier negative meanings.

In a sense, then, it has found a place, although by left-handed means (I'm left-handed, so I can use the phrase non-prejudicially), as a useful adjunct in story-telling.

But there has been fallout.

Consider one of the synonyms for *snicker*: *snigger*. According to some sources, it is simply a variant of *snicker*, differing in meaning from the original in the slightly increased sense of disrespect it suggests.

Yet....

On one of the social forums, I found this comment:

> I don't know where I heard it [*snigger*] first, it has just always been part of my vocabulary. I never once linked it to the N word, which I find horrendously offensive (I have black relatives, and I just like people and don't like derogatory terms in general!), but when I just typed it into a forum I'm a member of, it censored the middle arrangement of letters. I never use the word

"snicker" because it reminds me of the candy bar, and the LAST thing I need to do is create a craving for... oh, drat. Too late. Now I want a candy bar.

Regardless of its meaning, *snigger* was censored merely because of an adventitious arrangement of letters. The obvious message: MUST NOT USE.

The next post on the forum was explicitly angry, not that *snigger* had been misused but that it had been used *at all*:

I am offended when I come across this word. Why do authors use it when it is so close to the "n" word that it is uncomfortable to say? The word "snicker" would have the same meaning and would be less disturbing to the reader. I'm positive that I'm not the only one who feels this way about the use of this word.

One person expresses offense; should *snigger* therefore be expunged from the language?

If *snigger* has experienced difficulties, imagine what life must be for the second "N-word": *niggard* and its adverbial, *niggardly*.

Their etymology actually goes farther back, to the 12th and 13th centuries. *Nyggard* in Middle English paralleled *hnøggr* in Old Norse, one of the contributory languages to English. *Hnøggr*, in turn, was cross-related to an Anglo-Saxon adjective, *hnēaw*, meaning 'stingy.' From the beginning, then, *niggard* and *niggardly* have carried a single meaning, one utterly divorced from race, color, or social opprobrium (except insofar as it is deemed antisocial to be stingy).

Yet....

I've been explicitly told *never* to use it.

I wrote it on the greenboard in my classroom once, and the entire class gasped in shock.

An associate of the mayor of Washington, D.C., was forced to resign for using it (appropriately) to describe a proposed budget.

A college student in Wisconsin complained that a professor used the word repeatedly during lectures on Chaucer, in spite of her being deeply offended by it.

A teacher in North Carolina was reprimanded for using the word during a discussion of literary characters and was required to attend sensitivity training.

Newspapers and magazines have officially banned the word, fearing the public consequences.

An accidental arrangement of letters that results in a near-homophone.

And the word is banned.

Curiously, a second near-homograph/homophone has largely escaped controversy. *Niggle* comes from the identical root as *niggard*—the aforementioned Old Norse *hnøggr*. It has a related meaning: Whereas *niggardly* means 'parsimonious' or 'penurious,' *niggle* means to criticize repeatedly, albeit in a peevish, petty, rather miserly way. It is, admittedly, not common in contemporary English, although J.R.R. Tolkien used it magnificently in one of his lesser-known stories, "Leaf by Niggle." Niggle is the main character, appropriately enough described as a "little man." One of the points of the story is the way in which he is *niggled* by others, to the extent that his greatest artistic achievement—a landscape painting—is eventually allowed to deteriorate until all that remains is a small scrap with a single leaf…hence the title. In the end, the tale becomes a story of redemption and validation, and the name "Niggle" becomes synonymous with Heaven.

I'm not aware of any particular fuss about him—or anyone else—using *niggle,* and the reason, I think, has largely to do with pronunciation.

Niggard ends with a low plosive—'d.' That means that the final sound literally explodes from the throat as the tongue drops from the palate and allows built-up air to be released. It cannot be prolonged, and for that reason, in speech, it frequently disappears, leaving behind only the lingering sense of the guttural 'r.' In that context, the unaccented *-ar* sounds exactly like the unaccented *-er*. In effect, *niggard* can become another word entirely when heard.

Niggle, on the other hand, lacks the final plosive. In fact, its final sound—the high liquid 'l'—allows the speaker to hang on to the word, to let it continue until the speaker simply runs out of breath if so chosen, and in doing so, it effectively defuses the implicitly negative sense of the first letters: *nigg.* The 'g' becomes less rough, less thick, and the physiological effect of the word is much lighter, much higher. *Niggle* becomes acceptable.

In both cases—*snigger* and *niggard*—the words' disrepute stems not from meaning but from sound. Neither is in any way related linguistically to the infamous *N-word*. Nor does either bear any connection to racial comments. Indeed, if embedded racism were the primary criterion for choosing which words to avoid, then the ubiquitous *boy*, given its usage history, should join the list.

Yet from the evidence provided by our society it would be difficult to tell which word is the most undesirable: *dinosaur, war,* or *niggardly.*

Fortunately, the New York City Board of Education's attempt met with the scorn I think it deserved. And attempts to ban *niggardly* from college campuses resulted, in at least one instance, in a *broadening* of freedom of expression rather than a narrowing.

Now to bring the discussion down to my ultimate purpose—talking about story-telling and fictions.

No words are too sacrosanct to use in a story; and no words are so horrific—especially in writing darkness, *horror*—that they cannot appear. Even the most socially inappropriate of words, used carefully and with the intent to characterize the moral failings, not of the subject, but of the *speaker* can become effective.

All that is needed is a clear understanding on the part of writers of four points:

* The way the readers might react to the words and how that will impact the story's reception—as can be seen from the case of *Huckleberry Finn,* merely using a certain word might be enough to turn a significant portion of the readership away;

* The possibility of using synonyms that lack the emotional charge but that will allow the story to remain true to itself—remembering always that there are almost *no* true and complete synonyms in the English language;

* The responsibilities writers have to themselves, to their characters, and to the world in which they live—in Maberry's novel, for instance, the word is almost required, given the choices that his characters will eventually have to make between Good and Evil...and his language is expressly designed to allow readers to see, understand, and accept those choices; and

* The freedom of writers to self-censor and choose responsibly, fully aware of implications and consequences; but when a society identifies certain words that *must never be used,* that society has overstepped its legitimate bounds.

Fortunately, in spite of NFL commissioners, boards of education, college administrators, and others who would restrict the language to meet their view of the world, authors remain free to choose and to explore.

Chapter 25

Why Fuck?

After what appears to be an ambiguous title (but technically is not), perhaps a word of explanation of what this essay is about.

Here is a word. It has been excoriated publicly and privately for centuries. Until about a hundred years ago, it could not officially—or legally—appear in print. It has been pummeled from the pulpit, the lectern, and the soapbox. It has been linked with the Decline of Western Civilization and decried as a symptom of the moral degeneracy of today's youth (and that for the past few generations now).

Even today, when its appearance in a novel or story barely causes a raised eyebrow, it cannot be spoken aloud on prime-time television— instead, viewers are treated to a ubiquitous, grating, and totally useless *bleep* that only alerts them to what has been said…especially if they are adept at lip-reading. Nevertheless, some celebrities seem unable to articulate a paragraph without it; and others—thinking now of a certain blonde, tall, British chef of apparently unstable temperament—cannot speak a single sentence.

It has been censured, edited, repudiated, ignored.

It still retains its principle meaning of 'performing the sex act' but is increasingly used more as an intensifier without a lexical definition than anything else.

It—and its variants—may commonly function as a noun, a verb, an adjective, or an adverb. It may be combined with other words (*mother* being perhaps the most common) to create even more emphatic, culturally disapproved utterances. It can be used by itself as an interrupter and an exclamation…a part of speech sometimes with wild appropriateness called an *ejaculation*.

With all of this opprobrium loaded upon it, century after century, and its uncertain etymology—no, none of the popular acronyms have anything to do with its actual linguistic heritage—with the combined weight of Church and School working against it, with its ultimate ambiguity as to precise reference in modern usage or its specific part of speech, one question inevitably surfaces:

Why do we not only still use it but, frequently, revel in it?

I don't like it. I've only used it in speech perhaps three or four times (when anyone could hear me, that is), and in my fiction twice…both times with malice aforethought and for precise effects. And for the longest time, I assumed that it was, as its known history suggests, essentially a signal of limited vocabulary and—possibly—limited intelligence.

Then, a number of years ago, something happened that altered my perception. I still don't like it and I still don't use it; but at least, I think, I *understand* it.

Sometime during the mid-1990s, my college hosted the Royal Shakespeare Society in several on-campus performances of bits and pieces from Shakespeare's plays. After the evening performances were completed, the actors offered to stay two days longer and come to classes to talk about Shakespeare, his plays, his times, his language, etc. Pretty much anything the students wanted to hear them discuss.

One came to my poetry-as-literature class, and, among other things, performed several sonnets, including the famous Dark Lady Sonnet #129:

> The expense of spirit in a waste of shame
> Is lust in action; and till action, lust
> Is perjured, murderous, bloody, full of blame,
> Savage, extreme, rude, cruel, not to trust;
> Enjoyd no sooner but despiséd straight;
> Past reason hunted; and no sooner had,
> Past reason hated, as a swallowed bait,
> On purpose laid to make the taker mad:
> Mad in pursuit, and in possession so;
> Had, having, and in quest to have, extreme;
> A bliss in proof, and proved, a very woe;
> Before, a joy proposed; behind, a dream.
>
> All this the world well knows; yet none knows well

To shun the heaven that leads men to this hell.

Please note that I said "performed." He didn't *read* it, the way a student would; he didn't *recite* it like a neophyte, standing before the audience, hands grasped tightly behind his back, body rigid.

He *performed it*, and during those few minutes, the full range of venom, fury, disillusionment, anger, lust, hatred—everything Shakespeare's speaker felt toward his betrayer and his beloved—boiled over into the actor's voice. He almost literally spat words like *spirit, savage, extreme, despised, proposed*. (It helped that so many of them contain one of the most explosive sounds in English, the aptly named plosive, 'p.') As I recall, he might even have completed the first twelve lines in a single breath, leaping faster and faster over the words, as if he wanted to be done with the whole experience—and every memory of it—as soon as possible.

Then...a pause, a deep breath, and in a voice tinged with acceptance, understanding, longing, and defeat, he completed the final two lines.

No one in the class spoke. The moment had been too emotionally charged, too overwrought...too exquisite.

Then, looking directly at me, the actor said something like, "And that reminds me of a word.... *The word*."

Now, my university was church-affiliated. Most of the students were also.

But when he said *The word*, I hadn't the slightest doubt that everyone in the class understood precisely *which word* he referred to.

Then he proceeded to explain why it is the most powerful, unforgettable, inimitable vulgarity in the language.

It all has to do, not with meaning, but with sound.

First, he had everyone in the class say the letter 'f,' and as they did so, he asked them to note how the letter was formed in the mouth. Lower lip just touching the upper front teeth, air allowed to build up behind the blockage, then a sudden release...a mini-explosion, if you will.

Then he had them pronounce the vowel 'u.' Vowels are formed in precise locations in the mouth. The short 'i' in *hit* is among the highest of English sounds—in fact, to pronounce it, the speaker has to lift both edges of the mouth, creating almost a smile. Words containing the short-'i' tend to be, if you will, happy, joyous, uplifting...and *lift* is an excellent example.

The remainder of the vowels are formed in increasingly lower positions and begin to use more muscles in the throat. The short-'e' in *bet,* for example, is almost mid-range, with lips extended, teeth separated, nothing to inhibit the sound escaping.

One by one, the vowels drop until only one remains: 'u.' It is harsh, a literal growl that pulls itself out of the larynx, vibrating as it works its way—sometimes laboriously—up and out. It is arguably the coarsest, most discordant, least harmonious sound of all the vowels. Think of words that rely upon it: *trudge, lug, fudge* (famous as a child's word-substitute in *A Christmas Story*), *drudge, nudge, sludge, grudge, drug, mug,* and others. Heavy, slow, almost inarticulate...and if the speaker has a bad cold, almost enough to strangle the sound completely.

It is as if the word wants to start as fast, as violently as possible then, with the second letter, is dropped into the mire and nearly choked.

The last two letters function as one: 'ck.' With the jaw still at its lowest possible level, mouth fully opened, teeth separated, the throat abruptly closes off all air moving outward from the throat in what is called a *glottal stop,* as if the *glottis,* the space between the vocal chords, were paralyzed. For an instant, there is no sound at all.

Then the 'k' sound bursts from the throat, a short, clipped, chopped, unvibrated consonant that almost immediately again severs all sound. No lingering over soft 'm' or 'n' sounds; no hissing, slithering 's' or 'z.' Just a single *pop*—'k'—and nothing.

Pow, and it's over.

And that, I think, may be one of the key reasons why the word persists even after centuries of disparagement by polite society. Certainly there is an element of challenge in the word; young people often use it merely as a way of asserting their (perceived or real) adulthood. There is—or was, at least—an element of shock; actually *seeing* the word on the printed page has, until recently, evoked far stronger responses than speaking it. And there is the embedded sense of emotionally charged, almost violent action; while most of the acronyms adduced to explain the word are false, it does seem to be related to a reconstructed Old Germanic root that led to the Middle Dutch *fokken,* 'to have intercourse.' All of these reasons—and probably more—have played a part in the continued use of the word.

But at base, I think the truth is somewhat more mechanical and technical: There are simply no other combinations of sounds in English that allow for the same—or even a similar—explosive release in the throat.

To see what I mean by that, consider some of the alternatives now used.

The most innocuous, perhaps, and certainly the most old-fashioned, is to simply allude to the word without using *any* word. *F****, *f—*, *f**k*, and *f—k* filled the need for most of the twentieth century. For twenty-first-century writers, the abbreviations may seem too cute, too precious. If one wishes to remind readers of the word, just *use* it.

A second alternative seems related: *Eff.* Technically, it is simply a short-cut, as are the first examples; but here the process has expanded. All that remains of the word is a representation of the first letter, and all of the physical force has been removed. Even the final sound—'f'—is diminished by the voiced vowel that precedes it and overwhelms it. Useful, but not as powerful.

Recently, *f-word* and the more imagistic *f-bomb* have become popular. Again they are useful, but they share the same deficiency—all of the vocal apparatus that goes into making the word strong are lost and all that remains is the rather pathetic (in this context) 'f.'

In addition to the cut-forms, a number of other words have emerged as alternatives, most of them attempting to re-create the unique pronunciation without actually resorting to it: *Frak, frick, flip, freak* (especially *freakin'*), *frig*, and *fug* are fairly common and in some senses more effective than the cut-forms. Several of them retain the low, rumbling effect of the original by coupling 'f' and 'r'; several retain the terminal plosive 'k' as well. But what changes is the source-position of the intervening vowel. If 'u' represents the deepest, the lowest, the throatiest of English vowels, 'i'—as noted above—represents one of the highest. In order to pronounce *frick* or *frig*, for example, the speaker must effectively smile, that is, widen the lips to form the vowel; and in doing so undercut the essence of the word. *Frak* and *freak* are marginally stronger, although there also the vowel is medium to high in the throat, a far cry from the grumbling rumble of 'u.' *Flip*, a preferred form among a number of my acquaintances, is probably the weakest of them all, phonically. The 'l' automatically raises the 'f' in preparation for the high vowel 'i'; and the potentially strong plosive 'p' ends up forming higher in the throat/mouth than usual.

Of course, there is always *fudge*. The 'dge' drags in the throat—witness *trudge*, which some writers consider among the slowest, most painfully pronounced word in the language. But again, even with that awkward combination of consonants, the final effect is a lightening, a lifting of sound. Besides, as noted above, when not used to define a particularly delectable candy, the word is now almost irreparably connected to comedy, thanks to *A Christmas Story*.

So...we are left with a persistent, continuing human need for a blunt, powerful, evocative, harsh, emotion-laden word to express a number of psychological and physiological states. The usual alternatives simply fail to attain the same level of phonic potency and—if truth be told—often leave speakers/writers feeling ineffectual and unfulfilled, at least as far as discharging a visceral barrage.

At our disposal, now and for uncountable centuries (the exact number is not known because before the fifteenth century the word apparently never appeared in print), a collocation of three specific sounds, each unique in power and force, representing a single, unchanging and, apparently, unchangeable word. In terms of functionality—leaving out entirely the morality, the wisdom, the appropriateness of actually *using* it—we are left with only one option.

A single word.

Euphemistically referred to as *The Word*.

I noted earlier that I dislike it. Even after the eye-opening revelations in my classroom, I still dislike it. I did not use it before; I do not use it publicly now. But in the privacy of my mind—and occasionally in the privacy of my room or my car—when the pressures of depression, tinnitus, and deafness grow too insistent—I *do* use it.

Not for any meaning it conveys, since I speak it only to myself and fully understand the multiplicity of possibilities it conveys...and ultimately am not interested in anything so intellectualized as communicating ideas or thoughts. But rather for the sheer cleansing power of the *sounds* themselves...harsh, angered, irrational, guttural sounds that rip from the throat and, for an instant, externalize internal anguish and pain.

And that, I think, is why it persists, like it or not.

Chapter 26

On Words…and the Etymological Fallacy

Words are fascinating critters.

They can grow and shrink. Then can revert, invert…sometimes convert. Some shift meanings easily and generate dozens, scores, even hundreds of possibilities; others, more niggardly with semantic change, hold rigidly to meanings a thousand years old.

But beyond all, words have *history*. Etymologists, philologists, and lexicologists spend countless hours scouring ancient documents to create and verify family trees of words and languages, even going so far as to apply laws of linguistic change to existing words and thereby re-creating long-lost originals.

All of this is fascinating…but the reality of historical antecedents leads to two opposite and equally dangerous approaches to words. Both approaches incorporate variations on the Etymological Fallacy, a stance that basically preaches that if one knows what words used to mean, one knows what they mean, or *should* mean, now.

Sometimes exploring the histories of words, with an etymological dictionary or—even better—the massive multi-volume *Oxford English Dictionary* close at hand results in intriguing insights into how words, as they reflect evolving cultures and societies, themselves evolve.

A few years ago, while sitting in church, I was suddenly struck by how frequently the various lay speakers used one word: *blessing*. Taking it in all of its forms—*blessing, blessings, blessed,* even an occasional antiquarian *blesséd*—probably every person used it at least once. As often happens when one actually begins to *think* about words, the more I ran it through my mind, the more curious it became. Odd. Alien-feeling, almost.

So, of course, as soon as I got home from church, out came the dictionaries.

Bless, I discovered, derives from the Middle English *blessen*; which in turn stems from the Old English/Anglo Saxon *blētsian* or *blēdsian*, meaning essentially 'to consecrate...with blood."

Blood?

And further, *blēdsian* derived from the reconstructed Indo-European root **blōdisōjan*, 'blood sacrifice.' (The asterisk indicates that the word does not appear as such in the historical record, but that it is a probable re-creation of an earlier spoken word.)

A long way to travel on a simple word. And how much that hidden history echoes throughout our contemporary, almost commonplace use of *blessing*. The facts implied by the history so stunned me that I wrote the following poem:

> Blood-blessing—germanic
> heritage of childlike
> blessedness
>
> recalling oak-grove
> sacrifices, druid
> blood
>
> pouring wine-dark over
> stone-hollowed pagan
> ritual
>
> [*God bless Mommy,*
> *God bless Daddy,*
> *God bless,*
> *God bless....*]
>
> Blessing-blood life-sap
> dripping from a world-ash
> cross
>
> the light behind a shadow
> trapped within
> a word

The danger in knowing this about a single, simple word arises if I at some point forget that the *meaning* of the original has shifted over the course of millennia and begin to agitate, for example, that the word *blessing* be expunged from all Christian dialogue since, at root, it defines a pagan concept (rather like those who denigrate *Christmas* by pointing out that the date it is celebrated originally commemorated a pagan holi/holyday). It *was* pagan; now it is Christian. A drastic shift in culture and society left a need for a new word to define a new concept—and the old word simply stepped into the void, altered its meaning, and became part of a new world-view.

That is the way most words work. They are rarely static. And those few that are—*he, she, it, is, was, a, an, the,* etc.—work primarily as function-words rather than carrying sophisticated dictionary-level meanings. Many of them are shared by languages older than English; *is,* for example, can be traced back to ancient Sanskrit. This is why it is so difficult to introduce new pronouns, articles, and copular verbs into the language, and why *he* remains for many a generic reference rather than a gender-specific one.

Moving in the other direction, many words are new, with virtually no history. English in particular has a predilection toward absorbing words from other cultures, then using them to name things that did not before exist within our society. A glance at etymologies in dictionaries will show that the language has picked up words from almost every other major language group, especially as English-speakers have come into contact with new ideas and new words.

And that is good.

Language—and taste buds—would be impoverished without the Nahuatl (Aztec) *chocolātl*; weather would be less refined, less precise without the Taini (Arawakan) *hurakán*; and language—and fashion— would be less descriptive without the Hindi *sārī*, which goes back to the ancient Sanskrit *śāṭī*.

But there is an inherent danger in taking for granted the ability of English to grow, adapt, and change. It becomes tempting to think that the words we use to define *our* world should have a one-to-one correspondence with earlier cultures and societies.

And the consequences of *assuming* that our words, our moralities, our ethics can be simply superimposed upon the past are invidious.

Recently, I have seen a number of references to a particular nineteenth-century American religious leader as a *pedophile*. The evidence: his marriage to a fourteen-year-old girl.

In a real sense, however, no one in the nineteenth century can be legitimately labeled a pedophile.

Or in the eighteenth century.

Or in the seventeenth century, when the greatly esteemed father of the scientific method, the highly vaunted creator of empiricism, Sir Francis Bacon, a bachelor of forty-five, married Alice Barnham, then fourteen years old (they had been engaged since she was eleven).

An old man marrying a fourteen-year-old. Still not pedophilia.

Why not?

Because the word did not then exist. Oh, there were probably words throughout those centuries to describe men with unhealthy—or healthy—attractions to girls, but *pedophile* was not one of them. To apply *our* word to men such as Bacon is unjust, since the exact, almost clinical definition of *pedophile* did not emerge until *after* the development and application to human society of *psychology* as we now know it.

In fact, the first references to the issue as a social aberration occur in 1905, when the general term *pedophilia* ('child' + 'loving') was created to define a specific psychologically derived state. *Pedophile* came nearly half a century later. To use the word now to define someone from previous centuries makes a huge number of unsupportable assumptions about that individual...and about the nature of words.

Still, the fact that words can be created and that old words can take on new meanings is essential to language. Most attempts to codify languages—especially to control them through blunt political processes, such as proscribing certain words—fail miserably as the speakers simply pick up and use non-native words and phrases; if enough of them do that, a new word enters the language.

About forty years ago, I spent some time in Germany. German was highly resistant to new words; historically, it tended to meet the needs of new ideas by forming new compounds of old words. One of my friends was responsible for booking air flights back to the U.S. The *formal* German word for *jet aircraft* at that time was *das Überschallgeschwindigkeitflugzeug*—the "above-the-speed-of-sound flying train." While I was there, Boeing introduced a new aircraft, the 747, an amazing behemoth for the time. By the time I left, my friend was simply booking flights on *das Jumbojet*...a word that, until then, had not existed in German.

English is not above the same technique...creating new words to fill real (or perceived) gaps in the language. Somewhere in the 1930s, a search began for the longest possible English word, and a new one was devised: *pneumonoultramicroscopicsilicovolcanoconiosis*, still the longest word to appear in an English dictionary. Its parts define the whole: a lung disease (*pneumo-*) caused (*-osis*) by inhaling very fine (*ultra* + *microscopic*) dust (*silico,* the primary constituent of dust + *volcano,* 'underground'). Or, in more common terms: *silicosis.* Or more common yet: *black lung.*

And the processes continue. Recently, an online dictionary included a new definition of the quite clearly defined word *literally,* originally meaning 'to the letter, exact, precise' and 'actually.' It now also means *figuratively* ('metaphorically,' 'virtually,' not really but it seems like it). In other words, it now means the exact *opposite* of what it once did. The fact that at this point it retains *both* meanings is bound to create some confusion.

Which brings me to the beginning. Words are fascinating critters. They writhe, they shift, they hide, they contain hidden cores, they emerge from all sorts of nooks and crannies. Consequently, it behooves (from the Anglo Saxon *behōfian* 'to need, to profit') us to pay close attention to what we say and what we write. One person may use a particular word that, at some point in its history, was positive; a listener or reader may associate it with a more modern, more negative meaning, and by doing so wrench what was said to meet a different agenda. Same word, different meanings…and from them can spring animosity, virulence, and hatred. And especially as writers, we need to constantly be alert to the possibility—if not the *probability*—that somewhere along the line, our readers will apply their understanding of words, meanings, and history differently than we intended, and the story, the essay, the dialogue will collapse in misunderstanding.

Chapter 27

When Clichés Go Bad

Clichés are bad, right? We all know that, don't we?

Well, as it turns out, only *some* clichés could be considered 'bad.' Others in fact serve a useful purpose.

Take social clichés, for example. You see someone you know and he greets you with, "Hey, how ya doin'?" To discover how important clichés are to social interactions, try answering…truthfully: "Well, I've got a bit of a headache and my back has been sore for three weeks now and even with physical therapy every other day it just stays the same and my car probably will need a new battery in the next little while because it sort of goes *gnnn-gnnn-gnnn* whenever I try to start it and…."

A few seconds into the dialogue/monologue, you will probably notice several things. The friend's eyes will glaze over, perhaps begin wandering to the left and right (anywhere but directly at you), and eventually he will try surreptitiously to glance at a watch or stifle a yawn.

Why?

Because "How ya doin'" is *not* a request for information. It is a social cliché, a phrase designed in effect to say, "I see you and acknowledge you as a fellow human being." And the proper response is not a thousand-word monologue but simply, "Fine. And you?"

Many of our day-to-day conversations depend on this kind of short-cut communication. Without clichés on this level, life would become intolerable.

The situation alters, however, when we look at writing.

Writing locks things—words, phrases, ideas—into place. Rarely does writing serve merely a place-holder function. And when we write stories, we can *never* descend to recycling a list of conventionally acceptable platitudes that essentially mean nothing (although, granted, a particular *character* might be predisposed to 'talk' like that in dialogue).

At the best of times, and even when dressed in their finest attire, written clichés tend to stop movement, to stifle conversation…and eventually to turn readers off. When the phrases are not only hackneyed but *incorrect*, however, things take a far more serious turn.

There are two fundamental causes for error when using clichés, one based on pronunciation and misunderstanding, and the other on confused or misapplied grammar and semantics.

PRONUNCIATION:

Tow the line: I'm starting with this phrase because it was probably the most frequently misused by my students, who had likely heard it incessantly from infancy but had rarely if ever seen it *in print*. The key word sounded like the common *tow*, so that is how they spelled it, never having served on an early nineteenth-century naval vessel. Sailors were then frequently an unruly lot, and when high-ranking functionaries came on board, ship captains attempted to create a sense of order and discipline by laying a rope (a 'line') tautly across the deck, then ordering the sailors to stand with their toes against the rope…thus "toeing" the line.

"Towing" is on one level a simple homonym for the correct word. The cliché becomes more problematical if readers actually stop to *think* about it when they see it. Almost everyone knows that the phrase means to 'follow the rules,' to 'behave correctly, often rigidly'; but what does throwing a line (whatever that might mean) or rope over one's shoulder and pulling it down the road have to do with that meaning. Manifestly, *nothing*.

Lest I give the impression that the misused word is the sole province of students, let me share a further example of the same confusion, this one suggested by a Facebook friend: "Notice on the parking lot behind my apartment building: 'Violators will be toed away at there own expense'" —actually a three-fer, given the misspelling of *their* and the redundancy of "their own." But it does provide an interesting visual experience—imagining the parking-lot police lining up at the front of a line of *violators* and nudging them unmercifully off the lot with their toes. "Alas, poor Meaning, I knew him…."

To wait with baited breath: My senior-year course in the History and Grammar of the English Language made this one memorable for me.

Professor McEwen kept a drawerful of three-by-five cards with English oddities written on them, and for the last few moments of each class period he would share a few with us. To this one he added an explanatory image: "The cat, having just eaten the Stilson cheese, waited outside the mouse hole with baited breath."

The correct phrase is, of course, *bated breath*, 'breath indrawn or held in anticipation,' from an older word, *abated*, 'lessened in intensity.' Still, it makes one wonder what to eat to have baited breath...just in case.

It's a doggy-dog world: Or, alternatively and more formally, *It's a Dog E. Dog world*. Either way, the phrase makes little sense and in fact works *against* what most people assume it to mean. *Doggy-dog* sounds warm and fuzzy; *Dog E. Dog* descends to the cartoonish, perhaps on the model of Wile E. Coyote. Neither even begins to suggest what the phrase truly says.

This one doesn't have a clear-cut history. Evidences of the idea go back in English to the sixteenth century, while "dog does not eat dog" goes back to the mid-1800s. The actual phrase, "It's a dog-eat-dog world" is attested from the early 1930s and refers to a social climate in which aggression is paramount, in which success comes through destroying one's rivals. Quite a ways from the cuddly "doggy-dog."

Music hath charms to soothe the savage beast: This phrase at least makes sense. One can imagine a musician—perhaps a flutist—drawing soft, sweet, and soothing notes from an instrument, while wild beasts range pacifically beside, calmed by the pleasant notes.

A beautiful picture. But incorrect.

The phrase as used by the seventeenth-century dramatist William Congreve in his tragedy *The Mournful Bride* (1697) actually reads: "Music has Charms to soothe a savage Breast,/To soften Rocks, or bend a knotted Oak." The fact that modern usage has already replaced the contemporary *has* with the archaic *hath* and more frequently attributed the line to Shakespeare than to Congreve suggests that eventually the "beastly" version might win out over the original.

It peeked my interest, *alt.,* **It peaked my interest**. Neither truly works. The first is essentially senseless...at the very least *peek* seems to require a prepositional in this structure ("it peeked at..." or "it peeked into..."), and in any case it carries suggestions of furtiveness, of quickness that the context generally cannot support. *Peaked* comes more closely to the mark, with its image of height, of a pointed top, as if "my interest" had arrived at a "peak."

But, alas, that is not what the phrase intends. "It has *piqued* my interest" means 'to excite' and stems from a word meaning 'to pick' or 'to prick at.' *Piquing* interest suggests a kind of tentativeness about the situation, that one's interest is being probed and possibly heightened, but not quite yet fully engaged.

He has a difficult road to hoe: Difficult indeed. Particularly if the road is macadamized, although even an unpaved dirt road would be difficult to hoe, since it would most likely be hard-packed to the consistency of concrete.

How much easier—in spite of the fact that the task at hand will be arduous—if he were to hoe a *row* in a fertile field. The row might be long, there might be rocks scattered throughout, he might even have to labor with nothing more than a long-handled, flat-bladed tool...but eventually the chore will be finished.

In the meantime, worker number one will still be struggling, just trying to break through the surface of that road.

Reeking havoc: I actually like this one—the image of havoc so wide-ranging that it creates a stench upon the earth, odoriferous, noisome (nothing to do with *noise* there), cloying, and ripe.

Alas again, the rather plebian homonym, an unlikely (in English) combination of letters to create *wreak*, simply means that: 'create, cause.'

GRAMMAR/SEMANTICS:

Often, clichés are unclear or ambiguous because the writer mistakes underlying grammatical or semantic structures. In these cases, the ultimate culprit is not simply decades or generations of mispronunciation but a fundamental error.

Being on the right side of history: This phrase is fairly recent but has already attained to cliché status, in that it is being used without—it often seems—speakers having a clear grasp of what it implies or what *history* is. The phrase suggests that history is a thing, almost a tangible thing, that exists unaltered and unchanged through the centuries, and that our contemporary society, alone of all the societies that have ever existed, understands it completely and can, in fact, project its view of history (past and present) into the future. A wrong decision today, a disagreement on a sensitive issue, and—*POW!*—someone is automatically "on the wrong side of history."

The difficulty is that history doesn't work that way. History is malleable, fluid, capable of being re-interpreted, re-written, even falsified when circumstances appear to warrant it...and this has been going on since histories began to be written. Each generation reports upon the world *it* defines; and almost always, the reports that survive are written by the winners in social, cultural, religious, or political wars. They alone get to declare what is right and true for their generation.

And then along comes the next generation and, dissatisfied with what the 'ancients' said about issues, re-interpret historical events to make them jibe with a new way of viewing the world. Sometimes this process takes centuries; sometimes it can be accomplished in mere decades. When I was in grade school, for example, "Columbus Day" was a positive experience, accompanied by school pageants, decorations in the halls, and cutouts on the windows. That *history*—that narrative about Columbus and his achievements—no longer stands unquestioned. Columbus has been re-evaluated and found wanting. His "Day" has become a source of acrimony, censorship, and blame. And history has changed.

For me to assert then, that at any given point someone may be on "the right side of history" merely asserts that that person agrees with me. It has nothing to do with how people of future generations *will* view us, only with how they *might* view us.

Sorry, but history consistently resists future-fortune-telling.

She gave 110%: This phrase requires a bit of math and a bit of lexicography. Its meaning is that—quite literally—she has done, not only her utmost, but *more than she is capable of*. If she had done her utmost, she would have only been able to give *100%*, since the number, coupled with the word *percent (per cent)* means 100 out of 100.

Granted that 110% or even 1000% suggests a higher degree of commitment than a mere 100%, numbers and semantics tell us that 100 is as high as she can go.

He made a complete 360: This one is tricky, since it can be taken two ways...one correct and the other rather absurd.

If the writer means that a character has returned to his old ways—returning from repentance back to a life of crime—then 360° is appropriate. Going full-circle and starting again from the point of origin. I did a 360 on the way to a conference once; it was during a snowstorm, and I ended up not only in the barrow pit but heading in the same direction I started.

So far, so good.

The difficulty here arises when a character becomes convinced that he is going in the *wrong* direction and reverses, to go in the *opposite* direction. That is not a 360°-turn; it is a half-circle, or a 180. To confuse the two phrases is to confuse the reader and—more often than not—to condemn the writer.

She could care less: There's a curious twist to this phrase, since it in fact says the opposite of what it wants to. Roughly translated: there exists the possibility of her caring less about the situation than she does. In almost every context the phrase appears, however, the unstated point is that nothing could make her care less about the situation than she does at present—that is, *she could not care less.*

He couldn't of cared less: Close, but no cigar. The negating particle is present, which brings the phrase closer to what was intended, but there is no auxiliary verb to make the sentence semantically coherent: *he couldn't have cared less. Of* does not mean the same thing as *have,* even though in rapid speech the latter may seem to degrade into the former.

She didn't plan ahead: This one is simple. *Plan,* v., 'to arrange for or prepare for in advance.' Unfortunately, one can only do that *ahead* of actually carrying out the project. All plans are, by definition, *ahead* of the completed project. A straightforward but often overlooked redundancy.

He will try and do it: The phrase contradicts and undercuts itself. It says simultaneously that he will *attempt* something AND that he will *achieve* it. If he has achieved/will achieve it, just say so: *he will do it.* If there is a question about his ability to achieve it, then say that: *he will try to do it.* He will make the attempt…but perhaps he will fail.

There are more phrases that I could talk about, of both categories: in the first, *for all intensive purposes* ('intents and purposes'), *butt naked* ('buck naked'), *a mute point* ('moot'), and *statue of limitations* ('statute'), for example; and in the second, *pre-exist* ('exist'), *pre-heat the oven* ('heat the oven'), *the reason is because* ('the reason is that'), and *unthaw* or *de-thaw* for thaw. And many more. Neither time nor space will permit.

I should, however, mention one final example of a phrase that has separated so far from its original that it has spawned *multiple* variations, all of them now acceptable. Two people sit diagonally from each other; are they seated *kitty-corner*? *Catty-corner*? *Caddy-corner*? Actually, any of the three would be considered correct. But none is the original, and none give any fundamental indication of meaning. The fourth possibility — *cater-corner* — is still current and contains embedded suggestions of an origin: from the French *quatr-*, referring initially to a four-spot on dice.

The points I am trying to make:

First, not all clichés are evil, perverse, and threatening. Some provide a serious social function;

Second, when clichés are used they should be done so with care and accuracy or they become inadvertently comic or confused;

Third, pronunciation has a large influence on how clichés change, since eventually we use them essentially without thinking and, thus, without particularly caring to get the wording right;

Fourth, historical changes in the language provide a slipperiness to many of the oldest clichés as we lose sight of the world that generated them; and

Fifth, when we don't pay attention to each word and use each appropriately, *meaning* will be the first thing to suffer.

[Note: Many thanks to more than a score of Facebook friends who reminded me of many phrases and suggested several new ones. I would have liked to spend time with each of them…both the friends and the phrases.]

Part Five: Grammar, Spelling, and Other Oddities

Chapter 28

Saying Much with Little

Prose writers normally don't concern themselves overly with compression—with condensing lines and phrases to generate the most meaning in the fewest words. Storytellers especially are often more concerned with the narrative than with the minutiae of structuring paragraphs, sentences, and phrases. While these concerns certainly play a part in story construction, they usually remain minimal.

Poets, on the other hand, characteristically tend toward compression. One hallmark of great poetry is that it communicates much more than the total of its words. Diction, image, metaphor, symbol—all combine to give poetry the sense of a flower unfolding, revealing more and more meaning the deeper we examine it. For that reason, for example, it usually takes far more words in prose to express the meaning of a poem than the poem itself used, and frequently, even after our best attempts, the poem still evades absolute explication.

Compression—the art of saying much with little—is fundamental to effective poetry and, in its own way, to prose as well. No form of writing is made better by wordiness, by superfluous structures that, if used too frequently, disrupt the flow of language.

Because poetry offers the most obvious examples of how compression works and how it might enhance what is being said—the 'story' that is being told—most of what follows will concentrate on verse. Please remember, however, that everything included in this essay can just as beneficially be applied to novels, to short stories, and to essays.

From haiku, which consciously avoid unnecessary words and concentrate on every sound and syllable, to longer, more expansive pieces, poetry struggles to expand meaning beyond mere word count.

And one of the most common difficulties a poem can encounter is the sense on the reader's part that it is wordy, bulky, flabby.

As a matter of practical application, there are two large divisions of words in English: structure words and lexical words.

STRUCTURE words function primarily as adjuncts of syntax and grammar. They do not carry significant meaning in themselves but instead provide important signals as to how other words relate to each other and to meaning. They are notoriously difficult to define specifically; most often, definitions tend toward the abstract. The simple preposition *for*, for example, can mean "with the object or purpose of," "intended to belong to or used in conjunction with," "in place of," "to the amount of or extent of," and literally dozens of other possibilities; its specific meaning in a given phrase depends entirely on the meanings of the words that surround it. In general, the category of structure words also includes prepositions, articles (*a, an, the*), and the copular verbs (*is, seems, becomes*, etc).

LEXICAL words, on the other hand, can be defined. They relate to specific things, actions, movements, qualities. Their meanings usually refer to image-making constructs: *walk, run, touch, tree, fence, boulder*. In most cases, these words are nouns, verbs, adjectives, and adverbs.

[CAVEAT: At this point it is important to emphasize that there is nothing inherently *wrong* with structure words or with using them in either poetry or prose; nor does the presence of lexical words automatically make for tight, lean, effective lines. Structure words do, however, frequently occur unnecessarily and add bulk, a sense of the prosaic, and a rhythmical flatness when not used carefully and consciously, just as lexical words can create a sense of vividness, imagery, action, and specificity.]

Let's begin by looking at the most notorious of the structure words: PREPOSITIONS.

An online dictionary defines *preposition* as

> any member of a class of words found in many languages that are used before nouns, pronouns, or other substantives to form phrases functioning as modifiers of verbs, nouns, or adjectives, and that typically express a spatial, temporal, or other relationship, as in, on, by, to, since.

The definition is long, abstract, and cumbersome, particularly since the words being categorized tend to be remarkably short and direct. For practical purposes, however, perhaps the best definition of a preposition is the half-joking assertion that a preposition is "anything a rabbit can do to a hill": *in* the hill, *on* the hill, *by* the hill, *around* the hill, *through* the hill. Only a limited number of words function as prepositions in English, yet at the same time they are among the most difficult class of words to use idiomatically and "correctly." In spite of all this, however, they are essential to creating meaning in English.

In terms of compression, prepositions almost always add words, often unnecessary words. By definition, a *pre*-position comes before something; therefore prepositions, when functioning as such, always have objects, words that function as nouns. These, in turn, are frequently prefaced by articles (*a, an, the*) which in essence simply announce "Watch out! Noun coming."

Three words. Only one of which carries specific meaning.

Let's look at several lines from one of my earliest poems, an elegy to my uncle:

> For in the soothing sounds of waters' whisperings
> As they turn a moss-encrusted wheel,
> He is present.

Ignoring other problems for the moment, look at the first two lines. Fifteen words—three prepositions (*for, in, of*), two articles (*the, a*), a vague pronoun (*they*), and a wasted adverb (*as*). Nearly half of the total devoted to telling readers how words—substantive, meaningful words—fit together or relate to each other rather than telling us anything about the subject. The poor reader has to make it to the fourth word before anything is actually said. An overly long, bulky, uninteresting set of lines.

To revise for compression and energy, let's first look for a verb. The sentence, as written, has one, of course: *is*, the weakest verb in English (more about that in a subsequent essay). In addition, it comes so late in the lines that the reader has to perform a juggling act just to keep all of the intervening parts straight.

If we look for an active verb—or a word that could become an active verb—a couple of things emerge. First, words such as *soothe*, *sound*, *whisperings* and *turn* could easily become verbs. And second, the sentence as it stands makes no sense; stripped of verbiage, the opening clause actually reads, "sounds turn a wheel"—not at all what I was trying for. Wordiness, precipitated by incessant prepositions, gets in the way of meaning.

So...in that opening clause, where is our true verb? Probably the most likely candidate is the noun *whisperings*—an artificially nominalized word, since if we remove the noun-making endings, we get a strong verb: *whisper*. What whispers? *water*. Where? *through a moss-encrusted wheel*. And we have a sentence: "Water whispers through a moss-encrusted wheel."

But we have more than that. What happened to "sounds"? In its noun form, *whisper* **is** a sound; the earlier, more abstract, more general (how many kinds of sound are there?) word is redundant. What about "soothing"? Don't whispers usually soothe unless otherwise described, especially in an elegy? And if water whispers through a waterwheel, doesn't it turn the wheel?

In essence "Water whispers through a moss-encrusted wheel" says everything implicit in the first two lines, using seven words instead of fifteen, one preposition instead of three, and eliminating "they" and "the."

What, then, to do with line three, which asserts bluntly the point of the image: "he is present." Again, *is*, the weakest of verbs, followed by *present*—vague, abstract, generalized, non-imagistic, boring. The only word truly working here is *he*, which in the context points specifically to an individual: my uncle. Three more words (bringing the total to eighteen); only one carries significance for the lines.

This brings us back to an earlier problem: what do these lines want to say? When I wrote them, I was standing beside a waterwheel my uncle had built perhaps forty years earlier, moss-encrusted as the line says, still functioning. Just seeing it, hearing it, brought him forcibly back to memory. So what should the subject of these lines be? *Water*, which seems at this point tangential; or *he*? Let's go with the latter. If we move *water* to a different place in the line, and replace *a* with *his*, we get:

He whispers through his moss-encrusted waterwheel.

More imagistic, metaphorical, possibly symbolic, certainly more interesting—in seven words, fewer than half of the original count but saying more clearly what I intended.

Are we finished? Perhaps. A judicious break might transform the line into creditable free verse:

> He whispers through
> His moss-encrusted waterwheel.

Or we could keep going, transforming and re-structuring:

> His moss-encrusted waterwheel whispers...*him.*

Possibly simply:

> His moss-encrusted waterwheel whispers....

Or transform it into a haiku-like sequence:

> moss-encrusted
> waterwheel—
> his ghost whispers

Or any number of other possibilities, none readily apparent in the first version.

Of all the parts of speech, then, prepositions (and their accompanying nominal phrases) most often work against tightness, compression, and clarity. Lines needn't be stripped down as far as I have taken this one, but on almost every level, particularly in early drafts, finding prepositions and prepositional phrases, identifying the underlying verb, defining the actor performing that action, and restructuring accordingly may at least present new alternatives for expression.

If we move from poetry to prose, we find a similar situation. Prepositions are useful and functional but they also tend to get out of control and by doing so slow the movement of sentences, paragraphs, and ultimately stories.

In many cases, the culprit is simple repetition: where one preposition would work, we use two. In the first sentence of one of my favorite novels, we find the following:

> The motorcycle roared out of [town], carrying the
> blond boy and dark-haired girl away from the horror
> behind them.

It is an ideal opening for a novel that blazes with action throughout, including the arrival of a spacefaring monster willing to devastate the entire town to attain its goal. We are introduced to two key characters, whose intertwined lives encompass the wider story. And we are told that there is a *horror*; to find out what it is, of course, we must read further.

It is a great hook, one that establishes tone and atmosphere for the entire book.

Except....

Notice the prepositions. "The motorcycle roared *out of* [town]...." Two words that essentially construct the same relationship between *roared* and [*town*]. There is a suggestion of wordiness, although the alternative, single-word prepositional probably is not as useful in this instance: *from*. Having pointed out the doubling, I am now going to partially reverse myself and say that in this case, it is not a serious problem.

That assessment is strained, however, when we finish the sentence: "away from the horror behind them." Six words total; three prepositions, an article, a pronoun (indicating that we already know who *they* are), and one substantive, the strongest word in the sentence, *horror*.

The motorcycle is carrying the boy and the girl *away from* the horror. All right so far, although two doubled prepositions in one sentence makes me a bit wary. My difficulty rises with the third preposition, *behind*. In essence, everything that word, and its accompanying object *them*, says is implicit already. The boy and the girl (*them*) are fleeing *from* the horror. If they are moving *away from* it, it is most likely coming from *behind*—north, south, east, or west, whichever direction they choose to move, *away* places the monster *behind*.

Why not "The motorcycle roared out of [town], carrying the blond boy and dark-haired girl away from the horror"? Just a bit tighter, and now the terminal word in the hook-sentence is *horror* rather than the neutral and unexciting *them*.

Still, there is nothing seriously awry thus far. Just a couple of extra prepositions that might have been eliminated—the prose might have been compressed just enough to give us the motorcycle, the two characters, and the horror.

The reason that I've gone on so long about these minor points is that three paragraphs later, we read: "Something rose up from the smoke directly in front of them." That is the entire paragraph. Obviously, it is intended to startle and shock...both the characters and the readers. But if we look closely at the way the sentence is structured, two things become apparent.

First, of the ten words in the sentence, four—or 40%—are prepositions; one is an article, for another 10%; and, as with the first paragraph, the final word, which should bear the burden of shock and fear, is the neutral pronoun *them.* That means structure words comprise 60% of the sentence and that the kernel—the frightening revelation—is compressed into two words almost lost at the *beginning* of the sentence: "Something rose." From that abrupt beginning, the sentence trails off into inconsequentialities.

Looking even more closely we find another of the doubled prepositions: "Something rose *up from* the smoke...." Here, I would argue, the first preposition is unnecessary, because of the preceding verb. When things *rise*, they can only move in one direction: *up*. It would be perfectly appropriate, and perhaps more suspenseful, simply to say, "Something rose from the smoke."

(Having read more than my share of fair-to-middling horror novels, I must congratulate the author here for having avoided "Rose up out of the fog"—a relatively common occurrence that demonstrates how easy it is to multiply prepositions.)

A next step might be to restructure the sentence to make it more suspenseful. One way to do so is to place the modifications first, allowing their neutrality to both announce and delay the revelation of horror: "From the smoke in front of them, something rose." Or: "From the smoke before them rose...something." Or other alternatives.

This might seem like nitpicking at its worst. This kind of intensive analysis may have its place in writing and revising poetry, where one expects every word to count; but in prose, especially in a horror novel of several hundred pages, why worry about such minor occurrences?

The answer is: anything that slows, distracts, or confuses the reader is dangerous, whether in a seventeen-syllable haiku or an eight-hundred-page novel. It takes little to upset the delicate balance between reader and story; why chance any disruptions?

And a corollary is that these two examples of wordiness, within the first page or so, suggest that more might follow. And sure enough, half a dozen paragraphs on, we find: "Rivulets of gasoline burned on the bridge, and the thing strode on through the streams of flame." Five prepositions, two of them doubled; and the final phrases of the second half are implicit in the first. "Strode *on through*" seems unnecessary. "Strode through the streams of flame" is tighter, but given the fact that we already know that the bridge is burning, and burning in *streams,* since that is what *rivulets* means, why not simply "strode on"? Again, ending the structure with a vivid, image-forming word related to the horror: "Streams of gasoline burned on the bridge, but the thing strode on."

As I mentioned earlier, these samples come from one of my favorite novels. I've read it several times, worn out at least one paperback edition, and am now starting to read—and enjoying—an eBook version. I don't mean by my criticisms that the book is horrible or that no one should bother with it. Quite the contrary; it is a masterful tale, told with clarity and suspense…that occasionally uses a few more words than are quite needed.

In the hands of other writers, however, the problem with prepositions can become more intrusive.

The opening paragraph of a recent werewolf novel consists of two fairly long sentences. The first establishes that the point-of-view character is a werewolf…and a wedding crasher. The second begins:

> Sitting at a table in the reception hall at the top of The
> Galt House, with a whiskey on the rocks in hand and his
> back to the crowd….

Twenty-nine words. Now watch what happens when I highlight the prepositions: "Sitting *at* a table *in* the reception hall *at* the top *of* The Galt House, *with* a whiskey *on* the rocks *in* hand and his back *to* the crowd…." Eight prepositions, just under one-third of the total.

By definition, prepositions require objects, nouns or noun-substitutes most often preceded by articles. Now highlight both the prepositions and the articles: "Sitting *at a* table *in the* reception hall *at the* top *of The* Galt House, *with a* whiskey *on the* rocks *in* hand and his back *to the* crowd…." Fifteen words—over half of the total—devoted to relationship-forming words and words that simply announce that a noun is coming.

This kind of sentence is often called a "shopping-bag" sentence, because it has no inherent structure, no overt destination, as it were. The writer can simply keep stuffing things into the back, using the standard preposition + article + noun format:

> Sitting on a comfy chair at a table in the back of the
> reception hall at the top of The Galt House, with a
> whiskey on the rocks in hand and his back to the crowd
> gathered in front of the bride in her satin dress, with her

bouquet in her hand, her other hand around the shoulder of a man dressed in a tuxedo with....

Quite literally, the sentence could continue for hundreds of words with nothing to stop it.

First aid? Remove as many prepositions and articles as possible while maintaining meaning and the sense that this is an English sentence. Revised, it might read: "At a table in The Galt House reception room, whiskey-and-rocks in one hand, back to the crowd...." I've assumed that if he is "at a table" he is sitting there; if it is crucial to the story that he already be standing, then specify that. And I am assuming that it is *his* hand and *his* back because, thus far, he is the only character mentioned. What remains is seventeen words that carry the same message more quickly and with greater vigor.

Please note that nowhere in this essay do I advocate removing *all* prepositions or *all* articles. These parts of speech are fundamental to structure and syntax. Without them, English begins to sound like gibberish...strings of nouns and verbs with no suggestion as to how they relate.

Instead, remove *as many as possible*. Compress, tighten, make every word count, no matter how many words are involved.

Chapter 29

Whatever You Do, Don't Let Them Dangle!

In the previous essay, I wrote at length about a super-prepositionalized introduction to a sentence:

> Sitting at a table in the reception hall at the top of The Galt House, with a whiskey on the rocks in hand and his back to the crowd....

In addition to the almost random sequence of prepositional phrases, the introduction demonstrates an additional oddity.

It has no subject. We know from the previous sentence that the character is a werewolf and that he is crashing a wedding. We assume from the pronouns in this phrase that all of the actions and other modifications relate to that character, especially since no others have yet been mentioned. Since the phrase itself contains no subject, we assume—and English grammar insists—that the subject of the accompanying sentence will *also* serve as the subject of the introduction.

This kind of introduction is called an "absolute." It consists of a noun or noun substitute—in this case the closest we come is the pronoun *his*—and a participle, an *–ing* or an *–ed* form of a verb. The participle does not function as a verb in this instance; it becomes an adjectival or adverbial telling us something about the subject of the completing sentence. *He* is *sitting,* etc.

The absolute is highly useful, since it can compress a great deal of information into a small packet without having to repeat basic sentence parts such as subject or verb. It is also, however, one of the most frequently misused kinds of phrase.

Often called "dangling modifiers," "squinting modifiers," and other less-than-formal names when misused, these structures can cause a momentary disjuncture between the introductory phrase and the sentence itself. And, as has been argued again and again, such disjunctures may cause readers to falter.

All right, back to the original phrase. What makes this a dangling modifier?

When we complete the sentence, we read:

> Sitting at a table in the reception hall at the top of The Galt House, with a whiskey on the rocks in hand and his back to the crowd, his crisp blue eyes studied the reflection of the guests in the high-rise window as they trickled in to celebrate the occasion.

Problems? Well, more prepositional phrases, and a repetition of "high-rise" that seems implicit in "top of The Galt House." But more critically, the sentence has the wrong subject.

In spite of the promises made by the introductory phrase, and in spite of the appearance of the now-familiar *his*, the grammatical subject of the sentence *and* of the introduction is...*eyes*. *He*, which should be the actual subject, has been transformed into a pronoun that simply modifies the incorrect subject. As a possessive pronoun, *his* cannot control a sentence by itself.

Now, we have true horror. According to the sentence, the character's *eyes* are sitting at the table, holding a whiskey, and facing away from the crowd.

Just the eyes.

A few pages later, the werewolf becomes aware of danger. He leaves the banquet room, dashes down a hallway, and opens the stairwell door. Using his hyper-sensitive sense of smell, he knows that his prey—in this case a pedophile—is already at the bottom and entering the lobby. It will take him too long to race down the stairs, even at werewolf-speed, so

> He searched for a quicker way down. Bolting to the elevators behind him, his claws extended as he spread open the elevator doors....

Another introductory phrase, this one hinging on the verbal *bolting*. Who or what is bolting? Well, we must wait for the subject of the completing sentence. When it comes, we get "his claws." Yes, they *extended* (the sentence verb), and that makes good sense. But before that, they *bolted* to the elevators. Just his claws, apparently, leaving the rest of him behind.

Another quick example, this time from a giant-prehistoric-shark novel. In a rather relaxed moment of exposition, the author indulges in several paragraphs telling readers all about the megalodon. Within a paragraph of each other, we find two problematical phrases.

The first reads: "As if the size and voraciousness of its feeding orifice were not enough...." While this is not quite the same kind of problem as the one above, it stems from a similar cause. In the process of modifying one part of a sentence, the writer essentially forgot how that phrase should relate to the rest. The sentence begins well enough. Stripped to its basics, the first half reads: "As if the size of its feeding orifice were not enough." In spite of the rather pretentious circumlocution for *mouth,* everything fits.

The problem occurs when a second modifying phrase slips between the two parts, hinging on *voraciousness.* If we again strip this part of the sentence to its basics, we read: "As if the voraciousness of its feeding orifice were not enough...." And suddenly, the creature is not voracious; its *mouth* is. A startling moment of illogic.

Then the sentence continues, and the underlying dangling modifier is revealed: "As if the size and voraciousness of its feeding orifice were not enough, *nature has endowed* this monster with a predatory intelligence, honed by 400 million years of evolution" (my italics). So who or what has a voracious feeding orifice? According to the logic of the grammar, nature has. Not precisely what the author intended, but precisely what the sentence states.

Two sentences later comes this:

> The predator's eyes contain a reflective layer of tissue situated behind the retina. When moving through the darkness of the depths, light is reflected off this layer, allowing the creature to see.

Again the question: who or what is "moving through the darkness of the depths"? Grammatically, *light* is. The true subject of both the introductory phrase and the completing sentence is, of course, *creature,* which finally shows up in a second modifying phrase tacked onto the end of the structure. First aid? Perhaps something like "When the creature moves through the darkness of the depths, light reflects from this layer...."

"But isn't it obvious whose claws they are?" comes the objection, "and who is sitting at the table? Not to mention what is moving through the darkness?"

The answer: sometimes. But in every case of a misused introductory phrase, there is a chance for the reader to catch the fact that the subject has been hidden away as another part of speech and stop, even momentarily, to clarify what is happening. And in that momentary hesitation, the impetus of the story may disappear.

Chapter 30

Articles

Articles, like all parts of speech, fulfill a useful function in English. They serve as placeholders, alerting readers that nouns or noun-functioning words, serving as subject matter for utterances, are coming, if not immediately—as in "the book"—then after an intervening adjective or two—"the red book," "the new red book." They alert us to pay attention. If we miss the noun, we may miss meaning as well. Other kinds of words may also announce nouns, usually possessive pronouns—"my new red book," "your new red book"—or demonstrative pronouns—"this new red book," "that new red book."

Unlike possessives, which indicate ownership or belonging, or demonstratives, which act to point to a specific thing, articles carry little direct meaning. Some nuances are possible. "The" indicates a certain one within an undefined group: "the book"; while "a" indicates an undefined one within an undefined group: "a book," any old book. If the noun begins with a consonant, we use "a"; if it begins with a vowel, we use "an," to make pronunciation easier: "an apron," "an uncle," "an ocean."[4]

Other languages have different ways of identifying nouns in sentences, usually by specific endings that not only identify a word as a noun but also tell how it functions in the sentence. Some function entirely without articles, allowing these endings alone to signal nouns. Originally, English used such endings—declensions—in much the same

---

[4] Curiously, the first two words originally began with "n." The earlier Middle English forms were *napron* and *nuncle* (preserved as an archaism in Shakespeare's *King Lear*). But gradually the *n* split from the word, slid across the page, and joined the indefinite article *a* to become *an*, and our pronunciation and spelling of the words altered accordingly. Fascinating.

way as ancient Latin. The Anglo-Saxon word for 'stone' was, for example, *stan*. But a thousand years or so ago, if someone was killed "by means of a" stone, that could be signified, not by a long phrase such as we would have to use, but by the addition of a single letter: *stane*.

The point of this is simply that our ingrained sense that nouns must be preceded by articles can easily spill over into our lines, sometimes creating bulky, unnecessarily wordy writing, both prose and poetry. These lines from an early poem of mine seemed, at the time, clear, concise, precise, and artful:

> Watching
> on the fractured rocky shore,
> immersed in misty coolness
> boiling through the heat
> of day,
> he stared into the fog
> as it moved
> in indiscriminate fluffs
> of ragged white
> upon the surface of the lake.
>
> Clouds like darkened petals
> swirling in pools of indigo
> glided through the silences
> between the flowing stars and moon
> and his probing eyes.

I would still argue that, even though they were written a third of a century ago, they have a flow, a musicality that I appreciate. However, from the perspective of those three decades, I would also argue that they waste a good deal of time in saying what they want to say.

Combining comments made earlier about prepositions with those above, it might be instructive to simply count instances of structure words in the passage. Boldface indicates preposition, italics indicate articles:

> watching
> **on** *the* fractured rocky shore,
> immersed **in** misty coolness
> boiling **through** *the* heat
> **of** day,

> he stared **into** *the* fog
> as it moved
> **in** indiscriminate fluffs
> **of** ragged white
> **upon** *the* surface **of** *the* lake.
>
> Clouds like darkened petals
> swirling **in** *a* pool **of** indigo
> glided **through** *the* silences
> **between** *the* flowing stars and moon
> and his probing eyes.

A casual glance suggests that there are a lot of emphasized words. Now for a little mathematics. The passage has sixty words, a nice even number. Of the sixty, eight are articles: *the* (7) and *a* (1)—at least they give the images a slight sense of the specific. Still, 13% of the passage is used primarily to indicate oncoming nouns, most often without intervening adjectives. There are 13 prepositions; 22% of the words primarily indicate relationships between verbs and nouns or between one noun and another.

Added together, these structure words account for 35% of the entire passage—over one-third of the words do not strictly carry identifiable meaning. And if we add the two conjunctions—*and*—that percentage climbs to 38%. Or conversely, the percentage of words that provide clear action or image amounts to 62%—less than two-thirds.

For the sake of argument, let us assume that instead of receiving payment for words (a rare enough event), writers must pay to *use* words. Clearly, the price exacted for the passage we've just read would be unnecessarily high. So how could we streamline it—concentrating for the moment on articles?

OPTION: ELIMINATION

English is built on embedded principles of redundancy. For example, we immediately recognize *books* as plural because of its final letter; yet it is perfectly proper in English to provide a second or third plural-signpost when we use such words. We might say, "I bought six books," or "I bought 300 books"; or more to the point, "These two books fell to the floor." For this reason, many non-native speakers, whose first languages may not contain articles or allow such redundancy, might feel comfortable eliminating some of the plural markers in the last sentence and simply say "two book fall to floor"—non-idiomatic English but perhaps a literal translation from a native language.

Articles—part of that redundancy—indicate approaching nouns, and we are programmed by conventional usage to include them as often as possible. As writers, however, we can frequently eliminate them without hindering what we wish to say.

Let's look at another line: "The shadow of twilight seemed to outline the tree." Nine words—two articles, one preposition, an infinitive-making *to*, three nouns, and two verbs or quasi-verbs.

With a bit of focus, we can eliminate several words right off. *Twilight* implies *shadow*—we probably don't need both, and of the two *twilight* is more evocative, more specific. *Seemed* as verb is weak; unless there is an underlying sense that what 'seems' really isn't, it wastes syllables. Besides, there is a perfectly useful verb in the sentence already: *outline*.

In one step, we've compressed the line radically. *Twilight* does not usually take an article, so *the* disappears, and we have: "Twilight outlined the tree." Fewer than half the words.

OPTION: PLURALS

If we wish, we can remove the remaining article through a simple expedient: English plurals often do not require articles. "Twilight outlined trees." If that seems too bleak, too blunt, we have the option of filling the now-empty noun-placeholder before trees with a more meaningful word: "Twilight outlined dark trees." Four words, all of them carrying meaning.

Then, of course, we could work further, replacing admittedly boring words with more image-forming, more specific, more concrete terms: "Twilight limned stark oaks," or "Twilight brushed weeping willows," or "Twilight scorched saguaros." Or whatever the passage requires.

OPTION: MORE SUBSTANTIVE WORDS

By far the most effective way to deal with excess articles (and the prepositions that frequently accompany them) is to substitute substantive words for the weaker ones. Another example, this time a haiku:

> the light of the moon
> falls upon leafless branches—

it makes me feel old

Idea: acceptable. Imagery: woefully lacking. Compression: laughable. We have the traditional seventeen syllables; but five of them, nearly one-third the total, are taken up with articles and prepositions. Again, a weak verb: *makes*. And most damning, the poem simply asserts without giving readers an opportunity to enter and imagine.

Now, compression. "The light of the moon" (five words) might become "moonlight." "Falls upon" (weak verb + preposition) could be replaced by a single, more vigorous word, possibly "twists." Now the first line—the first five syllables—might read, "moonlight twists leafless," and we are almost through the second line of the original version.

"Branches" only takes two syllables. If we wish to keep the 5-7-5 structure, we now have five new syllable spaces into which we can place image-forming words. Since all former prepositions have disappeared, let's allow one in at this point...purposefully:

> moonlight twists leafless
> branches into icicles—

Acceptable. But what about that flat final line. Yes, the image might *make* me *feel* old, but neither "makes" nor "feel" works strongly enough now to balance "twists." Keeping the meaning but communicating it through an image, we might get: "fingers rake white hair." And the poem now reads:

> moonlight twists leafless
> branches into icicles—
> fingers rake white hair

Perhaps not a great haiku but certainly far more effective than the original. And it brings with it a wider lesson: even though this essay focuses on articles, it is impossible to ignore the fact that frequently multiple articles in a line accompany multiple prepositions; and they, in turn, nearly always trigger weak verbs and flat nouns. It is not just a matter of going through a piece and removing or replacing *a, an,* or *the*. In most cases, excess articles—and prepositions—merely act as symptoms.

Now, back to lines I cited earlier:

Watching
on the fractured rocky shore,
immersed in misty coolness
boiling through the heat
of day,
he stared into the fog
as it moved
in indiscriminate fluffs
of ragged white
upon the surface of the lake.

Clouds like darkened petals
swirling in pools of indigo
glided through the silences
between the flowing stars and moon
and his probing eyes.

Some possible changes seem obvious: in the lines "glided through the silences/between the flowing stars and moon," both articles can simply drop out, leaving: "glided through silence/between flowing stars and moon" ("silence" sounds better and makes more sense than the earlier plural).

"On the fractured rocky shore" is wordy—and the more interesting and visual noun is not the generalized *shore* but *rock*, which has been turned into an adjective. Restore it to its position as a noun, make it plural, and a five-word line (one preposition, one article) becomes a three-word line: "on fractured rocks." That the rocks rest along the shore becomes obvious later, when we see the "surface of the lake."

Perhaps the most enjoyable exercise would be revising these lines:

he stared into the fog
as it moved
in indiscriminate fluffs
of ragged white
upon the surface of the lake

which now sound repetitious and bulky. "The fog" requires the next three lines as description. Making "fog" plural would remove the article, but the real problem goes deeper. There are simply too many words, too many prepositions, too many articles for the lines to generate interest.

So…"fog" is white, it cannot appear below the surface of a lake, it is by definition indiscriminate in that its edges are blurred and indistinct. Perhaps all we really need is:

> he stared as
> ragged fluffs curled
> upon the lake

or something similar. Then, if desired,

> he watched ragged fluffs curl
> upon the lake

One benefit of compressing this radically is that doing so forces underlying meanings to surface, to be tested for clarity, logic, precision, accuracy. And then, once we've penetrated the tangle of words, removed deadwood, and structured the poem's core, we can build onto that basic structure as needed/desired and expand through image, metaphor, and symbol. Not all poems are skeletal; not all poetic styles can adapt to sparse words/phrases dropping like rocks down the left-hand margin.

But even in more leisurely poems, or in metered poetry where articles and prepositions can function usefully in creating rhythms of stress, challenging, eliminating, transforming, or replacing empty syllables will almost always strengthen the final piece.

Chapter 31

Deadwood

What's wrong with a little *deadwood*?

When I first heard the term used in a composition class in high school, it didn't seem that threatening. In fact, my only experiences with the word outside of writing had been rather pleasant: going camping, cracking dead twigs and small branches from pines or firs, and using them to start warm, comfy fires. The trees did look a little better for my ministrations, but that wasn't the true purpose of the exercise. My own pleasure was.

Not until I began gardening as an adult, a husband and father, and a homeowner, did I begin to appreciate the deeper, darker suggestions of the word.

Deadwood can be *deadly*.

In one sense, of course, deadwood in nature—as in forests—serves a useful function. It provides unique habitats for plants, fungi, small animals, and insects that flourish in broken or split branches and trunks and provide food for birds and larger animals. Modern ecologists frequently speak of the need for specific amounts of deadwood to maintain forest health.

On the other hand, the dry, often splintery wood, coupled with ragged bark, creates an ideal nesting place for tree-boring insects and an invitation to diseases—what might be called the *internal dangers* of deadwood. Branches become brittle and may break, potentially causing damage, as recently in Idaho where a long-dead tree suddenly fell, crippling a camper.

There are also the *external* dangers of too much deadwood, particularly in dry conditions. Living trees often survive forest fires when the flames sear through underbrush so rapidly that the sap-laden upper branches are not injured. If there is too much deadwood, however, either on the ground or in the trees themselves, what was once an inhibiter becomes an accelerant.

In my garden I discovered that deadwood on plants such as roses could be just as harmful. The old woody canes crowd out the living growth, forcing new canes to develop farther and farther down the stem. When they begin emerging below the graft line, all of the advantages of the graft are lost. The result is spindly, vine-like bushes crowned, not by beautiful, large, fragrant blooms, but by simpler, smaller and (to most rose fanciers, at any rate) less attractive flowers. Eventually, the wild rose stock will take over and destroy the grafted cultivar.

Over the years, the term *deadwood* has transferred to writing as a metaphor. It now describes words and phrases that, rather than encouraging clear communication, inhibit it—much like the fire-prone deadwood in forests. Everyone uses such words and phrases, especially in first drafts, where the important thing is to get the story down, not to fine-tune how it is expressed.

And, again like deadwood in nature, literary deadwood can occasionally serve useful functions. Characters might speak loosely, non-grammatically, with no particular concern for crisp, precise speech. In its essence, dialogue should suggest (but not always re-create) the characters' rhythms and patterns of daily use...and we all use grammatical and syntactical fillers when we speak, we duplicate plurals ("a pair of twins"), we multiply prepositions ("come on out of the house"), and commit any number of other writing "sins." Fortunately, there is usually no one around to preserve what we say for posterity, and we get away with it.

(If you want a kind of lab-practical test, just listen to any public employee being interviewed by the media and notice how much deadwood—jargon, passivity, clichés, trite phrases, circumlocutions, and general vagueness—infects their speech.)

Sometimes, a bit of deadwood can help avoid repetition. I once asked students to define a word in an essay, leaving the choice up to them (the last time I made that mistake). Unfortunately, one of the students chose *meaning*. The first paragraph used the word or its variants at least twenty times—the first sentence used it over half a dozen: "The meaning of the word *meaning* is to mean...." The essay would have been stronger by using what would otherwise be considered deadwood: "drive at," "hint at," "speak of," all two-part, relatively general verbs.

And, of course, deadwood can help shape utterances for specific audiences. We often feel uncomfortable when speaking to—or writing about—those who have had someone close die. We don't like to say, "Sorry, but your husband of sixty years just died." That seems brutal, blunt. So we call upon our supply of deadwood phrases to soften the blow: "I am sorry to hear that your husband has passed away," or "…gone to his reward," or any number of other easily editable versions.

As with deadwood in nature, however, when allowed to get out of hand, literary deadwood can be devastating.

Consider the following paragraph from an imagined horror novel:

> The thing moved on down the long hallway. It rapidly made its way past all of the closed doors. It turned into the last room on the left at the far end of the very dark hallway. Engle felt his breath putting compression on his lungs as he tried hard to catch his breath. He immediately considered his choices. Then he moved along on down the hallway as well. As Engle entered the last room at the end of the hallway, his eyes quickly looked into every corner of the room. The thing was not in the room. The room was empty. But it had to be in the room. It *had* to be. He knew instinctively that he had seen it turn into the empty room. Where was it? Where could it be hiding?

(I admit that I've made this a bit more egregious than most samples, but in my defense, I have edited manuscripts, reviewed ARCs, even read published novels that came perilously close to this. If memory serves, the "Meaning" essay was demonstrably worse. At least the passage above has the virtue of making the problems obvious.)

I would like to suggest several steps to identify and remove deadwood, along with some examples.

ELIMINATE TWO-PART VERBS:

In the first sentence, "Moved on" is the verb, even though it looks like a verb plus a preposition. It simply wastes space. The second word, "thing," indicates that the writer is talking about something unknowable; the following verb could provide an opportunity to begin defining "it" more specifically. Does it *rustle,* or *scamper,* or *skitter,* or *galumph* (probably not the best choice but better than the almost static *move on*)—any number of words could start visualizing the horror that is otherwise amorphous.

ELIMINATE VAGUE NOUNS AND VERBS:

To begin with, "thing." By the end of the paragraph, readers still have no notion what "it" looks like, how it moves, what noises it might make. The character, Engle, might not have any notion either, but the writer should, and here is an opportunity to begin specifying so that when readers finally *see* the thing, they are prepared and will feel a certain satisfaction.

Two additional nouns—"hallway" and "room"—appear far too frequently in the short span of 135 words. They become monotonous, rather like Lovecraft's "eldritch" when it is repeated too often. Other possibilities carry stronger connotations that might be useful in characterizing the story: "corridor" or "passage" for the first, "chamber" or "cubicle" for the second. Any of them, in conjunction with "hallway" and "room" would individualize the setting.

Then there is the vague, almost useless verb, "tried," propped by a second word, "hard," when the sentence cries for "struggled" or "labored." The precise nouns are out there somewhere; it just requires that writers look for them.

MAKE THE TRUE VERBS THE ACTIVE WORDS IN THE SENTENCE:

No, Engle's breath didn't "put" anything anywhere; it would, in any case, lack the appropriate volition to do so. What it could do, however, is "compress," or "squeeze" if something less formal is needed. Often in writing replete with deadwood, sentence objects or objects of prepositions provide the *action* words, although they have been forced into noun positions.

ELIMINATE UNNEEDED ADVERBS:

Not all adverbs are evil—make that *ee-vill*, pronounced the way stage villains do. They are a legitimate element of speech and have been part of the language for over a millennia. They do not, however, need to accompany *every* verb, especially weak verbs that need propping. "Rapidly made its way" has two flaws: first, the putative verb is *made*, yet the creature didn't *make* anything, it *moved*; and second, however it moved, it did so *fast*. So…reduce a multi-part verb to one word that encompasses both the prepositional phrase and the extraneous adverb. It "hurried," "glided," "swept," or "slipped," depending upon what kind of creature it is—something the writer has yet made no effort to explain.

The phrase "He immediately considered" comes between one precipitous action—Engle having difficulty breathing—and another—his moving ("racing," "stumbling," even "running" is better). In the narrative scheme, "immediately" is unnecessary. Junk it.

The same holds with "quickly looked." "Looked" is vague; "glanced," "scanned," "scrutinized" are specific, or any other word that defines precisely what Engle does.

Sometimes adverbs are simply wrong, as with the use of "instinctively." Engle didn't intuit in some mystic way that the creature/thing had entered the last room. He saw it. No instinct is needed. Junk it.

How much darker than dark is "very dark"? While the intensifier has some legitimate uses, the majority of the time it simply gobbles space. Mark Twain is credited with having told a neophyte writer to replace every adverb with "damn," then remove all objectionable language. In almost every instance, junk it.

"As well" is also adverbial and also unneeded. The thing has moved down the hall; now Engle does so. There is no confusion as to who does what or suggestion that one goes in a different direction from the other. Wasted words. Junk them.

ELIMINATE UNNEEDED PREPOSITIONAL PHRASES:

Where to start? "All of the" becomes "past the closed doors"—the sentence structure implies "all" and its requisite prepositional phrase. "At the far end of the very dark hallway"—two prepositionals that can be deleted, since a previous sentence stipulated "last door on the left," encompassing both phrases. Ditto for the next "at the end of the hallway"—if readers haven't gotten it yet, they never will. "Every corner of the room"; the *room* is under discussion, so the specification is redundant.

ELIMINATE EXTRANEOUS PREPOSITIONS:

This problem is similar to the one above and arises from the same writerly impulse: to make everything perfectly clear. "The thing moved on down the hall." Why not "The creature raced down the hall," eliminating "on." Later, the writer tops this structure with "moved along on down the hall." Again, deadwood, and again, failure to characterize the action to build suspense, interest, or understanding.

Also to be considered—although not specifically a form of deadwood—is general wordiness. If the thing is not in the room, do we need a second sentence to tell us that the room is empty? If lack of furniture is crucial to the story, say it more economically. Otherwise strike the second iteration. Ditto with the final questions. They seem obvious, and it is usually dangerous to restate the obvious.

Having endured an English-professor, satisfaction-guaranteed-or-your-money-back hatchet job on the paragraph, now consider how it might read if handled more carefully. After considering all of the nouns, verbs, adverbs, prepositions, prepositional phrases, and repetitions, we might have something like this:

> The apparition flitted down the hall, passed the closed doors, and disappeared into the last chamber. Engle's lungs felt compressed; he struggled to breathe. He considered his choices, then edged along the corridor. As he crept into the final room, he scanned every corner. The ghost had to be there. It *had* to be. He had seen it enter. But the room was empty.

Not deathless prose, to be sure, but neither is it quite so worthy of being summarily executed and put out of its—and the readers'—misery as was the first version. It is tauter, crisper, with sentence structures suggesting action and suspense rather than merely describing and discussing. And—not the most important point, perhaps, but one to watch for—it uses only 64 words, less than half of the original. Yet not only is there no lessening of understandability, there is actually an increase. And the final sentences develop and continue the suspense one assumes the author intended.

Deadwood. It has its uses when it is understood and controlled. Out of control, it becomes deadly.

Chapter 32

Colons and Semicolons

Of all marks of traditional punctuation, colons (:) and semicolons (;) are the least understood, the most complicated-seeming, and certainly the most intimidating. I know people (including a fair number of my former students) who will probably go their entire lives without using either one. Some people hate them. Others fear them.

Actually, however, there is no need to do either. Both marks have specific, highly useful, and easily understandable uses. It just takes a few moments of thinking.

Both colons and semicolons have a similar primary function: to join syntactical structures, including *sentences*; *clauses* (word-strings containing both subjects and predicates, often dependent upon a preceding or following sentence); and *phrases* (simply put, word-strings *not* containing a subject and predicate). How they join them and when they join them are far less complex than the sentence you just read.

To begin, when used to join sentences, the *colon* introduces formality: It usually feels out of place in fiction since storytelling often works at the informal, often colloquial level. Its primary use is to connect two sentences, as in the example above, when the second sentence basically says the same thing as the first. In this case, the initial clause (the sentence controlling the structure) makes a statement about formality; the second clause refines, expands, or explains just what the first sentence meant. Note that the colon is followed by a capital letter. This provides readers with a clear sense that what they are about to read is a second statement. The combination of colon and capital just as clearly indicates that essentially no new information will be added that is not implicit in the first. Since few people think or talk this way, colons appear infrequently in prose.

Except for the exceptions. Those deal with paradoxically more specialized and yet more familiar instances that might be useful in fiction: introducing lists, separating hours from minutes; identifying Biblical phrases; and completing the salutation for a formal letter. (It can also be used to introduce an indented quotation, should that be useful.) For example:

> When he heard of the coming invasion of vampires, he stopped only long enough to gather the necessities: stakes, mirrors, and a necklace of garlic.
>
> He checked his clock—it read 11:52 PM, which meant that he was in mortal peril for the next eight minutes.
>
> He felt as though he should say something scriptural, but the only thing that came to mind was the Bible passage that showed up so often on banners at ball games: John 3:16—"For God so loved the world, that he gave his only Son, that whoever believes in him should not perish but have eternal life." Since vampires were immortal, that one didn't seem quite right.
>
> By 12:01 AM, all that remained of him was a fragment of paper and a single line of writing—"To whom it may concern:"—his last words.

Except for a few esoteric uses that most likely won't be needed for effective storytelling, that is it: colons join closely related sentences, they introduce lists, they separate numbers that deal with different things or quantities, and they conclude formal salutations.

Semicolons also join structures. Although they too look complicated and frequently seem intimidating, the convention for usage is quite simple: Semicolons join *syntactically equal structures* or *a series of structures containing commas*. That is, whatever arrangement of words lies to the right of the semicolon has the same structure as the words to the left.

Semicolons can join sentences to sentences. They are particularly useful when writers want to jamb two sentences together, to juxtapose them on their own merits, without an intervening *and, but, however,* or any other words or phrases that spell out the relationship between them. For example: "All along, he had hoped for some kind of help, some kind of aid; by midnight he had to accept the obvious…he was alone."

They can also join clauses (word-strings with subjects and verbs) to clauses or phrases (word-strings without subjects or verbs) to phrases if the individual units contain internal commas.

Here is a sentence containing a compound object, several syntactically similar elements in series, each containing an appositive (renaming the noun) separated from the noun by a comma: "I went to town and saw these people: Mrs. Green, the grocer; Mr. Brown, the dentist; Dr. Collings, the sometimes pedantic retired professor, all of whom were by now zombies." Number of zombies seen: three. If the sentence has been punctuated differently, using only commas to separate parts, it would read this way: "I went to town and saw these people: Mrs. Green, the grocer, Mr. Brown, the dentist, Dr. Collings, the sometimes pedantic retired professor, all of whom were by now zombies." The number of zombies seen: *six*. Punctuation counts.

There are innumerable permutations on the possibilities but actually only two large categories in common use: Semicolons join sentences to sentences; and they join equal syntactic elements containing internal commas.

One final hint.

Note that the marks, the colon (:) and the semicolon (;), differ only in the lower component. If it is helpful, think of the colon as a kind of *super*-period: The lower mark most often separates two utterances as sentences, like a period would; while the upper mark holds them together. They join while simultaneously allowing two sentences with similar content their structural individuality and independence.

Semicolons, composed of an upper dot and a comma, act like *super*-commas. They can join two sentences, something uncommon with commas without creating a comma splice; but they can also join *parts of sentences in series*, something usually reserved for commas—if there are already commas within the elements, the semicolon avoids any possibility of ambiguity in meaning.

Chapter 33

About Ellipses....

In reading manuscripts over the past few months, the single most frequent area of difficulty I have noted deals with those pesky little points, the *ellipsis*.

While they may seem minor in the big picture of a novel, or even within a short story, they are important for what they say and how they say it. So it might be interesting to take a few moments and review what ellipses are...and what they aren't.

Many years ago, when I was first married and just beginning my career teaching composition and creative writing, my wife and I had a number of enjoyable exchanges about grammar and usage. She is very much a people-person; most people she meets feel like she is an old friend within a few minutes. She is easy-going, informal, a delight in every way.

I am not. I suspect that I come across as stiff, formal, even snobbish — when in reality I am shy beyond belief and, for the past three decades, increasingly deaf. I do not mix well with groups. And in my writing, I am formal, considered, and as correct as possible.

So....

The fateful day came when she was writing her first letter to her mother after our wedding. I was, as was typical, grading papers. When she finished her letter she handed me the pages and asked if there was anything I wanted to add. Red pencil in hand, I took it and circled all of the 'errors' in it, wrote a hasty note to my mother-in-law, and handed it back. My wife shook her head resignedly (something I became used to in the ensuing years) and mailed the letter.

It took ten years for my mother-in-law to dare to *write* to us. During that time, she would only telephone.

The consequence of academic humor.

Now, this anecdote actually does have bearing on my stated topic: ellipses. Most if not all of the 'errors' I circled in my wife's letter were of two sorts—repeated punctuation marks and ellipses.

When Judi writes, she uses multiple exclamation marks to indicate excitement, hers and the reader's. Like this!!!!!!!! Or multiple question marks to suggest incredulity or—again—excitement. Really?????

She would give me rough drafts to check. I would dutifully remove all but one exclamation mark or question mark, according to the rules of grammar. She would take my revision and, grinning, add them back in, according to the rules of Judi.

When Judi and I joked about end punctuation, there were hard-and-fast rules of grammar to rely on. When it came to those pesky points, however, things suddenly seemed less fixed. After all, if *!!!!* could represent an extreme of excitement and passion and *????* a parallel extreme of confusion and bewilderment, why couldn't.........indicate a pause...a long, long pause.

In fact, the two situations are quite similar.

Question marks and exclamation marks, like periods (full-stops, in British parlance) are discrete bits of punctuation that in general have a single function: they tell us that a sentence (command or question) is finished. Colons and semicolons have equivalent functions; under certain conditions, they tell us that two statements have a close logical or syntactic relationship to each other, and that the first of the two has just ended.

No problem.

But ellipses..., well, they obviously work on slightly different levels than the others, even though technically, they are a single, discrete mark of punctuation as well.

What? you might ask. How can three be one?

It's quite simple.

An ellipsis is made up of three—and only three—points. They are not periods; in fact, some computers and printers have special symbols for ellipses. Some automatically replace three manually entered periods in sequence with three smaller, compressed dots. That set of three is considered a single unit.

And it is a highly adaptable and useful unit.

With it, writers may indicate that elements are missing in a quotation, for example. Ethical writers will be careful that the deletions do not alter the meaning of the quotation in any way, merely remove unneeded information to highlight what is critical; less ethical writers might choose to shift the purpose of the original words, at times even negating it. We've all seen reviews such as this—"This is…a masterful re-creation of…time and place." Perhaps we've wondered what those sets of three dots were replacing. Something like, "This is not a masterful re-creation of any conceivable time and place"?

Writers may be unethical. Ellipses are not. They simply indicate that something has been left out.

Or that the sentence is not finished, that it has simply trailed off into….

But wait. There are *four* marks at the end of that last structure. Yes. Three points for the ellipses, to indicate that the thought is incomplete, and a fourth point to complete the structure *containing* that thought. That fourth point is not part of the ellipsis; it is a *period*.

And that is it. Three points, or three points and a concluding mark of punctuation. Nothing more. Nothing less.

If the omitted material occurs in the middle of a compound structure, an appropriate comma may follow: "Tell me if you took that cookie or…, and don't give me that expression!" or "'I know I've seen you before…,' she said."

The conventions governing ellipses apply as well to the other concluding marks of punctuation. It is possible to omit material at the end of one sentence, then continue the next sentence following a semicolon: "I only saw three people…; I swear I only saw *three*." Or to conclude a question with omitted material: "Did she tell you that I…?" Or an exclamation mark: "If you don't leave this instant, I'll…!"

In each structure the convention is the same. An ellipsis of three points followed by concluding punctuation.

Occasionally writers wish to include fragments of sentences, as when reproducing bits of overheard dialogue. Again, the ellipsis comes to the rescue:

"…Wouldn't have believed it if…."
"…Never expected him to…."
"…This world coming to anyway when…?"

Note that the punctuation marks provide a wealth of information about the fragments. The quotation marks tell us that they are quotations; characters external to the action are being overheard by the narrator or narrative voice, but their communications are not complete. Such structures may provide a quick sketch of a mob's emotional responses to an action or character, among other things.

The ellipses remind us that we are not to expect complete communication, complete thoughts; rather, the phrases merely give us an estimate of the entire utterances. And—as with all ellipses—there are three dots.

The capitalizations do not indicate that the speakers' sentences begin at that point; the quotation marks and the ellipses tell us that we are breaking in on a speech line. However, regardless of the fact that a character's thoughts and, perhaps, personality are being captured by a fragment, the *author* is nonetheless creating complete structures; they begin with capitals and end with concluding punctuation.

The terminal ellipses confirm the fact that we are not hearing all of the communication, just the bit that the author believes will create the requisite effect.

Much is being said in few words, and several levels of communication are being explored—speaker, narrator (who is *not* the author and who thus does not have to complete the fragments) and author, who has independent structures to close and *does* have to complete them.

As with many of the 'rules' of English grammar, the effective use of ellipses ultimately make sense when broken down into a few easily remembered points.

1. There are only three points in any ellipsis;

2. Given their position in structures, ellipses may precede commas, semicolons, question marks, exclamation marks, or other appropriate punctuation;

3. And, when the structure concludes with a full-stop/period, there are *not* four elliptical points; there are still only three, along with the concluding period.

Useful things, those pesky dots...!

Chapter 34

"He Said," "She Said": Speech Tags in Narrative

Oh, no. Not another article on speech tags. Why?

Perhaps the best reason to talk about dialogue attribution is that when used inappropriately or unconvincingly, it can be one of the first ways readers differentiate between polished, confident, effective storytellers and less polished, less confident, less effective neophytes.

Let's explore how and why.

The fundamental 'rule' (meaning that it can be broken *when doing so is effective*) for speech tags is itself simple: "Simplest is best."

Basically, this suggests that in general the most effective verb one can use to identify a line of dialogue in prose is the one that most clearly, most directly defines the action involved: *said*. This, after all, is what the character in question has just done—*said* something. There are a number of successful short stories, novellas, and full-length novels that, with rare exceptions, limit themselves to the formulas "He said" and "She said."

Or, in the case of science fiction, horror, and other alternate-world tales, "It said."

When we think about it logically, nothing more is needed. If—and, admittedly, these are rather large *ifs*—if the dialogue rings true; *if* it firmly establishes such ephemeral but crucial information as emotion, psychological state, timbre of voice, and others; *if* it has been so carefully crafted that only one character in the story would have said it, all that is needed, at most, is the simple phrase.

Still, writers frequently feel the need to add more. At base, I suppose, this tendency reveals a lack of confidence in the dialogue as written. *I want the reader to* feel *her anger. I want the reader to* hear *the shout. I want the reader to understand the depth of the character's humiliation*, etc. So we move away from the base formula and attempt to underpin dialogue with often irrelevant, frequently redundant, sometimes outright irritating phrasing.

There are several directions writers may—and often do—explore.

FIRST, *an alternate, common word.*

Such words often automatically contradict themselves by introducing actions irrelevant—even inimical—to articulate speech. "'Welcome,' he smiled" is worlds apart from "'Welcome.' He smiled." In the first case, the verb used does not actually introduce speech but rather states an impossibility—one cannot 'smile' speech. In the second, the verb identifies an action simultaneous with or immediately following the speech which lends greater depth and understanding to the character and his actions. Used thoughtfully, such sentences become powerful ways of demonstrating emotion and involvement rather than merely asserting them.

"'You might lose your job,' she giggled." In this example, the key word again describes an action rather than a speech act. Correctly used, however, the same words can give us a needed insight into 'her' personality...and perhaps her motives: "'You might lose your job.' She giggled." I'm not certain that this *she* is a particularly nice person.

Breathed (breathing is necessary *for* speech but is *not* speech itself), *growled, simpered, grimaced, minced,* and other such alternatives might actually draw attention away from the contents of the speech and re-direct it toward themselves. And the narrative suffers for it.

Stuttered, asked, answered, lisped, hissed—in the case of words such as these, the speech itself may render them unnecessary and redundant. If the character stutters, reproducing the rhythms of stuttering is sufficient to *indicate* stuttering. The speech tag need not specify further. If a character lisps, let the sounds of the speech *show* that. There is no need to make the lisping any more explicit.

Hiss is interesting because, with the right sounds, it can in fact be an effective speech tag. "'So you seek me here, in this secret place,' she hissed" is possible (even if it is not particularly interesting). "'Leave!' she hissed" is not. There are no sibilants in the second utterance (i.e., *s, z, sh, ch, z,* and *j*) to be *hissed.*

Any utterance ending with '?' is a question and as such does not need to be identified with "she asked." Any speech responding directly to a question is an answer and therefore does not need "he answered." In both case, the speech tags do little more than slow the narrative.

In almost every instance of alternatives to *said*, the lines may become more effective if the speech is followed, not by a tag, but by an independent sentence describing an action, a reaction, an emotional outburst…something to make the speech itself more dramatic and visual.

Some words may try to split the difference between speech and action, but generally they only succeed when the related speech fits the action defined. "'Wait…here…for…me,' he panted" may work in a text. The ellipses give credence to the idea that his breath is unable to sustain more than one word at a time—he is panting. "'Wait here for me while I run to the hospital and bring back a doctor to see to your ankle, which a rattlesnake has just bitten,' he panted" does not.

SECOND, *a more sophisticated, exotic word designed to draw attention to the line of dialogue.*

The rule of thumb here is…*Don't.*

The words selected are almost always inappropriate to either the context of the novel or the experiences of the reader.

Probably the most egregious example is a term used frequently, and for them correctly, by late-nineteenth and early-twentieth-century authors. Both Agatha Christie and Edgar Rice Burroughs found it entirely acceptable, as did their audiences (even though the sentences make us smile, albeit uncomfortably, now): "'You've got me over a barrel,' he ejaculated."

A century or more ago, the primary meaning of *ejaculate* was "to speak forcefully, passionately." Now, of course, that has changed, and precious few audiences can stifle a slight—or even raucous—giggle when such tags appear.

Other words—almost all multisyllabic and Latinate—share a similar fate. They were at one time considered part of any educated person's vocabulary; now they smack of being too literary, too stiff: *articulated, remonstrated, expostulated,* and the like.

All of them are still perfectly good words…in the appropriate contexts. It is just that those contexts generally don't include speech tags.

THIRD, *phrases, most frequently adverbials, that* tell *readers how to interpret lines.*

Invariably this alternative to "He said" or "She said" becomes wordy and bulky, if for no other reason than that adverbial phrases frequently incorporate prepositional phrases.

"'I like you,' she said in a sweet manner" adds more words than there are in the speech itself...and not one of the extras is needed. *In* is a preposition; its sole function is to announce that a grammatical object is coming that will have some as-yet-unstated relationship to *said*. Similarly, *a* is entirely functional—indicating for a second time that a noun is coming—and carries no specific meaning. It merely assists the syntax of the sentence. Skipping *sweet* for the moment, *manner* is the object of the preposition, the point to which this long extension to the speech has been leading. And it tells us...virtually nothing. It is a flat, vague, generalized word that means 'in a sort of way'—more prepositions and articles.

More critically, it deflects attention from the most important part of the phrase: *sweet*. What should be highlighted is nearly hidden as an adjectival modifying the nominal object of a prepositional phrase.

Literally (and I mean this quite *literally*), almost every adverbial speech tag incorporating a prepositional phrase may be reduced to a single word. That word is almost never the noun of the phrase; and in many cases, it has been demoted to modifying an ineffective word that in some magical way is supposed to make the original speech stronger.

First aid? Strengthen the speech itself so that the adverbial is no longer needed to hold it up; or add a *sentence* incorporating actions that *show* readers what the speech means: "'I like you.' She clasped her hands demurely and fluttered her eyes." Again my sentence is pretty bad, but at least it gives a clear idea of what 'her' definition of *like* includes.

FOURTH, *and perhaps least common, no speech tags at all.*

Least common, perhaps, but often the strongest.
There is a simple reason for this.: If one writes an extended passage of dialogue between two characters—and even more so among three or four—then *each speech must be so carefully constructed that it could be uttered by no other character.*

This thrusts the responsibility for clarity and coherence directly upon the writer, who no longer falls back on the crutches of speech tags to identify speakers. *The individual lines must themselves identify their speakers.*

This is enormously difficult, as most of us know. Dean Koontz once explored the possibility of such extended passages in an early novel, *The Voice of the Night*, and was able to carry a conversation over several pages without *any* indications of who was speaking. He simply gave each character's utterance, then the next, and so. No "Fred said" or "Fred picked up a cup of coffee." He handled it brilliantly; but then he had been working on honing that skill for years.

Intruding names into the speech is generally unnecessary. After all, if only two people are present, who else could the other person be addressing? Handled well, it works. Handled ineptly, it results in dialogue that is often both arch and twee, reminiscent of bad British drama:

> "Rosalind, my sweet, please hand me the butter."
> "Here you are, Reginald, my love. Here is the butter you asked me to hand you."
> "Thank you, Rosalind, my dear. I am taking the butter you handed me and spreading it on my toast."
> "I am so glad, Reginald, my own, that I was able to hand you the butter."

Gaaack!

In the hands of a competent, confident writer, unattributed speech can become staccato, rapid-fire—the parallel term in drama is *stichomythic*—and impel the narrative forward. In the hands of less confident writers, it more frequently stalls and over-explains the obvious.

One final point relating to speech tags—and to every 'rule' in composition—is also simple: *If it works, use it.*

There are difficulties inherent in each of the possible approaches to speech tags...including the standard "He said," "She said," which, if used after every line of dialogue, become tedious. The trick is to understand those difficulties and consciously *choose* what will work best with the narrative. By and large, *said* is the most effective, but used judiciously, consciously, and carefully, the others are available for occasional variety or for special—usually comic—effects.

He exhorted.

No, wait..."He said."

Chapter 35

So You Want to Turn Your Readers Off—Its' Easy

There are rules, and there are rules.

Some, writers may break or ignore.

Others, writers ignore at their peril. Breaking these rules—"words to watch," actually—can carry serious consequences.

For about twenty years, I regularly taught Business Communication at Pepperdine, sandwiched with composition courses, literature courses, and Creative Writing. I had the opportunity to speak with presidents of businesses about the importance of writing and particularly of effective writing. Here are a few of the words they identified as crucial.

ITS, IT'S, AND ITS':

Confusing these three can be a death warrant in writing. One business leader I spoke with simply said that if these were not used properly on a resume, there was no chance the writer would be invited for an interview. As an editor, I respond much the same way. One misapplied term in a manuscript, and I am willing to accept it as a typo. Another, and I begin to question the writer's skill. A third, and the manuscript faces major revision and re-writing, at the least.

In fact, these words are not complicated, confusing though they might seem.

Its is a possessive pronoun: "The bear raised its snout and growled." *Bear* is treated as neuter since its sex is irrelevant in the sentence; and the pronoun referring to it is *it*. No problem there.

The difficulty arises from the fact that in English, almost all possessives require an apostrophe: "This is the boy's book." The apostrophe indicates that letters have been omitted. In this case, the omitted letter(s) actually disappeared centuries ago, when English shifted from being a synthetic language (meaning determined by word-endings; word order in part irrelevant) to being an analytic language (word endings largely irrelevant; meaning determined by word order).

Much like Latin, Old English had a number of endings to indicate whether a word functioned as subject, possessive, object, indirect object, etc.; whether it was grammatically masculine or feminine, which had little to do with gender; whether it was singular or plural.

Most of these endings have dropped from the language. Most words retain the simple *–s* or *–es* to indicate plural: *tree/trees, box/boxes*. We generally do not have endings to differentiate subject from object: "Mary hit the boy," "The boy hit Mary." Word order alone identifies hitter and hittee.

The one place where endings remain is in showing possession. Almost all nouns require the apostrophe, frequently replacing an Anglo-Saxon *–es* ending, as in *stān* (the stone) and *stānes* (of the stone or the stone's). The concluding *–s* has nothing to do with plurality; it is a remnant of older two-letter possessive endings. Thus, today we have a kind of linguistic dinosaur in our midst, the possessive apostrophe.

Except for one small class of words: pronouns.

Pronouns stand for nouns, so one might reasonably assume that they would have similar grammars, including the possessive apostrophe. That assumption leads to the mistake: *It's* instead of *Its*.

Actually, the opposite is the case. While nouns are notorious for changing form and meaning over the centuries, the pronouns have remained remarkably stable. And NONE of them take the possessive apostrophe: *my, mine, his, hers, yours, theirs, ours,* and—perhaps regrettably, considering the number of writers who seem to wish it different—*its*. Few writers slip the apostrophe into any of the other possessive pronouns; *its* seems singled out for that dubious honor. I think for this reason we do not see *hes* as a possessive for *he is* or *shes* as a possessive for *she is*, but we do often confuse *its* and *it's*.

Therein lies the problem. *Its* looks like a pronoun, even though it is not.

It's contracts several phrases: *It is, It has, It was*. The first is the most common by far, but I've seen all three. They all have in common missing letters: the *i-* in *is*, the *ha-* in *has*, and the *wa-* in *was*. In each case, the missing letters and the empty space between the words have been replaced by a non-possessive apostrophe.

The best test to make sure whether *its* or *it's* is appropriate is to speak the phrase or sentence containing it aloud, saying "it is" rather than "its" or "it's": "The book is mine. *It's/It is* mine, I say!" Makes sense, and the form chosen is correct. "That is my book. *It's*/*It is* cover is missing"—makes no sense, so the form chosen is incorrect and should be replaced with *Its*.

As to the third—*Its'*. This one is a dead giveaway, since it does not exist in English. It is a fabricated structure that does nothing more than tell readers that the writer has no idea what is going on. I suppose that if one examined it for meaning, it would come closest to being the plural possessive of a singular pronoun; but even if that were somehow intended, the word would have to be spelled *Its's* and pronounced 'It-zez.'

Back in the bad old days of handwritten essays, I frequently came across a fourth permutation on the words: *Itś*, with the comma strategically placed *over* the *s*, presumably so that I could put it wherever seems most appropriate to me. Fortunately, with computers, that subterfuge has died a well-earned death.

THEIR, THERE, THEY'RE:

The problem with these three is analogous to the difficulty with the *It*-family. They look pretty much the same; they sound the same; but they mean entirely different things.

Their, like *its*, is a possessive pronoun: "This is my side of the road; that is their side." As with all possessive pronouns, it *never* takes an apostrophe, even when it is completed with an –*s*: "This is my side of the road; that is theirs." One mnemonic device that might be useful is to note the appearance of *heir* within the word. Both *their* and *heir* relate to people.

There is an adverb of place: "He's searched here and there and still not found his machete." As the sentence indicates, it is frequently used to define a place further from the speaker than "here." And the mnemonic for this word is even simpler than the one for *their*. *There* contains *here*; both refer to place only, not to people.

They're, like *It's*, is a contraction, this time for *they are* or *they were*. The mnemonic—simply replace the term used with the full phrase *they are* and see if the sentence makes sense. "*They're*/*they are* coming at noon" as opposed to "I will meet you *they're*/*they are*." The first is meaningful; the second is not.

THEN, THAN:

These two are often confused inadvertently, as accidental typos or because they sound similar in speech. As with each of the others discussed, however, they can change the meaning of a phrase or sentence if misused.

Then is an adverb of time: "They will meet us *then*." The mnemonic is based on the similarity in spelling and pronunciation between *then* and *when*. If *then* can be replaced in a sentence with *when*, and the result is a grammatically and syntactically proper question, the word has been used correctly. Using the example above: "They will meet us *then*" may be transformed into a legitimate question—"*When* will they meet us?"

Than is one of those words that can perform several functions. It is most commonly used when it appears in comparisons: "The whole is greater than the sum of its parts"—which, unfortunately, often becomes "The whole is greater then the sum of its parts," a sequence of words that makes no sense. Again, in spoken language, *then* and *than* would generally sound almost identical in these examples, and that similarity carries over into written language, causing the error.

There is a mnemonic for *than*, although it is less direct than most of the ones suggested so far. The principle indicator of comparisons in English is *as*, in phrases such as "as far as," "as much as," "as rich as...." Both *as* and *than* are comparators...and both contain the letter *a*. Not very witty perhaps, but it sometimes helps writers remember.

WHEN/WHERE:

The prime difficulty with these two words is conceptual rather than grammatical; they frequently appear where they simply have no justification for appearing. Usually, the sentences in question are truncated attempts at definition.

"What is freedom?" someone asks, and most common answers begin either "Freedom is where..." or "Freedom is when...." Actually, *freedom* is neither *when* nor *where*. When and where, in this context, denote either "time when" or "place where," and freedom is defined by neither. In fact, the more accurate definition would begin, "Freedom is a state of being in which...."

We find much the same kind of misuse when writers approach generalizations and idealizations. "*Democracy* is when," or "*Democracy* is where"; actually, "*democracy* is a form of government in which...."

What looks to be a rather wordy, certainly more formal statement, is necessarily so to complete a valid definition. *When* and *where* are not designed to do the job.

The key to effective usage: Remember that *when* and *where* rarely do other than what they claim.

When tells time: "When should we three meet again?" "Meet me at ten o'clock."

Where tells place: "Where should we meet?" "At the corner of Fifth and Main."

ALL RIGHT/ALRIGHT:

The proper phrase is two words: "All right." It is adverbial, indicating something about the accompanying verb: "All right, the genetically engineered slime monster is dead!" The trick is that this form finds itself most at home in formal prose, in edited writings that attempt to present the speaker at his/her best.

When writing dialogue, however, writers frequently slip into a secondary spelling, *alright*. The spelling is little more than a century old, developed most probably by analogue with similar-looking words: *altogether, albeit, already*. In a sense, this is the preferable form for certain moments in dialogue, since we can more easily envision the victorious monster-slayer stabbing the air with a fist and screaming, "Alright!" — probably pronounced more like *awwright*—than we can imagine the same person, rather finically enunciating two words.

A LOT/ALOT

One of these phrases is possible in English; the other is not. Formally, *a lot* may indicate a vacant stretch or land or a place where one might buy a Christmas tree or a used car. Informally, it may indicate a superfluity, an excess. *Alot,* on the other hand, does not exist, except in weak or careless writing.

There is no mnemonic here. Just never use *alot*.

English can be tricky. Any number of words come with baggage that makes them difficult. The words discussed here are not particularly cumbersome or unusual; in fact, their commonness and the frequency with which they appear are in part underlying causes of the problems they create.

Fortunately, a little thought, a bit of careful proofreading, and most of the false starts can be easily removed.

It's easy…more or less.

Chapter 36

Redundancies That Repeat Themselves Over and Over Again

Redundant—'to flow back, overflow, be excessive.'

The first definition most aptly speaks to the subject of this essay: The use of words that inadvertently repeat themselves. They are not *wrong* in the sense that a misspelled word is wrong or that *its* has been used when *it's* is needed; indeed, at one time the *conscious* use of multilingual redundancies constituted an elegant style in English prose.

During the sixteenth and seventeenth centuries, writers could choose whether they wanted to write in Latin or in English. Students at all levels would have at least a grounding in Latin. Grammar, when it first began to be taught, meant *Latin* grammar; and English was used primarily as a tool for teaching Latin. Students would read a Latin passage, translate it into English, then translate it back into Latin. The accuracy of the final translation, that is, the degree to which it was identical with the original, constituted the scale for achievement.

For many professional writers—especially those addressing the larger European audience of scholars—important works first appeared in Latin. Only later might they be translated into English for the more limited parochial audience.

By 1700, much of that had changed. Latin was still taught in the schools, but now English might receive as much or more attention. And writers were writing directly in English, with occasional Latin translations following. English had finally superseded Latin in literary prose, just as English had three centuries earlier become the court language in 1399 when Henry IV opened Parliament in English rather than in French.

During that century or so between the mid-1500s and the late-1600s, however, it was possible to use either language almost interchangeably. Sir Thomas Browne, one of the great stylists of the period, often purposely used two modifiers linked by *and*, one of which was pure English of Anglo-Saxon stock and the other, which meant exactly the same thing, Latin. It was an artificial style, to be sure, but surprisingly influential.

Elements persisted in formal English for centuries. It was not accidental that Lincoln's "Gettysburg Address" included several technical redundancies: "It is altogether fitting and proper that we do so," and "But, in a larger sense, we cannot dedicate, we cannot consecrate, we cannot hallow this ground."

Fit comes from the Middle English *fitten*; *proper* can be traced back to Latin, *proprius,* meaning "particular to itself," and that goes even further back to *pro privo* "for the individual." By Lincoln's time, most listeners would not have immediately understood the bilingual echo, but since his time, it has entered into almost common use in formal speech.

Similarly, *dedicate* stems from the Latin *dēdicātus,* meaning..."to consecrate." *Consecrate* stems from the Latin *consecrātus,* "to make sacred, to make holy." And *hallow*—no surprise at this point—comes directly from the Old English verb *hālgian,* "to make holy," from which our modern word *holy* also stems. Three key words in one sentence. Two are derived from Latin; one is derived from Old English; and all three mean exactly the same thing.

Was Lincoln simply so poorly educated or so dull-witted that he didn't notice that he was saying the same thing...three times...in a row...in the same sentence?

Of course not. He was speaking in the highest, most polished oratorical style of his day; and had the speech lasted significantly longer, it would probably have included even more such pairings.

So, there is nothing *inherently* wrong with using two or more words that mean roughly the same thing.

The problem arises when the writer seems not to be *aware* that they mean the same thing. When that occurs, the writing is made weaker rather than stronger by the repetition.

There are several classes of particles, words, and phrases that, more often than others, trick writers into needless redundancies.

WORD PARTICLES:

Re- means "back." *Reduce*, for example, comes from two Latin roots that, taken together, mean, "to lead back"—when one reduces one's weight, one leads it back to where it was earlier. *Regenerate, reread, retype, retort, retrace, revert, return, rewrite, reject*...there are scores of possibilities in English.

Using such words does not constitute redundancy; using them unthinkingly with *back* or *again* does.

Return means "to go back, to send back." Thus the phrase, "*return* the letter *back* to its owner" would mean something like "to send the letter back back to the owner."

Reward means basically "something given in return, for services, for unusual dedication, etc." *Reward again* would mean "give something in return back," and that leads us again to the redundancy of *return again*.

Refer simply means to carry back, sharing the same root as *transfer, infer,* and others. To *refer again*, then, is to carry back back.

Regurgitate, itself a rather intimidating word, harkens back to the Latin, *regurgitates*, "back + to swirl, as in a whirlpool," which is part of what makes it such a visceral word. The fairly common phrase, "regurgitate my food back up again," however, is so rife with redundancy that it becomes almost absurd: *to swirl back back up again.*

(As an interesting irrelevance, I wonder why no one ever *gurgitates*. If something is *regurgitated*, it must once have been *gurgitated*. I likewise wonder if people are ever *gruntled* or *combobulated*. Ah, well, the mysteries of language never cease.)

Sometimes the context will allow for an apparent redundancy. "The failing novelist rewrote his final word again and again," suggesting a continuing series of rewrites or revisions. But even in such cases, there is an unsettling feeling that by the time we get to the final *again,* we have heard this too many times.

MODIFYING PHRASES:

The phrases that present the most difficulty tend to be propositional; that is, the phrases are introduced by a noun or adjective that is then further modified by—usually—an *in*-phrase. For example: "The witch's hat was *conical* in *shape*." Now, the problem here is actually two-fold. First, *conical* is, by definition, a *shape*; to specify that that is what *conical* is becomes repetitive. And second, since witches' hats—at least when used in that particular phrase—tend to look pretty much the same, the modification might not be needed at all: "The witch's hat blew off her head in the horrible storm." Probably everyone reading will have a clear picture of what happened. If the hat was not conical, of course, then the image would be running counter to expectation, and a clear description of size and shape (without using either of those words) might be needed.

Then come some of my favorites:

"The table was square in shape." *Square,* like *conical,* is a *shape.* This one everyone who has passed beyond kindergarten knows. Why not "The table was square"? And then, since the sentence doesn't say much of importance, perform an adjective-transformation; put *square* in front of *table*—"the square table"—and then say something significant about the table, explain why it is important enough to the narrative to be mentioned.

Another favorite:

"The car was red in color." Same objection. *Red* is a *color.* In fact, I'm not sure that it can be anything except a color; so why specify? The remedy is identical to that in the previous example; transform it to "the red car" and then give the phrase a verb and a completer to make it into a pertinent sentence. Or better yet, identify *which* red car it was—a candy-apple-red Volkswagen Beetle does not have the same connotations as a fire-engine-red 1978 Mustang convertible. And now we have indeed come a long way from the blunt redundancy, "the car was red in color."

Or another: "solemn in mood." *Solemnity* is a *mood.* Rather than "The mourners were solemn in mood," put *solemn* where it naturally belongs—"the solemn mourners"—then have them *do* something.

But wait. Aren't *mourners* always *solemn,* at least in American customs? Is *solemn* even needed? Might a description of the setting or of the mourners' clothing sufficiently carry the idea of *solemnity*? Think about it. Then write what is needed…and only that.

ADVERBS AND ADJECTIVES:

Writers—especially neophytes—frequently distrust their nouns and verbs…and often for good reason. When sentences seem lax, writers tend to add, not better, more vigorous nouns and verbs, but adjectives and adverbs designed to prop up the faltering words. So we consistently find sentences structured around verbs such as the flat, vague *walk* (to transport oneself by use of the lower limbs) coupled with crutch-adverbs: *walk quickly, walk slowly, walk awkwardly, walk truculently, walk proudly.* Why not at least consider changing the verb: *trudge* (perhaps the slowest verb in English because of that heavy *udg* lodged in its middle), *amble, meander, stumble, stagger, stomp, stump, strut, march,* and a host of others.

Sometimes, however, the opposite occurs. A perfectly good, vigorous, specific verb is needlessly paired with an adverb, apparently intended to strengthen something that doesn't need strengthening. The result, paradoxically, is that the verb—and the sentence—is weakened by the insertion.

Some examples:

Whispered softly, whispered quietly: to *whisper* is, by definition, to speak quietly or softly. To specify that quality, then is to take away from the power of the verb.

Similarly: *shouted loudly.* Try shouting any other way some time—shouting *softly, quietly, restrainedly*—and it becomes clear that the adverb is not needed.

And a couple more: *darted briefly*—to *dart* is to move rapidly here and there, never stopping to rest at any one place; thus, *briefly* is implicit in the word itself. Or *pick carefully,* as in "she picked her way carefully through the thorn bushes." *Pick* carries the implication of *carefully* in this context, so the adverb becomes redundant. In another context, however, the adverb has more justification, as in "She carefully picked only the ripest, most beautiful peaches." Note that *carefully* extends beyond the verb to modify the entire phrase—she was careful to select only the best.

If there is any question whether an adverb is actually adding meaning to a verb or merely repeating the verb's basic meaning, try replacing it with its opposite—"blood pounded *loudly* in his ears" with "blood pounded *softly* in his ears." Note that the new phrase makes little or no sense. *Pound* implies *loudly*; no adverb is needed.

The situation is not so common with adjectives and nouns, although it still requires that writers consider (I almost wrote "consider carefully") what they are saying. Some of the following adjectives are trite, others create clichés, all to at least some degree become redundant.

Blood-sucking vampire. Really, now, what other kind of vampire is there? Doesn't the fact of *sucking blood* pretty much sum up what a vampire is? There is the small point of its being one of the unDead, but the blood-sucking is really the key issue, the reason why vampires are feared (I'm not talking about the sparkly ones, of course; they can be loved).

Ravening werewolf fits the same pattern. The apparent adjective is so closely connected to the meaning of the noun that there doesn't seem to be a need for it. And again, are there any werewolves that—at least in their transformed state—are not ravening?

Soulless zombie and *ghostly apparition*: Again, the adjective merely confirms a key element implicit in the noun and need not be intruded. Doing so weakens the noun itself.

Slavering saliva. This one is interesting. If you look up *slavering,* the definition is "to generate saliva"; apparently, then, in the phrase, the saliva is busy generating saliva. Not quite what the writer might have intended.

WORD COMBINATIONS:

Certain word combinations are organically redundant.

I remember years ago (when typewriters were still fairly bulky items and had not yet been entirely supplanted by laptops and tablets), one advertisement wanted to ensure that it made its point. It proudly proclaimed "The portable typewriter that you can carry." In other words, it was trying to sell "A that-you-can-carry typewriter that you can carry." A bit nonsensical.

One that is still with us is the idea of a *new innovation. Innovation* means "introducing something new"; *new* ultimately comes from the Latin *novus,* which means "new." A *new innovation* is literally a "new new."

COMPARATIVES AND SUPERLATIVES:

Certain words in English are, by definition, impossible to use in the comparative or superlative. Most adjectives have separate forms to indicate when one thing is *more* than another—*red, redder; old, older,* etc.— and when one thing is *most,* or *more* than three or more others—*red, reddest; old, oldest.*

There are a few words, however, that do not allow that kind of grammatical manipulation.

Essential means, as its form suggests, "pertaining to the essence, that which is indispensable." It does not allow for either comparative—*more essential*—or superlative—*most essential*—since it refers to those elements without which the entity could not exist.

Absolute also lends itself neither to comparison nor to superlative. It is the totality, the unconditional, the complete (another word that does not have degrees).

What happens, then, when the two are combined into a single phrase: "absolutely essential." Both words are superlatives that cannot logically be modified, yet one is used to suggest that the other is incomplete and needs bolstering.

Similarly, *unique* has a specific meaning: "the sole example, the single specimen, one of a kind." If there is only one, how can it be made comparative or superlative? The answer—for some writers, at least—is to create phrases such as: "It was the most uniquely one-of-a-kind I had ever seen." Really?

As noted at the beginning of the essay, the issues I've discussed do not quite fall into the category of grammatically incorrect or outright wrong. They do, however, suggest that the writers involved (and I've seen every one of these, in class essays, in manuscripts, in published novels and stories) are not, for the moment at least, paying full attention to what they are writing. Many of these words and compounds are so common in the language that they slip easily from the pen. A few are increasingly acceptable in informal English, spoken or written colloquialisms (and thus might be useful in characterization); but in most instances, when readers encounter them and there is no evidence that the usage was intentional, for a specific purpose, writers bear the brunt of the blame.

As with every element of writing—apply care, consideration, and thought.

Chapter 37

Seven Grammar Rules You Can Safely Ignore

Whenever I taught English Composition and Creative Writing in the same semester, I was forcibly reminded of one important rule in writing: "There are rules, and there are *rules*." Writers of expository essays and other non-fiction have, at ground, a single task—to communicate an idea effectively. This generally means following a series of conventions developed over the centuries to allow readers to understand such writing, evaluate its success, and decide whether or not the thesis and supporting materials are acceptable. To do that requires a number of elements: clear, precise, and complete sentences, each identifying agent, actor, and acted-upon; consistent use of the conventions associated with spelling, grammar, punctuation, and syntax; logically arranged evidence, with specific, concrete detail; and an overall structure guiding the reader from stated thesis to conclusion—no suspense is needed.

Everything that happens in a composition class, from grammar school to graduate school, serves this primary principle: to communicate an idea.

Unfortunately, too often the dicta established to help writers *and* readers become codified, lithified actually, and seem more important than the communication itself. I have had colleagues who would readily fail a twenty-page paper for a single fragment, for example, or allow only a certain number of punctuation errors before returning the essay as "unreadable." And I taught any number of students who emerged from high school English courses convinced that every essay had to have four paragraphs—no more, no less.

In actual practice, English grammar, spelling, punctuation, and syntax have had a long and extravagantly checkered career, to the extent that many of the "rules" learned by rote in school—and often continued in the workplace—have little relevance to the language as actually used. Some grammarians accept this. One of my favorite texts for Freshman Composition reprinted a list of key rules on the end papers, concluding with one in bold-face, capitals, and red ink: "BREAK ANY OF THESE RULES IF IT WORKS!" Other purists stick to their linguistic guns and enforce any criminal offenses with ruthless thoroughness. I still remember when one of my favorite professors (from whom I perhaps learned more about literature than anyone else before graduate school) handed back an in-class exam. He had circled one phrase and made one comment: "Why did you split this infinitive?" My only answer was unacceptable to him: "It felt right."

I know better now.

In the fundamental rules of writing (they're rather like the Pirate's Code, though; they're actually more like guidelines), the differences between *expository writing* and *storytelling* become crucial.

The storyteller's job is not to communicate a specific idea. That may result *through* the story, but it is not the *purpose* of the story. The story must entertain or no one would bother reading it; but at heart, it must speak Truth. Not factual data, although facts incorporated into it should be accurate; but the deeper, more honest Truth of human existence. Sir Philip Sidney placed writers of fictions (he called them "poets," but in his day the two terms were largely synonymous) above philosophers, mathematicians, theologians, musicians. Because, he argued, the others were wedded to the truths of this world. Only the poets were free to explore the Truths of a wider world. Nature expressed herself in *brass*; Poets delivered *gold*.

As a result, many of the rules devised for exposition do not fit with narration. I would like to point to seven that, however useful they might be in formal communication, might not be that important in writing fiction.

1. NEVER SPLIT AN INFINITIVE.

Briefly put, an *infinitive* is a grammatical structure that allows a verb to function as a noun. It is formed by joining the infinitive-particle *to* to the first-person present-tense form of a verb. "I dive for fun"—no infinitive, and the verb is *dive*. "To dive makes me happier than anything else." The *subject* of the sentence is the infinitive *to dive*; the verb, a weak one at that, is *makes*. The strongest verb-like word in the sentence, *dive*, has been placed in the strongest structural position, as the subject, the thing the whole sentence promises to talk about.

Splitting an infinitive, according to traditional grammarians, occurs when one slips an adverb *between* the infinitive particle and the verb: "To gracefully dive." Oops. Mistake!

The problem with this position is that in English, infinitives are *already* split. That is what the space between the *to* and the verb indicates.

In fact, the origins of this rule go back, not to the beginnings of English, but to Latin. In Latin, "I sing" is expressed by a single word: *cantō*. The *-ō* identifies the first-person form. The infinitive form is *cantāre*, with *–āre* identifying it as such. Notice that the two meaningful parts of the infinitive are connected; in Latin they cannot be separated without altering their meanings, or perhaps better said, without turning them into gibberish.

During the Renaissance, when English grammars were first constructed, scholars believed Latin to be the superior language, so instead of developing a grammar based on what English actually did, they tried to force it into the mold of Latin. Unfortunately, English has strong Germanic roots and doesn't fit. That didn't hamper the scholars, however. They cut and pasted until they created parameters for the grammar, then imposed it upon the language. And for centuries, students were taught not to do something that the language had always done.

There are times, especially in narratives and in conversation, when the adverb makes more sense coming between the *to* and the verb. "Boldly to go" or "to go boldly" effectively diminishes the adverb *boldly*; "to boldly go" places the adverb on a par with the verb (a rather insipid one) and the combination becomes stronger than either part.

(By the way, please note that the split infinitive creates a nearly perfect iambic structure. Neither alternative—"**Bold**ly to **go** where no **man** has **gone** before" or "To go **bold**ly where no **man** has **gone** before"—creates a clear rhythm. The split infinitive does: "To **bold**ly **go** where **no man** has **gone** before." The single exception to an iambic rhythm, the double stress in "no man" emphasizes a key phrase.)

The stricture becomes even less defensible when the infinitive is 'split' by an adverbial phrase. "The deficit is expected to more than triple in the next four years" makes sense. Neither "The deficit is expected more than to triple..." nor "The deficit is expected to triple more than..." does. There is no option for the phrase other than to split the infinitive.

In narratives—and especially in dialogue—the key is not an archaic rule but the rhythms natural to the speaker. To return to the *Star Trek* example, I'm sure the writers knew that they were breaking a rule; I'm equally sure that they chose to do so on the basis of emphasis, rhythm, and cadence.

And we as writers are free to do the same—to carefully choose when to break the rule.

2. NEVER USE FRAGMENTS.

A sentence, according to the books, consists of several parts: a *subject* (the actor), a *verb* (the action), a *complete thought*, an initial capital, and end punctuation. If any of these parts are missing, the result is a *fragment.*

The prohibition against fragments makes a certain amount of sense in expository prose. The purpose of such writing is to *explain.* That requires identifying something to speak about (subject), saying something about it (verb), and, if needed, adding any additional information to ensure understanding.

A sentence may require only two words: "Jesus wept." There is a subject, a verb, and a complete action. That is, by the way, one of the most intense and effective—as well as the shortest—verses in the King James Bible.

In certain cases, a single word may qualify as a sentence: "Go!" There is a subject (*you*-understood), a verb, and a complete idea...especially with the exclamation point.

In writing narrative, however, complete sentences may not be necessary. We do not always speak in complete sentences. When writers construct dialogue, therefore, they may wish to truncate a statement to replicate colloquial rhythms. "I don't know what to do next. Or where to go." The two could be joined, of course—"I don't know what to do next or where to go"—but doing so changes the rhythm of the utterance, makes it sound more thoughtful, more considered, which might jar with the emotional overtones the fragment makes.

In narration, the same is true. A fragment may concentrate attention on a particular thought or idea: "He was being herded by the zombies toward the open gate of the pen. The last place he wanted to go." Separating the latter from the former gives *last place* more emphasis. There is no subject, there is no sentence verb (*wanted* is part of a subordinated clause); but the idea is clear and complete.

A fragment composed out of ignorance may weaken a story; a fragment *chosen* for its emphasis, its jarring effect, its contribution to characterization may strengthen it.

3. Never Use a Preposition at the End of a Sentence.

My favorite version of this rule runs: "Never use a preposition to end a sentence with." My favorite anecdote relates to Sir Winston Churchill's purported response when an over-zealous editor put all of his prepositions into *which*-phrases: "This is nonsense, up with which I will not put!"

Either way, the suggestion is strong that there is something wrong with this rule.

In one sense, there is not. A preposition is, by its very name, a *pre*-position, that is, it comes before something, that something being its object, a noun or a noun-substitute. In its easiest definition, a preposition is intimately linked to that object: "A preposition is anything a rabbit can do to a hill"—*in the hill, on the hill, to the hill, beyond the hill, around the hill.* Of course, there are many more prepositions in English, not to mention prepositional phrases, but they all share that one element—they are connected to an object.

Thus, one literally cannot end a sentence with a preposition. For example, "I hit my brother with." A fragment—no complete thought.

The difficulty is that not all prepositions are *merely* prepositions. Many also function as separable verb particles. That is, they do not connect with an oncoming object but rather with the *preceding* verb, completing it and giving it its full meaning. For example, if I mean, "Hurry up the stairs," omitting the object (*the stairs*) and concluding the sentence with the preposition completely destroys that meaning. No one will know *what* must be hurried *up*.

If, however, I mean, "You are lagging behind, so hurry up and catch up to me," both *hurry up* and *catch up* would be incomplete without their separable particles: "You are lagging behind, so hurry and catch." *Catch* now means something completely unintended, since the verb almost always requires an object. *Catch up* does not.

This structural ambiguity suggests that writers need to be aware of *what* preposition-like words are doing at the end of sentences and *why* they are there. But there is no need to restructure every sentence to place them inside. In other words, "Get on the bandwagon and come on—prepositions are fun."

4. Never use a Conjunction to begin a sentence.

Conjunctions are short words (occasionally phrases) that join structures. The most common are *and, or, but, for, nor, yet,* and *so*—note that *for* can be either a conjunction ("I bought glasses, for I needed new ones") or a preposition ("I bought glasses for my sister"), so be wary of it.

Joining structures, be they phrases, clauses, or sentences, in most cases requires two elements.

First, a mark of punctuation—generally a comma, a semicolon, or a dash—primarily to indicate that the first structure is closing. A punctuation mark *other than a period* lets readers know that something will follow that first structure and that they must prepare their minds for it.

Second, coordination requires a coordinator. If you choose *and,* you tell readers that the sentences are equally important, one following logically from the other: "I woke up, I stretched, and I dragged myself out of bed." *But* indicates a contradiction between them: "I liked her, I even thought I might love her, but I decided not to ask her for a date." *For* indicates cause and effect or, as in the example above, *because. Or* suggests alternatives. *Nor* indicates a negative connection, a denial, a reversal: "I do not like him, nor will I ever like him." *Yet* and *so* also indicate cause and effect, although weakly: "I ran out of food, so I went to the store." That *so* often seems weak is evident in the frequent but redundant structure, "and so...."

General rule of thumb: think carefully about using either *yet* or *so,* and even more carefully about *and yet* or *and so.* Where possible, replace the weaker conjunctions with the stronger, more meaningful *and, but,* and *for.*

Traditionally—and more formally—conjunctions were held to be valid only within a larger structure; that is, joining two sentences with ", and" was acceptable as long as the conjunction appeared in the middle of the structure. After all, the words were called *conjunctions,* as in 'to join with, to join together.' And two sentences are *not* joined if the first concludes with a period.

In contemporary prose, however, the uses of conjunctions have expanded sufficiently to allow the second sentence to begin with *and, but, nor,* etc., *as long as* the logical connection between the two is clearly defined and unambiguously supported by the conjunction: "I tried and tried to move the dead branch. But to no avail." The *but* accurately defines the relationship between the two; and the concluding fragment (see Rule #2 above) emphasizes futility and reversal. In a very real sense, it is not only beginning the second structure but, more importantly, bridging the momentary white space demanded by the period—the momentary pause in thought—to make the abrupt reversal that much more compelling.

5. NEVER USE DASHES; THERE IS ALWAYS A BETTER MARK OF PUNCTUATION.

I was tempted to punctuate this rule with an internal dash but thought better of it. The internal debate did remind me of an incident in high school, however, that has effectively influenced my attitude toward dashes.

As a senior, I attended the Advanced English class, thirty-some students who, because of test scores and grades, had been moving through high school rather as a homogenous lump, seeing each other year after year not only in accelerated English but in similarly accelerated math and science courses. We knew each other well, and we recognized the awkward fact that in some ways we knew as much or more than some of our teachers (especially one poor substitute in Math who spent six weeks with us, despite the fact that her specialty was English; we were cruel to her in countless small, petty ways).

We received our just comeuppance, however, when we began Senior English. The teacher, married but nevertheless an archetypal "old-maid school marm" type, would not let us slip anything by her.

When we entered the portion of the class devoted to grammar, she stood before the class and intoned in her best manner, "Never use dashes; there is always a better mark of punctuation."

"But what if…," one student began.

"Never."

"But how about…?"

"Never!"

"Not even if…?"

"*Never!*"

We finally got the point. I think one of the students tried to slip a few dashes into an in-class essay, and the result was disastrous.

We learned the lesson well.

Then I graduated, went to college (where the rule still applied), and, while serving as a missionary for my church, began to write poetry.

And discovered that, indeed, the dash has its uses. Traditional punctuation, primarily semicolons and parenthesis, were simply too formal for the kind of colloquial verse I wrote. Periods were too final. Ellipses interrupted rhythms.

Dashes worked—and I've used them in informal writing ever since. I chose to avoid them in writing my Ph.D. dissertation since the style sheet indicated that they were still in disfavor in expository prose, but after that, when no was one *grading* my prose, in came the dashes.

There are, however, several considerations when using them, primarily typographical.

First, the appropriate mark is what is technically called an "em-dash," a single line the width of the letter *m* in Times Roman font. It is created by typing two hyphens. Most computers will automatically transform double hyphens to —, eliminating the possibility of ambiguity.

If the computer does not change the mark, simply leave it as two hyphens--readers will understand that they indicate a break in thought between the first part and the second part. Some writers include a space before and after the em-dash -- doing so emphasizes the fact that a logical, syntactical, or conceptual break has occurred.

Problems arise when writers use a single hyphen instead of an em-dash and consequently create a hyphen-bridge rather than a structural break.

Hyphens *join*—dashes *separate.* Because the two marks are so similar, it is easy to confuse them. And confusion is the last thing effective writers want to invite.

6. NEVER USE RUN-ON SENTENCES.

Run-on sentences—the infamous *RTS* (run-together sentences) of strict grammarians—occur when two sentences are joined with the improper conjunction, usually *and* without the preceding comma: "It was raining and I went outside to smell the fresh air." Technically an RTS, although in this case, the meaning is clear.

RTSs become problematical when they create structural ambiguity, that is, when they allow a sentence to be read in either of two ways, with no clues as to which is preferred. For example inadequate punctuation for an adverbial conjunction: "The night was dark and foreboding, however, no zombies were in sight." The problem arises with *however*. To which part of the structure does it belong, the first or the last? Either way makes sense: "The night was dark and foreboding, however. No zombies were in sight" or "The night was dark and foreboding. However, no zombies were in sight." The reader is confused and will probably have to go back and start the sentence over—never a good thing.

On the other hand, judicious RTSs may give a passage a sense of urgency by forcing readers to rush through it without a stop, may characterize a narrator/speaker by education or intelligence (as Mark Twain does brilliantly with the persistent *and*-RTS in *Huckleberry Finn*), or may create short, pithy parallelisms all the more memorable for their flaw ("I came, I saw, I conquered," which, without the *and*, is technically incorrect).

Case in point: during my first year teaching composition at UC Riverside, I assigned a narrative essay; students were to tell me about an important event in their lives. (While the incident has already been mentioned above, the essay was so powerful that it deserves repeated attention.)

While grading the results, I picked up one paper, noted that the first sentence was an *and*-RTS, and started to lower my red pencil. Then I saw that the second one was also. And the third. The pencil dropped, and I simply read the essay.

The student told about the night of her brother's celebration for having been accepted at the local college, the first member of her family to do so. He went out, intending to pick up some additional sodas at a nearby convenience store. She followed him.

Midway there, he was accosted by several former friends, drug dealers who felt that he should not have quit the enterprise and while she watched from shadows a few feet away they stabbed him to death.

She had never told the story before. The essay was both a response to an artificial assignment and an act of catharsis. She *had* to get the words out as quickly as possible, and to do so she simply dropped the connective commas.

It was a perfect essay.

I spoke with her about it later and told her how impressed I was by what she had accomplished and quietly requested that she *never do this to me again*. For the next assignment—a definition paper—she wrote in nicely punctuated, objective sentences, appropriate for the content.

Run-ons can work. But as with all of the 'rules' discussed here, only when the context is appropriate.

7. NEVER USE ONE-SENTENCE PARAGRAPHS.

Right.

This rule also stems from expository prose. In exposition, a paragraph is a unit of meaning, a part of a controlled series of thoughts providing evidence for a particular point of view. Each of those units in turn recapitulates the structure of the essay in small. Where an essay has a *thesis*, each paragraph has a *topic sentence*. Where an essay has several *paragraphs* supporting the thesis, the paragraph has *body sentences* supporting, modifying, defining the topic sentence. And where an essay has a *concluding* paragraph, each paragraph has a final *sentence* rounding out the argument just made.

Hence, multiple sentences.

Writing fiction is different, however. There is not—or should not be—an overriding concern for making a point. Fiction is about story. While it may use expository structures to facilitate that story, it depends primarily upon *showing* events in motion, characters in crisis. It may be impelled by dialogue, which has no need for a specific number of sentences to make its point. A single word may suffice.

* * * * * * * *

Just as I was completing the draft for this essay, I picked up Joe McKinney's taut story *The Crossing* (Print is Dead, 2012) and began reading. The first paragraph contained an example of McKinney adroitly and effectively ignoring one of these 'rules'; the second paragraph provided an example of him ignoring a second one.

Just for fun, I decided to keep count and see how long it would take to find an excellent author creating better fiction by *ignoring* the seven traditional 'rules.'

Answer, fewer than six pages.

Here are some samples (my italics added):

Rule 1: "Jessica hunkered down in the corner to get out of the seething wind. She had a tattered bath towel wrapped around her shoulders, but it was too threadbare *to even warm* her, withered as she was from starvation." (p. 1)

McKinney has placed the adverb *even* between the infinitive *to* and the verb *warm,* the best position for the word. The phrase "too threadbare even to warm her" places *even* closer to *threadbare* than to *warm,* creating a momentary ambiguity as to which word it modifies; its relative distance from the verb tends to de-emphasize its impact. "Too threadbare to warm even her," the alternate way of avoiding a 'split infinitive,' changes the meaning of the sentence entirely. Jessica is now one of several and the most likely to be warmed—not at all what the passage indicates. "To even warm her" is the only acceptable position, even though it violates a conventional stricture.

Rule 2: "I was scared like I'd never been in my life, but I wasn't sorry. *Not a bit.*" (p. 3)

"Not a bit" is a fragment; it contains no subject, no verb, and no complete thought. In fact, it completes the S + V + COMPLETER in the previous sentence: "I wasn't sorry." Yet it is the ideal structure for McKinney's purposes. To incorporate it into the previous sentence, perhaps including intensifiers, would paradoxically weaken it: "...but I wasn't sorry, not even a bit" detracts from the solid impact of the phrase when it is given the full rhetorical weight (indicated by capital and closing punctuation) of a sentence. For the duration of those three words, pace slows; the plosive *t* sounds in *not* and *bit* come to the fore; and the increased stress on the two words parallels the narrator's resolve and courage.

Rule 3: "Sam it is. *Come on*, let's try to get you *warmed up*." (p. 4)

A twofer! In the second sentence (which is actually a run-on sentence composed of "Come on" and "Let's try to get you warmed up"), neither preposition-like word—*on* or *up*—functions prepositionally. *Come on*, taken as a unit, is the first verb; there is in fact no possible object to be modified. Similarly, *warm up* is a two-part verb.

The simplest way to verify this is to complete each statement with a modifier. "Come on into the house"; note that the modifier is a prepositional phrase. Likewise, to complete the second sentence, we have to add another prepositional phrase: "...to get you warmed up by the fire." Since *on* and *into*, like *up* and *by*, contradict each other as prepositions, one of each pair must be functioning as something else, in each case, as a verb-particle.

Rule 4: "I never really believed, even as a little girl, that a place could be haunted. *But* if ever a place had a right to be, it was that shack." (p. 2)

Here, the conjunction *but* does two things: it negates the previous thought and it connects the second sentence *conceptually* to the first. They remain separate, each given the impact of a full sentence, yet the *but* completes a bridge between them.

Rule 5: "The place smelled of stale beet and sweat, mildew and rot, and the dim morning light revealed a lot of ice-encrusted trash on the floor—broken beer bottles; tin cans; a scattering of cigarette butts; an occasional spent shell casing—sad markers of others, like Jessica and me, who had taken refuge here." (p. 1, para. 1)

There really is no other way to craft this sentence and maintain the sense of dereliction and dissolution required. There are actually two intruded phrases. The first, beginning with "broken beer bottles," is an appositive further clarifying "ice-encrusted trash." Traditional grammar would set it apart from the main sentence with commas. However, the intruded phrase(s) contains internal punctuation, and the comma separating the two parts might read as a continuation: "ice-encrusted trash on the floor, broken beer bottles...." The bottles do not necessarily create a subset of "trash" but rather could be the second element in the series. The dash between the two structures makes it clear that the second provides examples of the first.

The phrase beginning with "sad markers" similarly modifies the preceding element. *All* of the things listed, the accumulated trash on the floor, act as "markers"; yet to separate the two with a comma would increase the ambiguity: "an occasional spent shell casing, sad markers of others...." Here, *shell casing* and *markers* function on the same level, and the final phrase merely indicates that there are other, unnamed and unenumerated, bits of trash.

To create precisely the meaning he needs, McKinney must separate the first and the second elements. A parenthetical intrusion won't work, because then "sad markers" would grammatically look back to "trash," ignoring everything in between. The only option for this sentence is the pair of dashes, linking all three elements yet identifying how each relates to the other.

(I would quibble with the semicolons in the second part. Since there is no internal punctuation within phrases, and since the series is clearly set off from the first and third parts, commas would suffice.)

Rule 6: "Be the reporter, I told myself. Watch, observe, soak it all in." (p. 2)

Here is a Julius-Caesar sentence: Three short clauses (with the subject *I*-understood), closely related, rhythmically complete. To add the requisite *and* would create a more formal sentence, as if she had the time and the leisure to contemplate her choices: "Watch, observe, and soak it all in." It would also give the last phrase perhaps too much emphasis by the addition of one word.

Instead, McKinney opts for a more telegraphic approach. Reduce words, eliminate the understood subject, let each verb stand on its own, and let the final object—"it all"—stand as the object for all three, undisclosed until the end. Suspense, tension, tautness.

(Note that *soak in* is a two-part verb and that this sentence does not end with a preposition but with a separable verb particle.)

Rule 7: "We didn't know who was in the other shack, but every once in a while one of them jabbed a sharpened stick through the walls at the crows." (p. 2)

The single-sentence paragraph establishes tone: fear, curiosity, the unknown. And it impels the narrative forward. The previous paragraph had described in detail the first shack, its inhabitants, the actions of the zombies surrounding it, the screams and shrieks emanating from it. The next paragraph could have been fully developed, with details of what the narrator saw and heard; but to do so would simply be to repeat what readers already know from the previous one. All that is needed here is a reminder of the threat, of the desperation of whoever is in the second shack.

The same desperation experienced by the narrator.

Seven rules 'broken' within six pages. And every one of the choices made for stronger sentences, more appropriate to the narrative.

This is not to suggest that McKinney agonized over each one, mentally going back and forth, exploring every option. Rather, it is to suggest that as a writer he knows the 'rules' so well that he can almost instinctively twist them, turn them, break them, perhaps even as he drafts his story, knowing that in each case, the story is enhanced.

After all, there are rules, and there are *rules*. And some of them are made to be broken.

Chapter 38

On Writing Reviews

Several days ago, someone approached me to ask a question, prefacing it with that terrifying phrase, "With all due respect...."

Now, in normal parlance, that phrase introduces a question or comment at which the respondent will probably take offense. In my case, my first thought was "Okay, what did I do wrong *this time*?"

As it turned out, the situation was not as dire as it might have sounded. The question was about a recommendation I had recently made for a story. My questioner—and apparently others—wondered why I had given it a strong recommendation, which, after reading it, they felt that it had not merited.

We spoke for a while and eventually came to an understanding.

Still, the question concerned me, and I decided that this might be a good time to discuss writing reviews, particularly from my perspective as both literary scholar and novelist/short story writer/poet.

For me, a review has a single purpose: **To impel the reader to the book**. If the reader has not yet read the work in question, the review should provide assessment, backgrounds, and matrix for reading and understanding the work. That might include historical or biographical backgrounds that the reviewer has gleaned over years of reading; or it might relate to the genre in question; or it might deal with particular difficulties in the text that the reviewer might be able to unravel.

If the reader has already read the book, the review should provide additional information about it that would enable the reader to engage more completely with the text on a second reading. It might give insight into themes and images; it might direct attention to characters, motivations, and actions; it might suggest alternative ways of viewing the book. But in any case, it presents the book—*as written*—in such a light as to emphasize its strengths while, if necessary, defining any crucial flaws.

I have a number of self-imposed rules about reviewing that have helped me through the years.

FIRST, I DO NOT LIKE WRITING NEGATIVE REVIEWS—I have never performed a pure hatchet job on a novel or story. When I write books about writers, for example, I try to contact them to let them know several things: 1) I emphasize the fact that I do not waste my time writing about books that I do not like; 2) I promise not to take up their time with needless questions but request permission to ask for help occasionally; and 3) I assure them that I do not write articles, reviews, or books in which I talk extensively about the books I *wish* they had written. If I have a critique, I will base it on the text; if I find something valuable, I will likewise base it on the text.

With reviews, these rules become even more important. When I began my poetry-writing classes at Pepperdine, I would generally ask students to raise their hands if they had ever written a poem. Since the course was explicitly on poetry, nearly everyone would. At which point, I would congratulate them for committing a major act of courage and state that by virtue of writing a poem, each was in fact a superior human being.

And I meant it.

To put oneself on paper—in a poem, a story, a novel, a screenplay—requires courage and commitment; to place the resulting words before the public requires even more so.

As a result, I will generally excuse myself from writing a review if there is nothing I can find worthwhile about a book, particularly if other reviewers have found the book of value. They obviously approached it from different perspectives than I, from different backgrounds and from different purposes, and found something in it to recommend. I won't argue with that.

SECOND, I RESPECT ANYONE WITH THE COMMITMENT AND PERSEVERANCE TO COMPLETE A SHORT STORY, LET ALONE A NOVEL. Therefore, I will treat that work with the greatest consideration I can. I may disagree with details of writing style or expression; but if the writer approaches the subject from a unique or important perspective I will concentrate on that. I may find the characters flat, but if they manage to communicate a theme or explore a serious topic, I will emphasize the latter over the former. If the flaws reveal a depth of incompetence that overshadows all else—as in the case of a recent novel that read more like a freshman composition essay than a professionally written narrative—I will excuse myself.

THIRD, I BELIEVE THAT MY BACKGROUNDS IN TEACHING AND SCHOLARSHIP OFTEN GIVE ME UNIQUE PERSPECTIVES ON BOOKS. In writing a piece on Stephen King's *Desperation,* for example, I found that several lines and phrases in the book suggested certain 17th-century metaphysical poets. I knew that King was widely read; his allusions to writers past and present in *The Shining* and other stories demonstrate that. Linking those references opened the book to me in ways that—in most likelihood—other readers might not have noted.

Similarly, a recent review of a zombie tale was heavily influenced by readings I had done on the Black Death in 13th-century Europe and other epidemics throughout history. This colored the directions I took in the review while—I hope—giving readers of my piece and prospective readers of the story a hook, something to link the story with wider implications.

FOURTH, I UNDERSTAND THAT NEITHER I NOR ANY REVIEWER IS INFALLIBLE. Reviewers are (mostly) human. We (frequently) make mistakes. We may like a book that everyone else thinks is a bomb. We may dislike a book that eventually becomes a classic. Novelist Dan Wells recently posted a link to "11 Early Scathing Reviews of Works Now Considered Masterpieces" that demonstrate the chilling fact that even the most adept of reviewers can miss the point entirely.

Conversely, one has only to read sterling reviews of long-forgotten bestsellers to realize that praising a book may not necessarily mean that it is good...or that it has staying power.

FIFTH, I TRY TO BE HONEST...EMPHASIS ON *TRY*. While reading a book or story, and immediately after finishing it, I ask myself one question: "Did you enjoy reading that?"

If the answer is "no," I try to figure out why...and usually the answer rests on writing skills that are not capable of handling the plot, characters, and setting well enough.

If the answer is "yes"...*ahhh*...then I allow myself the luxury of figuring out why and, in the process, of re-living the best parts of the book. *Those* are usually the parts that end up on reviews.

Reviews are *re-views*, 'again-looks' at works to determine what might be valuable in them. And ultimately, they are self-centered: they concentrate on what *I* think potential readers might find useful or, in the best of cases, entertaining.

Chapter 39

Editor versus Reviewer

As a writer, I don different hats: novelist, short-story writer, poet, critic, reviewer, editor.

Occasionally—and frustratingly—the hats collide when one function strays over into another. For example, I am the Senior Publications Editor at JournalStone Publishing, which means that when working with a manuscript, I need to be alert to anything that impedes the flow of the narrative while simultaneously remaining as true as possible to the words and rhythms of that most marvelous of creatures, the author.

I am also a reviewer for my own site, *Collings Notes* (michaelrcollings.blogspot.com), for *Hellnotes* (hellnotes.com) and for *Dark Discoveries*. When I wear that hat, I am responsible for assessing the effectiveness of narrative, taking into account as many elements of writing as possible.

Once in a while, however, I find these two hats at odds with each other. I recently read a novel that had compelling characters; a well-constructed story; a clear setting; and a distinct beginning, middle, and end—in a nutshell, the author had conceived of an intriguing story, structured it imaginatively and interestingly, and told it well.

Or almost well.

By the time I finished the novel, I was frustrated.

The reviewer in me wanted to conclude that this was a strong story that deserved an equally strong review. The editor in me, however, balked.

The problem rested, not with the story *per se,* but with the words used to tell it. At the level of editing—correcting grammar, spelling, punctuation, syntax that might otherwise create distractions and derail the story—there were so many problems that they eventually took over. The story as story dissipated and finally disappeared.

In this instance, the problems dealt primarily with punctuation, with the all-too-common sense among many authors and editors alike that little things like commas and hyphens really don't matter that much. If you want a pause in a sentence, throw in a comma, regardless of how that actually changes meaning. Or, if you wish, just leave such trivialities out altogether.

At the moment, there are two popular memes on the social networks, designed to remind people that punctuation counts.

One is a sentence that reads:

> I enjoy cooking
> my pets
> and my family.

Writing the words on a single line reveals the essential problem: "I enjoy cooking my pets and my family"—a truly horrific meal in progress, presumably. The solution to the problem: two small commas: "I enjoy cooking, my pets, and my family"—three creditable activities although, one hopes, listed in reverse order of importance.

The second meme is similar but even shorter: "Let's eat kids." Again, a rather carnivorous, not to say cannibalistic comment worthy of Jonathan Swift at his most satirical. Add a comma, and we get: "Let's eat, kids." An entirely different statement.

As I thought about the problem, I came up with six words that, depending on how one punctuates them, are capable of several meanings:

> He watched the grandmother eating bear.

Surface level, as punctuated—a man is watching an elderly woman consuming the flesh of a bear. Perhaps from a historical novel, perhaps from a novel about survival in the wilderness, but either way, perfectly acceptable.

Add a comma, however, and the meaning shifts:

> He watched the grandmother, eating bear.

Now the man, whoever he is, is contentedly observing the elderly woman while he chows down on his evening meal of bear steak. Same words; different action.

To ring yet another change, delete the comma and add…a hyphen:

He watched the grandmother-eating bear.

By indicating that *grandmother* and *bear* are connected as a two-part adjective, the sentence now asserts that the man is hot on the trail of a man-eating (or grandmother-eating) carnivore and, having located it, is watching it…presumably prefatory to killing it.

[By the way, the possibilities of ambiguity and misunderstanding increase if *homonyms* come into play: *bare* instead of *bear*—something a spell checker won't pick up.]

Granted, these sentences are contrived. In novel after novel, story after story, however, it is fairly easy to find parallel structures that— through the positioning of a comma or a hyphen, or the lack of same— assert a meaning wildly at odds with the tone and movement of the story.

"But the context will make it clear," some will say, impatient at what appears to them as nitpicking.

True. It will.

But in the period, however brief, between initially reading such a sentence and fitting it into the context of the story, there is necessarily a pause, a break, a moment's hesitation that for that instant fractures the story. And enough of those small moments, enough of those uneasy junctures, and there is the danger that the reader will not only back up sufficiently to put the sentence into context but will back out of the story completely.

That is a danger no writer should be willing to risk.

Part Six: Walls and Roof—
Sentences, Paragraphs, Dialogue

Chapter 40

A Rose by Any Other Name—Some Types of Sentences

A sentence is a sentence is a sentence.

Actually, it would be more to the point to paraphrase George Orwell's trenchant comment in *Animal Farm*: All sentences are created equal, but some are more equal than others.

By this I mean that any sentence—and here I include fragments and run-ons—may be effective when used in the right context. Every form of sentence structure offers something than none of the others do.

SIMPLE SENTENCE: I read the book—Subject + Verb + [Completer]

This is the basic sentence in English. The first word establishes who is performing the action; the second identifies the action, and subsequent words or phrases can define a number of elements, in this case, to whom (or what) that action was done.

Such sentences are ideal for a quick, perhaps cutting, often startling statement of fact that in itself might create a climax in a paragraph, a passage, a chapter: "The butler did it!" No further discussion, no modification to limit the possibilities of meaning. Just a plain, straight statement. Such sentences are often perfect after a long passage of more complicated, more developed structures.

COMPOUND SENTENCES: I read the book, and I saw the movie—Subject + Verb + [Completer] + [, and/but] + Subject + Verb + [Completer]

Here two simple statements have been coordinated using *and, but, or, nor, yet,* or *so.* Compound sentences allow writers to present two ideas as equal; whatever is on one side of the coordinating phrase (and the comma is a crucial part of that phrase) has precisely as much weight as the idea on the other side. Neither reading a book nor seeing a movie is preferable.

Of course, choosing a different coordinator shifts meaning. *But* indicates that two equal statements oppose or contradict each other: "I read the book, but I didn't see the movie." Simple opposition of equalities.

Lest anyone think, however, that because such structures are called by grammarians and linguists "simple" they are thereby simplistic. A series of simple coordinated sentences can go far in creating tone, feeling, mood, atmosphere, even in characterizing and defining speakers. Take, for example, the opening paragraph from Mark Twain's *Huckleberry Finn*, Chapter 40:

> WE was feeling pretty good after breakfast, and took my canoe and went over the river a-fishing, with a lunch, and had a good time, and took a look at the raft and found her all right, and got home late to supper, and found them in such a sweat and worry they didn't know which end they was standing on, and made us go right off to bed the minute we was done supper, and wouldn't tell us what the trouble was, and never let on a word about the new letter, but didn't need to, because we knowed as much about it as anybody did, and as soon as we was half up stairs and her back was turned we slid for the cellar cupboard and loaded up a good lunch and took it up to our room and went to bed, and got up about half-past eleven, and Tom put on Aunt Sally's dress that he stole and was going to start with the lunch, but says:
>
> "Where's the butter?"

Everything is equal, coordinated. No single action, observation, or thought is any more important than another, even though several of the structures contain information that will influence the story. It is perfect...if your narrator is an uneducated boy who, unlike his friend Tom, reacts to things as he sees and hears them. He doesn't plan, he doesn't construct elaborate "effects." Things simply are. He floats through time and space as unhindered as does the great river itself.

No one has ever sustained this kind of structural definition of character as masterfully as Twain.

COMPLEX SENTENCES: I read the book before I saw the movie—Subject + Verb + [Completer] + Subordinator + subject + verb + [completer]

Notice that I chose not to capitalize the last three elements in complex sentences. I did so because the act of subordinating, of creating a complex sentence, automatically informs readers that one part is more important to the narrative than the other. "I read the book" is independent; it stands on its own and receives the most focus. "I saw the movie" is now dependent, contingent upon the first element and, without that first element, cannot stand as a sentence: "Before I saw the movie." The word *before* requires more information than the clause can provide.

It is possible to reverse the order of clauses, but doing so still does not make the subordinated element more important than the independent one: "Before I saw the movie, I read the book." Note two things. First, a comma is now necessary to separate the two structures; and the fact of reading the book actually becomes even more emphatic.

COMPOUND-COMPLEX SENTENCES: I read the book before I saw the movie, and I liked the book better even though the movie offered interesting visual insights—Subject + Verb + [Completer] + Subordinator + subject + verb + [completer] + Coordinator + Subject + Verb + [Completer] + Subordinator + subject + verb + [completer]

Here, the writer balances at least four separate thoughts, indicating through structure that two of them—"I read the book" and "I liked the book"—are exactly equal in force, while the remaining two—"I saw the movie" and "The movie offered insights"—are contingent upon the first two for their full meaning. There is a lot of information being presented, but chances are good that the reader will automatically use the compound-complex structure to create a mental hierarchy of importance.

In terms of writing skill, complex-compound sentences suggest greater sophistication on the parts of writer and/or narrator, greater awareness of how elements of the world fit together, and a greater sense of observation and discrimination (a much- and unfairly-maligned word, by the way).

PASSIVE SENTENCES: The book was read by me—Completer + was + past-tense verb + [subject]

Passive sentences are also much maligned. I've seen any number of writing manuals and rule lists that begin with something like "Avoid the passive."

In general that is good advice, if for no other reason than word count. "I read the book" is two words shorter than "The book was read by me," and the difference lies in a prepositional phrase that may often be deleted: "The book was read."

Now, however, there is no sense of who performs the key action. A passage written using active sentences tends to be stronger, more vigorous, more action-oriented (obviously), and readers generally have no difficulty in figuring out, in the words of William Lanham, a scholar from UCLA, "Who's kicking Who?" (He follows that question with, "I know it should be *whom*, but that is just being pretentious.)

Who is doing it? What is he/she/it doing? And to whom/what is it being done? Key questions in every sentence…except the passive.

Of course, there are times when the passive is entirely appropriate. "I was bitten by a ferret" suggests that the recipient of the action—I—is in some critical sense more important than the actor. We really don't care much about the ferret—its homelife, its struggles as a misunderstood ferretling, its motivation, its deep psychological traumas. I was bitten, for heaven's sake!

If, however, there is something aberrant about the ferret, it might be wise to shift to active: "A rabid ferret bit me." I've been bitten, bad enough; but the blasted ferret was rabid. That crucial point deserves first place in the sentence.

The basic rule for passives, then, is straightforward: is the receiver more critical than the actor? If so place him/her/it first.

There is much more to be said about passive sentences—and please note that they are often the *best* choices—but in terms of how the structure works, this will have to suffice.

There are two additional structures that can be of particular value in writing narratives, primarily because they not only contribute meaning and information (as do all sentences) but they also build or release suspense and tension, and control pacing in the story.

LOOSE SENTENCES:

Simply put, in a loose sentence the basic sentence is completed in the first phrase, even though the structure itself may continue with additional modification. If not controlled, loose sentences threaten to end up meandering aimlessly and bonelessly through piles of information, never giving readers any hint as to which bits and pieces are relevant or important. Consider the following:

> I read the book by my favorite author in the new library down the street, across the block from the desolation of the burned-out rubble of the old library, built at the end of the Civil War and dedicated by General Ulysses S. Grant after the end of the war but before he became President of the United States.

Information there is aplenty, but which parts should readers retain as significant? After all, the sentence, shorn of modifications, merely states, "I read the book." The rest is built of prepositional modifiers of key nouns in the previous prepositional phrases: by the A in the B of the C for the D between the E of the F and so on.... Such shopping-bag sentences can continue for as long as the prepositional phrases keep coming.

When handled more carefully, however, loose sentences are anything but loose. They may begin with a straightforward statement—subject + verb + [completer]—and continue with strings of modification, but the strings themselves may be arranged to create a rising motion in the story, or generate the sense that the action is speeding up. The following example is taken from "Space Opera," a story of mine that appeared in a Lovecraft-in-Space anthology:

> He started to move closer to her, infusing his bodily stance with all of the subtle signals of hatred for her stubborn, presumptuous species that he could—tarsi fully extended, as if he would rip her body covering from whatever structures supported it; carapace divided just enough to reveal the ichor-green of his wings; mouthparts quivering with suppressed rage; eyen glistening as his compounds flared toward her.

The sentence is simple: "He started to move." All that follows hinges upon that, but we know from the beginning the significant action and the specific actor—in this case an insectoid alien. If the sentence were to stand alone, it could probably be compressed into a two-word structure: "He moved." Since subject and verb are parts of a much longer expression, however, the shift from "moved"—which identifies a particular, completed action—to "started to move" is warranted by the lengthy series of elements that must occur before he actually approaches her. The tail, as it were, that is wagging this short dog is itself an assemblage of phrases identifying precisely how he moves: "infusing his bodily stance," which is further defined by the prepositional phrase "with all the subtle signals." That, in turn, is amplified by a series of parallel noun phrases: "tarsi extended," "carapace divided," "mouthparts quivering," and "eyen glistening" (in the context of the story, *eyen* is the correct word).

All of that, all of the detail and emotion and horror, is controlled by the initial phrase: "He started to move."

On a less dramatic scale, and therefore perhaps more directly effective, here is a short but well-crafted loose sentence from Benjamin Kane Ethridge's fine mythic/horror novel, *Bottled Abyss*: "He peeled off, weaving through traffic, looking for the next available exit, praying the fire had not spread to his closet, to the shoes." Again, the kernel structure is completed at once, in the first three words: "He peeled off." Everything else modifies that statement through a series of subordinate clauses hanging on "weaving," "looking," "praying." The final element is then sequentially modified/extended, bringing us from the vague generality of "traffic" to the increasingly specific and localized "exit" and "fire," and finally to the rather rushed-seeming but appropriate compression of two prepositional phrases, "to his closet" and "to the shoes"; the lack of conjunction or subordinator ("that") between them adds to the tension. The shoes, by the way, play a significant role in the plot; hence the character's sense of urgency in reaching them. Even though the structure is technically a simple sentence—Subject + verb + completer—it is complex in the levels of information that it conveys and perfectly appropriate to the heart-stopping anxiety the character experiences.

Dr. Michael R. Collings

PERIODIC SENTENCES:

These structures work in the opposite direction. While there may be many words at the beginning (see the examples below), the sentence itself is not completed until the final syntactical unit. The author begins with a subordinate modifier, moves on to another, then another, then another, and so on until—finally—revealing the subject and action of the statement. By doing so, the author can generate interest, curiosity, suspense, and build toward a climax, a revelation, a discovery.

My favorite example of this kind of structure appears, not in prose, but in the opening lines of John Milton's magnificent epic *Paradise Lost:*

> Of Mans First Disobedience, and the Fruit
> Of that Forbidden Tree, whose mortal taste
> Brought Death into the World, and all our woe,
> With loss of Eden, till one greater Man
> Restore us, and regain the blissful Seat,
> Sing Heav'nly Muse....

The sentence continues for another few lines (which in fact construct a second crescendo for the sentence), but this is sufficient for my purposes here. Note that each of the first five lines begins with an unstressed syllable, creating the general effect of blank verse (unrhymed iambic pentameter): *Of Man's, Of that, Brought Death, With loss, Restore.* Then suddenly, as if out of nowhere, the sixth line crashes down with three heavy stresses—*Sing Heav'nly Muse*—and at the same time completes the prepositional phrase that begins in the first line. By the time readers discover who ("Heavenly Muse") and what ("sing!"), Milton has presented all of the preparatory information necessary to know what his epic will celebrate: Adam and Eve's disobedience, the Fruit of the Tree of Good and Evil, loss of Paradise, eventual restoration through Christ, and final unity of the faithful with God.

Milton's age was intensely interested in style. Poets, dramatists, preachers, politicians, scientists—nearly everyone involved in letters had opinions about the correct use of style. For the rigid Puritans, the plain style was best; present God's words directly, simply, with no mediation between speaker and audience. Their obsession for simplicity was reflected in such activities as whitewashing interiors of medieval churches to remove distracting murals; crating away stained-glass

---

Dr. Michael R. Collings

PERIODIC SENTENCES:

These structures work in the opposite direction. While there may be many words at the beginning (see the examples below), the sentence itself is not completed until the final syntactical unit. The author begins with a subordinate modifier, moves on to another, then another, then another, and so on until—finally—revealing the subject and action of the statement. By doing so, the author can generate interest, curiosity, suspense, and build toward a climax, a revelation, a discovery.

My favorite example of this kind of structure appears, not in prose, but in the opening lines of John Milton's magnificent epic *Paradise Lost:*

> Of Mans First Disobedience, and the Fruit
> Of that Forbidden Tree, whose mortal taste
> Brought Death into the World, and all our woe,
> With loss of Eden, till one greater Man
> Restore us, and regain the blissful Seat,
> Sing Heav'nly Muse....

The sentence continues for another few lines (which in fact construct a second crescendo for the sentence), but this is sufficient for my purposes here. Note that each of the first five lines begins with an unstressed syllable, creating the general effect of blank verse (unrhymed iambic pentameter): *Of Man's, Of that, Brought Death, With loss, Restore.* Then suddenly, as if out of nowhere, the sixth line crashes down with three heavy stresses—*Sing Heav'nly Muse*—and at the same time completes the prepositional phrase that begins in the first line. By the time readers discover who ("Heavenly Muse") and what ("sing!"), Milton has presented all of the preparatory information necessary to know what his epic will celebrate: Adam and Eve's disobedience, the Fruit of the Tree of Good and Evil, loss of Paradise, eventual restoration through Christ, and final unity of the faithful with God.

Milton's age was intensely interested in style. Poets, dramatists, preachers, politicians, scientists—nearly everyone involved in letters had opinions about the correct use of style. For the rigid Puritans, the plain style was best; present God's words directly, simply, with no mediation between speaker and audience. Their obsession for simplicity was reflected in such activities as whitewashing interiors of medieval churches to remove distracting murals; crating away stained-glass windows (or in the worst cases, shattering them); dismantling or destroying elaborate, centuries-old organ cases; and replacing ornate pews with plain, often backless, benches. Nothing, whether in art, architecture, or speech, should come between God's word and the congregant.

At the opposite extreme, High-Church Anglicans often argued that God's word should be presented in the highest, the noblest, the most exalted of styles. Milton was clearly of this party. They found art and architecture a form of the sublime; contemplation of such beauty, they argued, would lead to God. On the continent, this attitude resulted in Baroque churches, in which every inch of every surface was painted, gilded, studded with sculptures and reliefs of angels, cherubs, so that everywhere the eye rested, it could revel in the amplitude of God's abundance, power, grace, and creativity.

Even prose styles reflected the sense that words could almost literally carry listeners through this world and into the greater one beyond. In discussing the need for order in all things, for universal laws to govern every level of God's creation and hold all in balance, the great prose stylist Richard Hooker wrote:

> Now if nature should intermit her course, and leave altogether though it were but for a while the observation of her own laws; if those principal and mother elements of the world, whereof all things in this lower world are made, should lose the qualities which now they have; if the frame of that heavenly arch erected over our heads should loosen and dissolve itself; if celestial spheres should forget their wonted motions, and by irregular volubility turn themselves any way as it might happen; if the prince of the lights of heaven, which now as a giant doth run his unwearied course, should as it were through a languishing faintness begin to stand and to rest himself; if the moon should wander from her beaten way, the times and seasons of the year blend themselves by disordered and confused mixture, the winds breathe out their last gasp, the clouds yield no rain, the earth be defeated of heavenly influence, the fruits of the earth pine away as children at the withered breasts of their mother no longer able to yield them relief; what would become of man himself, whom these

things now do all serve? (*Of the Laws of Ecclesiastical Polity*, Book I, Chapter 3.)

One. Periodic. Sentence!

Yet if we look at it closely, we can see that it is structured to contain and reflect the idea of universal order that it discussed. It begins with the broadest, most general of issues: If nature should cease following her own laws. Then it narrows: If the elements themselves lost their essential qualities. Then narrower and closer to earth: If the heavens should dissipate; if the sun should cease shining. And closer still (given the cosmology of the time): if the moon ceased following its orbit. And now, as he approaches his peroration, he allows the tempo to increase by the simple expedient of deleting the introductory *if* and linking everything to the world beneath the influence of the moon: if the moon should wander, the seasons become confused, the winds cease, the clouds become dry, the earth separate from God, the fruits of the earth wither....

And finally his core: What would become of man?

The universe must be orderly; otherwise humanity itself would perish. He not only argues for the point, but he demonstrates it in the structures of the sentence itself.

Granted, prose of this sort would be woefully out of place in contemporary narrative, although occasionally Lovecraft approaches this kind of intensity. But the underlying structure, the rhetorical period, can be useful. Here is another example from my Lovecraft-in-Space story:

> As the Cwrth stood there in her triumph, her features twisted in pain, the grotesque swelling abruptly even larger, her covering more stretched, now burnished with a red deep beyond belief—even as she stood there; as a thin line formed from the jointure of her supports, questing upward with all of the determination of the universe of tentacles that now surrounded her world; as it quested upward and thickened until her covering split, some thing reached out with its own tentacles and wrapped itself around one of her supports and, still sticky and putrid with her scarlet ichor, lowered itself slowly, almost painfully, to the floor.

"Some thing reached out." The core structure, reached simultaneously with the moment of highest emotional impact in the sentence. Note also how, after that simple sentence, everything diminishes, declines, slows, literally drops "to the floor." Even the conclusion of that period is designed as part of the pacing of the language and the action of the story.

A sentence is a sentence is a sentence?
No, not for careful, alert, skillful, and effective writers.

Chapter 41

Periodic versus Loose

Tom Piccirilli's *The Night Class* is a dark, phantasmagorical cyclone of events, emotions, and discoveries. Covering something less than twenty-four hours during a college-senior's final semester, it concentrates on at first gradual, then incrementally rapid shifts in Caleb Prentiss' understanding of himself, of the handful of students he considers his friends, of the faculty that controls their lives in more ways than they know, and ultimately of the essential questions of life and death, good and evil.

Reading it, however, I found myself vacillating between engagement with the story—which whirls and pivots with each turning page—and admiration for the way Piccirilli tells it. One of the advantages/disadvantages of having taught English for over three decades is that often moments of strong writing impress themselves upon my reader's imagination, and I have to take a moment and figure out why that particular passage was so effective and how the writer managed it.

The first time this occurred during *The Night Class*, I had just begun Chapter 3. Cal is considering breaking into the school library basement during the daytime, where the effects of a murdered student are stored. He is pretty sure that no one will notice...or care.

Then comes this paragraph:

> But if you were around last year at about four in the morning at the end of March, and were awakened by awful panting and unknown noises heading up toward your second-floor window, and you happened to get out of bed and draw back your blinds to take a look— having dreamed of your sister again, reaching for you

with red arms—only to yell and hop a foot in the air when you saw this humongous milk-white ass shining at you in the moonlight, all 340 pounds of Fruggy Fred playing Human Fly on the wall, extremely agile actually, for a guy his size, keeping all his weight on his toes and hanging on to the brick like a rock climber, naked and smeared with something slick and glistening, maybe baby oil or Vaseline or maple syrup or even honey, silently scaling the wall covered with thick ivy in order to get back into the locked dorm, only minutes after having run from his girlfriend's room, making the grand escape during a vicious fight with the butter knife-wielding lady because he'd fouled the final moments of romantic milieu just before making love, having fallen asleep in the middle of foreplay again ... hey, now *that* was an attempt at some seriously surreptitious movement.

A grand total of 214 words crammed into a single sentence that tears its way across the page (or in my case the Kindle screen) with a speed and a ferocity that match the most violent moments in the book—of which there are many. It is a *periodic* sentence, beginning with an *if*-clause, then continuing through several parallel clauses (with the *if* deleted) before plunging into modifying phrase after modifying phrase, increasingly detailed, increasingly tactile, culminating in the image of the vicious attack with the butter knife before it breaks off abruptly, leaving the sense that the sequence of images might continue on and on. Then, finally, comes the clause to which everything else, all 202 words, is subordinate.

What most intrigued me was how adroitly Piccirilli incorporated additional information about Cal's surroundings and friends, with a brief glimpse at his sister, whose suicide haunts him throughout, while simultaneously embedding language that will resonate with the actions and themes of the novel: "awful panting," "unknown noises," "red arms," "naked," "slick and glistening," "locked," "vicious fight," "knife-wielding," "fouled," and "asleep." Each of them, and several of them in combination, looks backwards and forwards to other scenes, other confrontations. And in doing so, they unify the novel and intensify the force of those scenes. Yet in this instance, nothing is happening/has happened, other than a student climbing through a dorm window. Even that sense of the present past is central to the book, which spirals through past and present willfully and frequently.

While it is unfair to judge a book by a single paragraph/sentence, this passage clearly indicates the control Piccirilli exerts over his materials.

In Chapter 8, Cal visits a bar with the express purpose of getting as drunk as possible, not yet understanding that his need is part of larger manipulations. Again, we find a single sentence/paragraph that encapsulates the moment:

> No way to tell just how many girls there were with the lights flickering so wickedly, dancers appearing to move in mechanical stop-and-go motions, bodies twisting as they flung themselves across the stage, guys entranced, tits bouncing, chicks slinking over there, now here, there against other men, the music still driving.

This one works in the opposite direction from the previous passage. It is a *loose* sentence, with everything hinging upon the initial statement: [There was] *no way*…. The subject and verb do not actually appear, and the completer spins off from a prepositional clause several words later: *with lights flickering, dancers appearing, bodies twisting,* etc. The modifiers begin as relatively long structures, then compress to almost elliptical parodies of sentences: "guys entranced, tits bouncing, chicks slinking over there, now here, there against other men…." Note especially the repeated adverbials: "over there, now here, there against." The words contract until the word *there* by itself must bear the burden of meaning. And it does.

Then, without a final conjunction (one anticipates an *and*), the final phrase is simply slammed against the previous one, leaving the impression that the list of *–ing* verbs could be continued indefinitely: "the music *still* driving" (my italics).

What Piccirilli gives us is a sentence structure designed to slow, to expand ideas, being redesigned to do the opposite, to speed things up, to create a sense of an enclosed space exploding with barely controlled sensual/sexual energy…setting the stage for a crucial recognition scene that will in some ways tip Cal into near-insanity. The sentence not only communicates its necessary information, it does so in a way that puts the reader as much on edge as the character.

The sense of nightmarish, meaningless movement continues for several more paragraphs, never losing its impetus, until "from the floor came the hooting of boys and old men as they shouted and laughed like killers striking the mark." With that savage image, the paragraph ends. Followed by:

> The strobes blinked off and the houselights burned bright in one brutal moment of clarity that made Caleb dizzy. It took a minute to get used to it as he took in the anemia of everyone's skin, the bareness of the room, the lack of his own pity.
> And Willy over at a table.

Abruptly, in the space of three sentences (one of them a fragment, with neither subject nor verb), the frenetic actions dissipate. There is silence. Stillness. The sentence structures force things to slow down. In sentence two, we are fourteen words in—and the words are such banalities as *it, to, took, to get used to, took* (repeated)—before we arrive at the first key word, *anemia*, which looks forward to the emptiness, almost exhaustion of *bareness* and *lack.*

Carefully used, sentence structures may control readers' responses, speed up and then forcibly retard pacing, moving toward an overriding narrative purpose—in this instance, concentrating on a single, apparently innocent image of a boy sitting at a table in preparation for Cal's next and greater crisis of belief and awareness...for which, please read the novel.

Chapter 42

To Is, or Not to Is…Or Perhaps to Do Both

Some while ago, I attempted to write an essay on the uses and abuses of *is* (and its cohorts *are, was, were, be, being, been, seems*, and *becomes*) in poetry. I set out to do so without ever using the word except *as the word.* I could talk about the meaning symbolized by those two random symbols—*i* and *s*—but I could not use *is* as a sentence verb.

I had no idea how difficult doing so would be. It required that I revise sentence after sentence, struggle to find active ways to express state-of-being ideas. Eventually, however, I succeeded; the chapter is titled "Compression III—Linking Verbs" in *The Art and Craft of Poetry.* And I think it makes the point I wanted: writing can become stronger and more energetic without the linking (or *copular*) verbs.

But not always.

Is and its related forms are among the oldest in the English language. In its present spelling, *is* goes back over a thousand years in English and in slightly different forms is easily recognizable through the history of Indo-European languages: Dutch, *is;* Old Norse, *es, er;* German and Gothic, *ist;* Latin, *est;* Greek, *estí;* and Sanskrit *asti.* Given the changes that most words have undergone over the past centuries and millennia, *is* is remarkably stable.

Which suggests that it is also remarkably functional in the grammar and syntax of most Western languages.

Yet writers are frequently told "Avoid *is*" and, especially, "Never use the passive."

Why?

COPULAR STRUCTURES:

It is important to note that not all structures using *is* are identical in construction and function; that is, just because a sentence contains *is* or one of its forms does not mean that the sentence is therefore passive and to be avoided. In fact, I would venture to guess that most uses of *is* do *not* form passives but merely what might be called "copular" or "linked" sentences.

Simply put, in these sentences, the *is* functions as an equals sign — A = B. Whatever occurs to the left of the *is* is *identical* with whatever occurs to the right. For example: "My hair is gray." Both key words refer to the same thing: my hair. One is a noun (*hair*) and the other is an adjective (*gray*), but in the world of equivalences, they create an identity. Theoretically, the sentence could be reversed and still retain its meaning: "Gray is my hair." A bit poetic but legitimate as an English sentence.

As may easily be seen from what I have written thus far, there is nothing wrong with such sentences; in fact, it seems difficult if not impossible to write at any length *without* using linked forms. In narratives, however, they do have one insurmountable disadvantage: they not only fail to impel the story forward, but for the duration of the sentence, they halt any movement whatsoever while the sentence makes its state-of-being assertion: A = B. In most cases, therefore, *where possible*, it makes sense to replace the equation with an action.

Sometimes that may be as easy as shifting the B-term to its natural position as adjective and replacing *is* with an active verb: "My gray hair makes people treat me like I'm old." Not the world's greatest sentence, but at least something happens to someone. A further revision might result in this: "Because of my gray hair, strangers often open doors for me and offer me their seats." Much happens in this sentence, and the sentence-verbs are now more active and slightly more interesting, but it still contains the basic information, the basic equation, we started with, A = B.

IT-STRUCTURES AND *THERE*-STRUCTURES:

These structures fall somewhere between copular and passive, sharing superficial similarities but fully belonging to neither.

A simple test suggests that many sentences beginning with "It is..." and "There are..." are not copular. Try reversing one of them: "It is raining." The result: "Raining is it." While perfectly good Yoda-speak, the structure isn't English, nor does it communicate quite the same information. Or another: "There are good reasons for...." This becomes equally awkward: "Good reasons are there for...." Again, Yoda-speak.

The best way to consider these forms, perhaps, is to consider the positional subject (*it, there*) and verb (*is, are*) as placeholders doing little more than announcing that a statement is on the way, only the statement has not been allowed full strength as a sentence.

If you look back several paragraphs in this study, you will see this sentence: "It is important to note that not all structures using *is* are identical...." A little analysis shows us that we are seven words in before anything of specific meaning appears, and that the seventh word—*not*—simply indicates negation. "It is important to note that" does essentially *nothing* except alert the reader that in the writer's opinion (but then, the whole essay is the writer's opinion, isn't it?) the following assertion is *important* (but isn't that to be assumed, considering that the sentence introduces its own paragraph and all?).

The *true* meaning in the sentence, the kernel as it were, is almost hidden away as an independent clause attached to the subordinating *that*; in other words, the long introduction has as its primary *grammatical* and *syntactical* point to relegate the kernel to a secondary thought.

Probably the sentence should have been written directly and plainly: "Not all structures using *is* are identical...." In most cases, I would revise it to do so (and possibly go even further to eliminate *are* as the sentence verb), but if I did so, I would lose a nice example of wordiness, so I shall let it stand.

Note, however, that "It-is" and "There-are" can kill otherwise active, vigorous sentences: "In spite of the fear limned on his face, the awkward angle of his shattered arm, and the imposing arsenal the zombies had accumulated, *there was* no hint of fear or awkwardness in his voice as he raised it to clarion clarity and trumpeted, 'Die, zombies! Die!'"

Basic sentence structure controlling everything else: "There was." *True* subject of the sentence: "his *voice rang* with no hint of...."

Where possible, keep the kernel sentence the same as the actor/agent in the sentence; this means avoiding "It is" and "There are" when they slip too easily into writing.

(Note: I mentioned that "It is raining" is neither precisely copular nor directly passive. The test for passives reveals even more clearly than that for copular that these structures work differently—see below for further discussion.)

PASSIVE SENTENCES:

Finally, the dreaded *passive*. What is so horrible about this structure that writers and editors and critics decry it so vehemently?

Well, in a nutshell, it is that such sentences are *passive*. Nothing happens in them. And the core verb, which would normally denote activity, is demoted to a mere companion of, you guessed it, *is, are, was,* and *were.*

An example: "A zombie bit my arm." Subject = *zombie*. Action = *bit*. Receiver of the action = *arm*. Someone—or in this case, *something*—did something to something. A straight-forward English sentence.

In some languages, Latin for example, such a simple sentence as "The dog bites the girl" (*Canis mordet puellam*) can be reversed with no shift in meaning, since each word has an ending that indicates whether it functions as subject, object, or action. *Puellam mordet canis* means *exactly* the same as the original.

If we take the English sentence, in which there are no such endings, and reverse it, something peculiar happens: "The girl bites the dog." Not at all the same thing.

In fact, however, it is possible to reverse the order of subject (*dog*) and object (*girl*) and still retain the essential meaning. To do so, we transform the active sentence (S + V + O) into a *passive* sentence (O + [*is*-form + past participle] + prep + S). "The dog bites the girl" becomes "The girl is being bitten by the dog."

While there is nothing at all wrong with the sentence structurally, there are two difficulties with it in terms of driving a narrative forward. First, action has ceased. The action word (*bit*) is still present but is now an adjunct to *is/was* and *being*. And second, a five-word sentence suddenly has *eight* words, three of them in a prepositional phrase not required by the original ("by the dog"). That is not a problem by itself, but imagine the wordiness in a novella or novel in which most sentences are passives.

Earlier, I mentioned that "It is raining" is neither precisely copular nor directly passive, and gave the example of a linking-reversal, "Raining is it," which resulted in, at best, Yoda-speak. Transforming the sentence into a passive structure reveals even more clearly that *It*-structures and *There*-structures constitute a separate class. *It* (subject-position) + *is* (verb) + *raining* (completer) becomes "Raining is being by it." This is not even Yoda-speak—it is simply gibberish.

So…we have one of the most change-resistant verbs in English—or in any Indo-European language, seemingly impervious to the alterations that happen to most words over centuries and millennia. We have three separate structures in which *only* that verb and its related forms appear; and each of the structures performs a unique and at times necessary function.

And we have voices all around us telling us not to use them.

Instead, perhaps the 'rule' should read: "Avoid *is* and its forms *where possible* and replace them with active, one-word verbs; but use them *where the context requires it.*

For example, if the narrative consists of a series of long sentences outlining reasons why a character decides he should *not* enter a putatively haunted house at midnight on a dark and stormy night, the series might justly conclude with a simple—and therefore potentially powerful—copular statement: "He was right."

When the actor is unknown or irrelevant to the context, an *It*-structure or a *There*-structure can identify the effect of the action without struggling to find some way to identify the cause. Instead of something like "Because of an unseasonal conjunction of masses of hot air and equivalent masses of cold air, clouds formed across the sky, blanketing the moon and the stars and eventually releasing a deluge of water, accompanied by thunder and lightning," becomes "It was a dark and stormy night." After all, who cares why?

And when a character screams, "Help! I was bitten by a zombie!" the passive seems justified. In the active voice, the sentence would read: "A zombie bit me!" But the speaker/screamer is quite correctly less concerned about the zombie than about herself—consequently, in this context, using *I* as subject is appropriate. Conversely, "Oh look! My arm was landed upon by a butterfly" would be ridiculously wordy and inappropriate in almost any context.

There is nothing wrong with judicious and conscious appearances of *is*. After all, writers and speakers have been using the word since writing began.

Chapter 43

On Trying Too Hard

All literature depends to one degree or another on atmosphere—on tone, mood, feeling, ambience. It underlies the often more easily recognizable elements of characterization, plot, landscape, and action, and often—as in the case of such classic novels as *Wuthering Heights* or, to a lesser extent, the Mordor passages in *The Lord of the Rings*—becomes strong enough to act almost as a character itself.

Horror may depend upon it more fully than other genres, however, since the *feeling* of dread or terror or fear elicited in readers, the *frisson* that emerges as a physical manifestation of something essentially unreal—the content of the printed page—often supersedes other elements of storytelling, as in some of H.P. Lovecraft's tales, where the atmosphere *is* the story.

That dependence may itself become a danger. Frequently, horror writers work too hard to develop a tone, a feeling, and seem to believe that simply dropping more words into a passage will increase the reader's physiological responses. If one is writing a Lovecraftian tale, then, of course (the argument seems to go) the more often *eldritch* appears, or the more references to weird angles, rugose creatures, and other dimensions, the scarier the story will be.

Unfortunately, it doesn't always work that way.

The other day, while reading a collection of short horror fiction, intending to review the book (which on the whole was quite well done), I came across a paragraph that stopped me cold. Not because it enhanced the sense of the alien but because it—quite literally—overwhelmed me with words. The purpose was, I think, to create atmosphere. The effect was to stall the story and focus on ultimately irrelevant details.

The passage begins: "[She] drew in her arms and sat up in the sand. She felt its grit against the curve of her bare back." Not bad; certainly nothing in the two sentences that one might label "wrong" or "inappropriate." Two actions and a response, with a certain amount of visual and tactile imagery.

Then it continues:

> She could see, now, that the sand around her was of an almost metallic quality, like gold dust. But more of a bronze color, over there. And directly beneath her bottom and the soles of her feet, more of a dark sterling silver appearance. Perhaps it depended on how the light touched the heaped granules, or maybe these pulverized minerals had all been brought together to form this beach...the gold dust swept in from the ocean, all that remained of some crumbled golden city at the bottom of the sea....

It goes on for several lines, imagining sources for the silver and bronze, which have by now both become absolutes rather than images.

If we look at the opening sentences of the initial paragraph, we will find vivid, image-forming key words: *drew in, sat up, grit, curve, bare back.* In the middle of the third sentence (the first reproduced above), however, everything stalls. *Could* moderates the action in *see,* making the *seeing* less important than the *ability* to do so. *Now* seems to break up the flow, particularly when isolated by commas. Then we come to "the sand around her was of an almost metallic quality." Key word: *quality.* Neither vivid nor visual, almost indefinably vague.

She is on a beach; that there is sand around her need not be specified. And instead of "of an almost metallic quality," why not simply *metallic?* And we are left with something as direct as "The sand was almost metallic, like gold dust." Or perhaps better: "The sand glittered, like gold dust."

The wordiness, the vagueness, the over-wrought sense of that sequence by itself would not draw particular attention. But it is followed by...precisely the same thing. "More of a bronze color...." *Bronze* is a color; it does not need to be specified. But more importantly, gold has earlier been treated as a *thing;* now, suddenly, the metals are *qualities.* There has been a subtle but significant shift in thought. Perhaps this sentence might read: "But over there," (assuming that the directional is needed) "more like bronze."

In the next sentence, *directly* tries too hard, since she is sitting on the sand and therefore it is beneath her bottom and her feet (*soles* might not be needed, especially since it requires an article, *the*, and a preposition, *of*, that go nowhere). Then, another abstraction: *appearance* surfaces as the climax to the long, rather turgid "dark sterling silver appearance." Why not a more visual verb: "Beneath her, it shimmered darkly, like sterling silver."

In the next sentence, the passage gives up all pretense of telling a story and becomes declarative. In an attempt to become lyrical, it becomes wordy. "Heaped granules," "pulverized minerals" (silver and gold are, strictly speaking, not minerals but elements; and bronze is a non-naturally occurring alloy and therefore also not an element) almost overwhelm the pictorial sense, replacing it with something quasi-analytic, pseudo-scientific.

The final phrases simply surrender to the impulse to write words. Instead of the twenty-one forced words in the text, perhaps: "the gold, all that remained of a crumbled city beneath the sea" (twelve words). Everything else in the original is either a given (sand is swept in from the ocean) or redundant (if it is gold, then the city had to have been golden, and if it is dust, then the city has crumbled).

The point of this exercise is not to demonstrate that the author was unskilled or untalented; indeed, this passage is remarkable because it is an exception in an otherwise disciplined, controlled series of stories. Instead, it is to suggest that in those moments when we want so much to create something powerful, lyrical, imposing…we are more likely to succumb to the lure of words and—simply put—try too hard.

Chapter 44

Paragraphics and Speech-Breaks

On the surface, the guidelines for paragraphics and speech-breaks in narrative do not disagree much from the rules for writing in general. Briefly, a paragraph of exposition has three functions.

The first is to present a **topic sentence**, a coherent, compressed, single sentence defining what the paragraph will discuss. This usually occurs in the first position or immediately after a bridge-sentence providing a transition from a previous sentence, but in actual practice, it might be placed anywhere in the paragraph, depending upon the writer's rhetorical purposes.

The second is to provide solid, concrete discussion of the topic sentence. This might entail statistics, analogies, definitions, brief narratives, quotations, and any number of other literary approaches. Generally there should be three or four such sentences, depending upon the logical divisions of the topic sentence. A literal rule-of-thumb: if a paragraph extends longer on the page than the space you can encompass with your thumb and your index finger, it is probably too long. If it is only one sentence, it is probably too short.

The third function is to conclude, to draw together the elements of support into a single, convincing statement. It need not summarize the paragraph's arguments, since most readers will easily remember what was said a line or two before, but it should make it clear that the topic statement has been treated thoroughly, fairly, and—the writer hopes—convincingly. At times it might also provide a squinting glance at the content of the next paragraph.

Because in some senses the paragraph is a basic structural unit in expository prose, paralleling the stanza in verse, teachers tend to spend a goodly amount of time on the discovery, ordering, and expression of relevant data to demonstrate that the topic sentence is valid.

But in narration, the foundation is often **dialogue**, and dialogue does not place as weighty a responsibility upon the writer as does exposition. After all, an entire paragraph may consist of a single word: "No!" In the context of two speakers arguing, all of the needed context has been provided, and that curt paragraph succeeds.

Unfortunately, however, there is more to the mechanics of paragraphics and dialogue than that one-word sentence might suggest. Here are a few considerations that might be helpful in handling the various components of dialogue:

ONE SPEAKER PER PARAGRAPH:

This parallels the idea that in an expository paragraph there is only one topic sentence and *everything else* revolves around it; nothing may be introduced into the paragraph that does not modify, limit, examine, define, or otherwise clarify and 'prove' the topic sentence.

Similarly, in narrative, once a character has begun speaking, generally in the first word of the paragraph (indicated by its position following the initial quotation mark), readers will assume that the same person says everything in that block of dialogue.

For example, consider the possibility of ambiguity in this paragraph:

> "Second star on the right...," Lila began. "And straight on to morning," Ella finished, without any break in the rhythm.

There is quite literally nothing to indicate that Lila does not continue her thought following the speech tag. In fact, only at the sixth word from the second opening quotation mark does the reader discover that someone else is actually speaking:

> "Second star on the right...," Lila began.
> "And straight on to morning," Ella finished, without any break in the rhythm.

In order to forestall any confusion, which might tempt the reader to back up and, having begun the process, back completely out of the book, it is best to give Lila and Ella separate paragraphs. And, whenever a new speaker takes over, the opening quotation marks provide readers with a signal to be ready.

Within a specific paragraph the dialogue may be interrupted or broken off. If it continues later, however, readers expect to hear the same voice:

> "Well, yes. You caught me again. But seriously, I would be happy to show you. The driveway's a bit jungly and you might miss it. Then you would have to follow this bit of a creek" — she pronounced it *crick*, just as the others in the Valley had — "you might have to follow it for another five miles or so before you could turn around."

The most important consideration here, of course, is not to confuse readers.

SPEAKERS MAY CONTINUE FROM ONE PARAGRAPH TO ANOTHER:

A single paragraph may not be sufficient for the character to say everything necessary. When the dialogue spills into a second (or third or fourth) paragraph, readers depend upon writers to provide signals *not* to expect a change in speaker. This is done quite simply. The final quotation mark of the first paragraph is deleted.

That's all. That is sufficient to alert readers that the voice they are hearing in their heads (that is, within the dialogue itself — I'm not responsible for any other voices) will continue into the next paragraph:

> "Well, the state — my boss, actually — wanted to make sure that everyone involved got fair treatment…as fair as possible, given that the reservoir was *going* to be built and the people here were *going* to have to leave…regardless.
>
> "About three months ago, once all of the details for constructing the reservoir were completed, he organized a meeting here in Shadow Valley. In the old church."

Placing a concluding quotation mark at the end of the first paragraph would tell readers that a *different* voice will speak the next passage.

ONLY ONE MARK OF PUNCTUATION BEFORE SPEECH TAGS:

Occasionally, writers conclude a line of dialogue with a question mark or exclamation point, then, remembering that a line of dialogue needs a comma to separate it from the speech tag, they use both marks, as in:

"Get out of here right now!," the old man roared.

A general rule-of-thumb for all English writing is that any utterance gets only one mark of punctuation. That is, no "!?" or "?." In the sample above, the writer may actually choose which to use:

"Get out of here right now!" the old man roared.

or

"Get out of here right now," the old man roared.

In the first instance, the fact that *the* is not capitalized indicates that the underlying structure continues and that what follows is in fact a speech tag. The structure might be made more dramatic if the second part were separated from the line of dialogue and included an action that *shows* how angry the old man is:

"Get out of here right now!" The old man cocked his pistol and aimed it directly at the werewolf's eye.

The content of the line and the exclamation point both imply anger, fury, intense emotion…so *thundered* becomes irrelevant.

In the second instance, something similar occurs. The tone and content of the line communicate anger already, which is supported by the verb *thundered,* so the exclamation point might not be needed. If the result doesn't seem strong enough, transposing subject and verb might help:

"Get out of here right now," roared the old man.

The effect of the shift is to place a powerful verb, *roared,* next to the dialogue line, allowing the force of the verb to amplify the line's content.

Either way, the rule-of-thumb has been validated.

[Note, by the way, how different the effect of the dialogue-line would be with an alternative verb: "Get out of here right now," mumbled the old man. Now the old man is older, tremulous, uncertain of himself and of his ability to command.]

EXTENDING DIALOGUE WITHOUT SPEECH TAGS:

One fascinating use of dialogue is to create a sense of rapid-fire give-and-take between or among characters. The shorter the dialogue, the faster the interplay and the more intense the emotions, especially when speech tags are omitted altogether.

The result is what might be called stichomythic speech, from an ancient Greek dramatic technique in which alternating actors spoke single lines or parts of lines. In fact, the word simply means "to speak using alternating lines."

The technique is potentially powerful but for obvious reasons difficult to master. If the speech tags are eliminated, leaving only the lines of dialogue to identify speaker and emotion, the writer must craft those lines so carefully that readers are never confused about who is speaking. In addition, because the lines will tend to be quite short, no word can be wasted. If there is an introductory "Well," there had better be a strong reason for it. If there is an interruptive "Uhm," why doesn't the second speaker break in, as would probably happen in real-life dialogue?

In a 'Brian Coffey' novel, *The Voice of the Night,* Dean R. Koontz uses stichomythia, often continuing the dialogue for several pages without incorporating speech tags. To give an example (one of many possible in the book), Chapter 22 opens with two boys, Colin and Roy, apparently pretending to push a derelict pickup into the path of an oncoming train:

> When he felt the pickup moving, Colin jumped back, astonished.
>
> The truck stopped with a sharp squeak.
>
> "What'd you do that for?" Roy demanded. "We had it going, for Christ's sake! Why'd you stop?"
>
> Colin looked at him through the open cab of the truck. "Okay. Tell me. What's the joke?"
>
> Roy was angry. His voice was hard and cold and he emphasized each word. "Get … it … through … your … head. There … is … no … joke!"
>
> They stared at each other in the fast-fading, smoky light of dusk.

In these few lines, Koontz establishes context, characterizes the two boys, shows that one is aggressive and — in fact — sociopathic and the other is only discovering how dangerous his friend is.

Then the rapid-fire dialogue begins:

> "Are you my blood brother?" Roy asked.
>
> "Sure."
>
> "Isn't it you and me against the world?"
>
> "Yeah."
>
> "Won't blood brothers do anything for each other?"
>
> "Almost anything."
>
> "Anything! It has to be anything! No ifs, ands, or buts. Not with blood brothers. Are you my blood brother?"
>
> "I said I was, didn't I?"
>
> "Then push, damnit!"
>
> "Roy, this has gone far enough."
>
> "It won't have gone far enough until it's gone over the edge of the hill."
>
> "Fooling around like this could be dangerous."
>
> "Have you got concrete for brains?"
>
> "We might accidentally wreck the train."
>
> "It won't be an accident. Push!"
>
> "You win. I give up. I won't push the truck or you any further. You win the game, Roy."
>
> "What the hell are you doing to me?"
>
> "I just want to get out of here."

Imagine this exchange cluttered with speech tags and stage directions informing us precisely when Roy pounds on the door panel in frustration, or when Colin takes a step back from the truck to indicate his shock at what he has just realized, or any number of other bits of action that are implicit in the stark lines of dialogue. More, and the rapidity, the intensity, the near violence of the interchange would be diminished.

I'm not even sure that the repeated "Roy" is needed; even without Colin calling his soon-to-be deadly enemy by name, we know which is speaking each line, what the tone of voice is, and (in our imaginations at least) how each reacts to the other's words.

Paragraphics and speech tags — or in this case, lack of speech tags — are keys to effectiveness and strength.

Just as paragraphs build upon the power of each other in expository prose, so dialogue—when presented accurately and carefully—can become more than just reporting what characters say. It becomes a means to control the pacing of a passage, to keep readers informed as to who is speaking, and in general to allow the narrative to continue uninterruptedly.

Chapter 45

Transforming Terrible

Some years ago I wrote a terrible story.

At the time I finished it, of course, it didn't seem terrible. Hot off the typewriter, it seemed like a small, highly polished gem. It was one of the first pieces of short fiction I had written, so perhaps I can be forgiven for over-appraising its worth at the time. But as the years passed and I began writing more stories, something about that one never seemed quite right. And yet, given frequent opportunities to burnish it a bit, I didn't try to make it any better.

When the time came to assemble my first collection of short stories, *Wer* Means *Man, and Other Tales of Wonder and Terror* (2010), it didn't even make the initial cut-off. By then, I had long since acknowledged the awful truth.

It was a terrible story.

Then I was offered the opportunity to submit a story to an anthology of Lovecraft-inspired novelettes and novellas to be titled *Space Eldritch.* Lovecraft in Space! It was a chance I couldn't pass up, so I began writing.

It wasn't long before the idea I was struggling with shuddered to a halt. It just wasn't working.

That's when I remembered the terrible story.

I went back to it, thought long and hard about it...and decided that it in fact contained the essence of what I wanted to say. Why not re-work it? A simple revision wouldn't be sufficient because of the initial structural problems, but it still held promise. What it needed was a wholesale re-vamping.

Before proceeding any further, perhaps I should define what I think constitutes a story and how one can easily become *terrible.*

Stories have several foundational elements.

THEY HAVE CHARACTERS.

Occasionally a story succeeds with a single character, but in almost every case, that character must struggle against *something*—environment, inner demons, the natural world in the form of storm or cold or other threats. More commonly, there are two (or more) fully defined individuals, one of whom is the focus of interest and empathy for readers, and the other, who acts as a counterpoint, an antagonist, a villain. The focal character—the protagonist—wants or needs something crucial that is obstructed by the villain or is in serious jeopardy because of the villain's actions. Both characters need to be believable, vigorous (again, with a few exceptions), and multi-faceted.

In a *terrible* story, none of this happens. There may be performers, flat constructs who follow the writer's playbook, but they fail to come alive. The sense of threat may not be sufficient or may not even exist; and when it is sufficient, the pseudo-characters do not respond to it credibly.

THEY HAVE A PLOT.

That is, something significant occurs. There is a *legitimate* conflict between two forces, the outcome of which is *legitimately* in doubt and, if achieved, will *legitimately* justify one and condemn the other. In the most extreme cases, the outcome may be life for one character, death for the other. The plot is sufficiently complex to generate interest but not too complex for the confines of the story; short stories are particularly vulnerable to overly skimpy, straight-line plots or bizarre, tortuous plots that extend well beyond the limits of the page count. A successful short story marries sufficient action to engaging characters, with the result that, at the end, readers feel a sense of completion, of satisfaction that just enough has been told...no more, no less.

In a *terrible story,* there may be either no plot at all, or too much. Sometimes characters—who may in and of themselves spark some interest—simply talk at each other. Rarely *to* each other. They recite stock ideas as if the ideas themselves could replace action. They spend most of the time telling backstory or force-feeding readers apparently pertinent information and not enough *doing* anything. Or they are in constant motion, fidgeting through strongly telegraphed, predetermined events that build no suspense, create no tension, and ultimately signify...nothing.

THEY HAVE A SETTING.

Stories do not take place in a vacuum...and if they do, then the *vacuum* itself needs to be so clearly defined as to become virtually a character, as, for example, the emptiness of the moors does in *Wuthering Heights.* That story could not have taken place anywhere else; the same should hold true for any successful story. This does not mean that the writer has to describe every picture on every wall in every room of a house, but it does mean that readers should have enough of a sense of place to understand how it will become part of the conflict, how it will influence the characters. Far from being an ornamental excrescence or an exercise in willful description, setting should resonate with every other component of the story.

In a *terrible* story, setting is usually ignored. It is not uncommon, for example, to have a commonplace action-adventure plot arbitrarily set on one of Jupiter's moons and, without any serious adaptation for place, labeled as science fiction. Or—moving in the opposite direction—it may be that a tight, psychologically intriguing horror story is simply plopped into a stereotypic haunted house, on the assumption that the story will enliven the setting. Either way, the parts of the story do not meld.

THEY ARE CAREFULLY WRITTEN.

In a novel of 150,000 words, a single poorly handled sentence, a misturned phrase, or an infelicitous word choice will probably be forgiven, if even noticed. In a story of 1500 words, that same sentence, phrase, or word might destroy verisimilitude, create distrust in a character, turn an intense action into momentary parody, or in any number of other ways disrupt the story's flow. And thus kill the story. Successful stories allow readers to come to the end without even noticing the level of writing. Every word is such as to support character, plot, and setting. Change a key word or phrase, and the illusion of life might dissipate.

In a *terrible* story, writing is peripheral at best; sloppy, inaccurate, inadequate, or distracting at the worst. Without getting into such proofreading issues as spelling, grammar, and punctuation (although they are critical), the care—or carelessness—with which a story is told can undercut excellences in any of the other elements.

THEY ARE ENTERTAINING.

After all, why else would readers work their way through page after page? Successful stories—no matter whether they simultaneously communicate important ideas or suggest crucial themes or reflect our world either optimistically or pessimistically—*successful stories* entertain.

Terrible stories simply don't. Enough said.

All right, so why was my original story so *terrible*?

As I re-read it, I realized that—although it actually contained in embryo the possibility of a Lovecraftian Great Old One, something I wasn't consciously considering when I first wrote it—it was woefully undeveloped in almost every element of storytelling.

It was pretentious from the first words. The original title, "'Fortitude to Highest Victory'" reflected my Ph.D. work with John Milton's *Paradise Lost* and, as I now saw, really had nothing to do with my story. It was just an opportunity for me to boast about having read the poem. As if that weren't enough, on the final page, one of the characters actually *quoted* Milton...even though she/it was an alien on a planet light-years from earth, millennia separated from earth. She also spoke Greek. Quite the knowledgeable creature.

It had no true characters. The story had actually begun accidentally. As I was looking up something else in the dictionary, I stumbled upon the Welsh word *cwrth* (pronounced like *cooth*), 'an archaic stringed musical instrument, bearing a clear resemblance to the classical lyre, with the addition of a bow.' For some reason the word caught my imagination. It *looked* alien, and the definition triggered an image of pregnancy, of swelling, so, logically enough, I started with a pregnant alien. And that was as far as I went in characterization for her/it. The antagonist, I decided, would be somehow bug-like—you know, a "bug-eyed monster" also made literal. And he would be male. Other than that, and the stated fact that he represented an intergalactic Empire, I had no idea where he came from or what he was doing there. In the short space of the story, neither character had an opportunity to change in any substantive way. By the end, they were precisely what they had been at the beginning; there was, in fact, no story about them. Just authorial assertions.

It had no conflict. Almost everything that actually happened occurred outside of the heptagonal chamber and was reported second hand. The Cwrth—my protagonist—began by asserting a belief and never wavered. In the end, of course, she was proven right; but up until the final phrase, there was no warrant for her adamancy.

There was an intrusion of something potentially interesting on the last page. A cloud appears on the distant (but undefined) horizon. It draws nearer:

> Before Torcius could move, it had resolved itself into a fog, a mist, thick and impenetrable, but definitely inorganic—although there seemed to be a central core of darkness into which Torcius could not see.

Reading this now, perhaps twenty-five years later, I have no idea what I was trying to say. The passage seems to function as little more than an introduction to the quotation from *Paradise Lost* containing the phrase "Dark with excessive bright" (III, 375-381). But when I approached "'Fortitude'" with the idea of salvaging what I could and transforming terrible into something better, it struck me that this *might* be how a Great Old One would appear if It were to sweep down upon a world. In the original, however, nothing happens that illuminates, as it were, the darkness.

Ultimately, the tale had no plot. It was a single episode, not a story, two characters without backgrounds or clear motivations talking to each other until the final paragraphs, when something finally happened. In addition, the story was stilted. Nearly every sentence was wordy, overburdened with information, some necessary, much tangential.

The story had no landscape, no setting, other than the seven-sided room in which the two meet. I think the "heptagonal chamber" was chosen as much for theological resonance as for anything, as if either alien would automatically respond to Earth-norm theology and symbology.

It was, perhaps worst of all, *boring.*

Actually, when I think about the story, I'm oddly impressed. It missed on *every count*. Pretentious. Overwritten. No plot. No characters. No setting. No conflict. Wow! am I good, or what?

Yet out of the wreckage that was "'Fortitude to Highest Victory'" came "Space *Opera*," a story I am proud to have appear along with fiction by D.J. Butler, Robert J Defendi, Carter Reid and Brad Torgerson, Nathan Shumate, Howard Tayler, and David J. West.

What happened? What made the difference?

First, a new title. The call for stories had specified an anthology incorporating space opera *and* H.P. Lovecraft's mythic structure of Great Old Ones. The new title actually came *before* any key re-writing: "Space

Opera." I'm a great believer in italics; in this case, they indicate that the title means something more than the standard phrase. The story was going to be about a violent clash between cultures, both obsessed by religion and utterly convinced of the rightness of their respective—and antithetical—causes. *Opera* suggests a certain level of drama, if not actual melodrama; it hints at ecclesiastical echoes through its root in ancient (human) languages; and it fits the characters' mindsets.

The next thing to go was the obvious and gratuitous in-text reference to Milton. Allusions can be powerful; they invite into a story entire levels of additional storytelling. They remind readers of other characters and plots and settings that thematically or imagistically amplify the story being told, lend it greater depth and fullness. They do, however, need to be germane to the story. They need to point to something in the larger universe of storytelling that will make *this* tale better. If not, they are at best wasted words, at worst misdirection and pomposity. In a Lovecraft-based universe, Milton has no place.

For a story, one needs authentic Characters. "Space *Opera"* still focused on Torc and the Cwrth, but now they needed to be expanded. What were their motivations? How did their actions reflect their personalities? Which of the two seemed stronger? Which actually was?

Since both were aliens, a fair amount of anthropomorphism entered in. Both are functionally bipedal. Both are bilaterally symmetrical. Both recognize the visible symbols of pregnancy. Both can access spoken language (although I must admit to having some fun with the traditional space-opera convention of a translation-computer).

At the same time, however, they must also be *alien*, that is, *other*. How do they differ from *us*? How can those differences be incorporated into the plot? Which ones are crucial? Which incidental? To what extent do they simultaneously understand and *mis*understand each other?

The next stage was to remember the basis of storytelling: Plot. A story might be defined as characters in conflict; taken as a whole, these two points constitute the action of the tale, its plot. "'Fortitude'" had no action, so probably the most crucial step in transforming it was to establish that both characters wanted something critical and that their desires were mutually exclusive. One must win, the other must lose...in this case, die.

That required knowing much more about Torc. Who is he/it? What is this nebulous Empire he represents? He must react in certain ways to the pregnant, female Cwrth; why would he do so? How would his presuppositions and assumptions make inevitable the clash between them?

Similarly, what would be the assumptions of a culture represented by an obviously pregnant female? In which, in fact, there are no significant males present? How would such a culture respond to the intrusion of the alien, the unexpected?

Answering these questions required both society-building and planet-building...which turned out to be the most enjoyable part of writing "Space *Opera*."

Then there was the issue of setting. One was no longer sufficient. In order for readers to understand each alien as representative of a species, a culture, a civilization, without huge blocks of assertion and interruptive back-information, it seemed best to show each in its own matrix. Torc is a space voyager; he appears in the opening paragraphs on the bridge of his ship. The Cwrth is a planet-dweller; she confronts the alien intruder, Torc, in the confines of a room sacred to her people...and critical to the Lovecraftian theme.

As to writing and entertainment value...well, trust me on this one— given where "'Fortitude to Highest Victory'" ranked on either chart, the only way "Space *Opera*" could go was up.

"Space *Opera*" is a fundamentally different story from "'Fortitude to Highest Victory.'" For one thing, at 10,000+ words it is three times longer. It took substantially more time, effort, and ingenuity to deal with than did the original. A huge portion of the labor, in fact, related to deciding what and how much of the original was even worth salvaging, beyond Torc and the Cwrth. The process, though long, was satisfying. I came to know both Torc and the Cwrth more fully than before; I understood more fully what each had to lose or to gain; and I wrote from the beginning with the Lovecraftian theme in mind, even though it doesn't appear until late in the story. But when it does...wow!

Is it still a 'terrible' story? Not to me, at any rate.

Is it a 'great' story? I don't know.

Is it a 'better' story? Yes. And all it took was hours of re-imagining, re-writing, concentrated effort, and care.

Chapter 46

Using Allusion

One of the first "great" books I remember being assigned to read in school was Thornton Wilder's 1928 Pulitzer Prize-winning novel *The Bridge of San Luis Rey*. As a sophomore in high school, I was probably too young to appreciate the many subtleties and nuances of the novel, but I can recall vivid and extended discussions among the students (we were all in accelerated/Honors English, all had top GPAs, and all had vastly inflated conceptions of our own intellectual depth and awareness) about the novel's basic themes: fate versus chance, meaning versus meaninglessness, cosmic justice versus cosmic indifference. And, of course, we *knew* that we, perhaps alone of all mortals throughout time and space, had fully unraveled and resolved the ambiguities of the story.

I recall the discussions, yes...but not much about the novel. As I noted, it was probably too sophisticated for us, and we were far too assured of ourselves to allow any questioning of what was and was not important in the book. As a result, I have probably only thought of *Bridge* a handful of times during the intervening half century, usually as a result of a chance reference in a book or television show. I certainly don't brood about it or look for allusions to it in every book I read.

So it was with a bit of surprise that, a couple of chapters into Michaelbrent Collings' recent horror novel, *Darkbound*, I found myself wondering—*à la* those long-past discussions—about the same issues. Six people waiting in a subway station; six people board the end car and take their positions scattered through it; six people begin to experience things inexplicable, uncanny, and ultimately horrifying.

Why *these* six people? Was there any common thread(s) to unite them, to justify the terrors they were facing? If there was, what was it? and if there wasn't, where was the sense of order, of control, of meaning in *Darkbound*?

A few chapters later, and the questions shifted. One character—clearly the most despicable and degraded of the six—dies (or perhaps doesn't) in ways almost too awful to be imagined (but the author succeeds in imagining them and making them gruesomely visual for readers, extending the description—quite justly, as it turns out—over a number of pages).

As one, the survivors become desperate to leave the end car and, after great pain and not a little bloodletting, they succeed. Then, when another of their number falls victim to an excruciating, bloody, and wholly unnerving attack, the survivors again seek sanctuary in the next car.

And the next.

And the next.

And echoes of *The Bridge of San Luis Rey* give way to hints of Poe's magnificent parable, "The Masque of the Red Death." Room by room, subway car by subway car, the characters move through a staged sequence of terrors—from the FIRST STOP posted on a wall map to the LAST STOP, which might mean redemption for the survivors...or utter damnation.

There is no superficial, obvious connection to the Poe story—no vague awareness of color symbolism attached to the rooms, no ambiguous feeling of pseudo-oriental pageantry—but the sense of progression toward something final, something unanticipated, permeates the middle portions of *Darkbound*. What waits in the final car? and who will live long enough to see it?

And then, my underlying concerns again shifted. Midway through *Darkbound*, Michaelbrent initiates a series of transformations/revelations that force us to review everything that has thus happened, to rethink our conclusions about the six passengers. Some of those assumptions alter only marginally; the first victim remains despicable and degraded, but inexorably, we understand that what happened to him—however horrible—was both fair and just.

From that point, characters undergo similar transformations and revelations, defining not who they *seem* to be but who they actually *are*. "Is there justice in an unjust world?" evolves into more fundamental questions: "Is there a world beyond this? and if so, does it—*can* it—interact with this one?"

And we become aware that the transformations/revelations of a film such as *Sixth Sense* are also at work in *Darkbound*. Beneath, and through, and all around the horrors—and there are many—are unimaginable levels of meaning and existence. This understanding should come as no surprise in a novel that begins, "Jim's first indicator that he should have waited for the next subway was the skull driving the train"; but Michaelbrent nonetheless handles transmutations of setting, time, and character adroitly and effectively.

So what does *Darkbound* offer readers?

One part *The Bridge of San Luis Rey*, with its underlying questions about the essence of life and death;

One part "The Masque of the Red Death," with its sense of inevitability and horrendous fatalism;

One part *The Sixth Sense*, with its evocation of things normally unseen and unseeable;

One part startling imagination that goes places most of us would never even approach in our worst nightmares;

And one part solid, crisp writing, focused on storytelling, promising much and delivering much.

Blend thoroughly...and you have *Darkbound*.

Completion

Chapter 47

Literature, Genre, Horror…and Mormons—What?

The debate over the relationship between "literature" and "genre fiction" is, in some senses, doomed from the start. Supporters of belletristic fiction see nothing whatsoever of worth in those groveling little tales based on plot and character, emphasizing as they do one element of, one perspective on, the "human experience," and often ignoring the darker parts—the suffering, the pain, the tragedy—that make humanity (and one sort of literary expression of it) great.

Genre writers, on the other hand, frequently look with disdain on much of what is touted as "great literature," particularly by establishment critics and reviewers. They may harbor secret loves for Chaucer, Shakespeare, and Milton, of course; but when it comes to fictions that are relevant to *our* times, *our* conditions, *our* age, they find "establishment" stories and novels to be dull, boring, driven by style, symbolisms, or image and lacking in—you guessed it—plot and character.

The situation is particularly tense, I suspect, when it comes to horror as a genre. It is, in some ways, diametrically opposed to mainstream fiction. It often deals with the patently impossible…or at least the wildly improbable. It may easily reduce itself to clichéd images and figures: ancient castles, shadowy groves, sometimes ridiculously one-dimensional characters, and, perhaps worst of all, *monsters.*

Just as a number of first-class authors in the past rejected booksellers' attempts to place their books in the "science fiction" or "fantasy" shelves, arguing that they were merely using the *tropes* of those genres to write metaphors about essential humanity; so some of my friends and colleagues hesitate to come right out and say they write "horror." I frequently use the euphemistic "dark fantasy" when speaking to audiences that I know have little contact with horror beyond seeing previews for the latest buckets-of-blood slasher films. I especially use it when, in a church setting, people ask me what I write. It somehow seems too much of a disjuncture to say that I am the church organist—have been for fifty-five years—and that I write *horror*. The disjuncture becomes even more obvious when I admit that on occasion, when my hearing problems have made it impossible for me to get anything from the service, I have *written horror...in church.*

Most of the time, these various threads—writing, debates between genre fiction and literary fiction, the intersection of one's spiritual life and one's chosen form of literary expression—stay safely apart, often surfacing only in my own mind, where I deal with whatever issues arise and live with the fallout.

Recently, however, something happened that brought all of these issues, and more, to something approaching national attention.

When it was announced that the film adaptation of Orson Scott Card's multiple-award-winning science-fiction novel, *Ender's Game*, would be released in November, 2013, there were several immediate groundswells. One was unanimously positive. For nearly three decades the novel had helped form the imaginations of readers young and old, winning acclaim for its author. Regardless of the fact that it contained some intense scenes of real and imagined violence—not *horror*, precisely, but bordering on it—the story became one of the most highly anticipated films of the year.

One swell was distinctly negative. Based on versions of what Card was supposed to have written, sometimes years ago, about same-sex marriage, groups supporting it orchestrated grassroots boycotts of the film. According to their statements on the social media, many were distraught that the book should even continue to be published. One commenter said that she did not wish Card dead, but it would be nice if he were on a plane that was shot down on a desert island and all he had to read were the works of William S. Burroughs.

One swell was more ambivalent. The movie would be a SCI-FI EXTRAVAGANZA (and I use the term intentionally), full of special effects and topped off with a stellar list of actors...and the novel would get lost. Here people spoke of favorite scenes that would just *have* to be in the film or it would destroy the story. And with the term *sci-fi*, the issue of genre fiction entered the fray.

In mid-November, 2013, Mark Oppenheimer published an essay in *The New York Times* that brought all of these elements together and, for me at least, forced a moment of soul-searching. After identifying Orson

Scott Card and Stephanie Meyer as members of the Church of Jesus Christ of Latter-day Saints (Mormons), Oppenheimer rapidly segued into a discussion of why so many members of that church in particular choose optimistic, "sunny" literary forms—more specifically, science fiction and fantasy—rather than opting to struggle with the grit and nastiness and tragedy of real life to seek literary greatness.

His argument rests heavily on his interpretation of comments made by Shannon Hale, an LDS young-adult writer. In particular, he relies on "Ms. Hale's theory…that literary fiction tends to exalt the tragic, or the gloomy, while Mormon culture prefers the sunny and optimistic." That Pollyanna-like perspective—resulting in what another source in the essay calls "faith-affirming and uncomplicated-type writing"—finds its natural expression in escapist genre fiction, "Because when you write sci-fi and so forth, things aren't as messy as with realistic fiction."

While there is much to quibble about in Oppenheimer's article, including his leaving out any significant investigation into the complex moral questions raised by *Ender's Game*, with its less-than-sunny conclusion, one major lapse lies in the fact that he completely ignores perhaps the darkest, arguably the most uncomfortable genre, one that (perhaps for him, inexplicably) thrives among authors along the Wasatch Front.

Horror.

Granted, horror is explicitly a form of genre literature, and, further granted, most readers of the *NYT* might hesitate to accord it "great literature" status under any circumstances. In a recent Facebook conversation, however, one participant commented that although

> [a]cademics dismiss horror writing…writing about terror and horror in human experience is one of the most serious things a writer can address. Fear, anxiety, and isolation are what drive us to our most cherished extremes. It is what forms the foundation for so much of our desperate achievement and scramble toward height and light. Even the crudest reach for significant themes is better than the most sophisticated sigh of emptiness, apathy, and despair. Let the blood spatter and the screams echo and revel in what is revealed as shadows flee. (—Samael Gyre writing as Gene Stewart)

While horror writers would certainly applaud these sentiments, critics, reviewers, and "establishment" types would more frequently side with the academics. In the hierarchy of literary writing (limiting it to the three genres in question) fantasy ranks low; science fiction ranks lower; and horror ranks lowest. Even its most eminent practitioner, Stephen King, appears to accept this estimation with his three grades of horror: *terror*, with its frisson of anticipation; *horror*, with its monsters creeping about in the darkness; and the *gross-out*, the physical representation of the gruesome and the gory—the visceral. And, he frequently notes, if all else fails, he will go for the gross-out.

All this may be true, but the fact remains that a specific geographical area, a specific shared culture (or sub-culture), and in many cases, the same writers Oppenheimer wishes to associate with simplistic, highly optimistic, uncomplicated, less-than-sophisticated writing (if not his words, then the ones he chooses to quote) have written some intensely disquieting fiction.

He could, in fact, have looked no further than the first Mormon author he mentioned, Orson Scott Card. A multiple *New York Times* bestseller, winner of the Hugo and Nebula Awards back-to-back for a novel and its sequel (an unparalleled achievement), Card was in all likelihood the source of Oppenheimer's interest in LDS fiction, particularly because of the brouhaha over his authorship of the source novel for one of the year's most anticipated movies, *Ender's Game*. That novel itself is sufficient evidence to refute many of Oppenheimer's claims: it is tough; it acknowledges both family togetherness and the tensions that rip families (and individuals) apart; it deals with complex issues revolving around the relationship between the individual and the community; it deals with aliens that are at once science-fictional and horrific in their non-humanness, and at the same time it urges readers to see beneath the surface and confront ugly, unpleasant realities about them…and about us.

But it is a walk in the park on a calm summer's day compared with some of Card's other works. "Eumenides in a Fourth-floor Lavatory," "Fat Farm," "Unaccompanied Sonata," "The Porcelain Salamander," and—for my money his finest, most disquieting, most horrific, and most sublime short story—"Kingsmeat" sufficiently indicate how deeply Card has penetrated into "our cherished extremes." In fact, a number of his early shorter works garnished not only praise but severe censure among LDS readers for their graphic depictions of horrors. And novels such as *A Planet Called Treason* (1979; extensively revised as *Treason*, 1988), *Lost Boys* (1992, expanded from an earlier short story), *Treasure Box* (1996), and *Homebody* (1998) show him fully capable of extending the tropes into full narratives.

Card is a far more complex, more sophisticated writer than the blurb in the *NYT* essay might suggest. His writings range from biography to historical fiction, from how-to books to essays on contemporary LDS life, from scripts for religious tapes and films to full-scale theatrical productions. At one point, in fact, he told me that less than one-third of his total output could be considered sf/f. Yet in almost everything he writes, genre or not, there is an element of darkness, of awareness that life is more than a sunny outlook and an optimistic religion.

If Card were alone in his dedication to the darker elements of fiction, this essay would be superfluous. But he is not. For well over thirty years, writers throughout the Wasatch Front (southeastern Idaho through northern Utah) have organized symposia, hosted conferences and conventions, created workshops, encouraged writers groups that have produced a remarkable number of writers of fantasy and dark fantasy...and horror.

Just last night, a friend of mine, Dave Butler, posted a self-proclaimed screed on Facebook that included the following: "Big Storytelling (Broadway and Hollywood, and maybe to some extent Publishing) is in a serious rut. They rehash the same stories over and over. As an investment strategy, I get it—big dollars go into these things, so investors want to place bets on sure (or very likely) wins." He then lists, by name, authors whose works he sees as providing "more diversity of stories, more quirky stories, more local stories, more unique stories. I want stories that are awesome, not stories that are commercial." His list includes:

Angie Lotfhouse's "syncretistic-Mormon science fiction";
Steven Peck's "weird west lit fic";
Bill Housley's "libertarian first contact stories,"
Danyelle Leafty's fairy tales;
Paul Genesse's "romantic epic fantasy";
Michaelbrent Collings' "serial zombie survival epic";
Tom Carr's independent films;
Platte F. Clark's *Bad Unicorn* series;
Eric Patten's Hunter Chronicles;
Dan Wells' "I am not a serial killer" trilogy;
Robison Wells' YA science fiction

To which could easily be added:

Larry Correia, *New York Times* bestselling author of the Monster Hunter International series, the Grimnoir Chronicles, and others;

Eric James Stone, Nebula Award winner and Hugo Nominee;

Brandon Sanderson, Hugo and Whitney Award author of the Mistborn series and completer of Robert Jordan's *The Ring of Time;*

Jeff Savage, the first to publish clear-cut horror through an LDS publisher;

Wilum Pugmire, an accomplished Lovecraftian;

Jaleta Clegg, specializing in sf/f and silly horror—some of the best and silliest.

Two years ago, a remarkable anthology was published by Wm Morris and Theric Jepson, *Monsters & Mormons* (2011). Anyone unaware that the West has produced an enclave of Mormon horror writers might take a look at this 500-page tome containing stories, poems, graphic comics and illustrations…many emerging as if from the landscape itself. Some are humorous, others are straight-line extrapolations from present to future, but most at least touch upon darkness—even Jaleta Clegg's, in which the "monster" is the infamous green Jell-O reputedly served at all LDS functions.

A year ago, a second remarkable anthology appeared, this time a group project spearheaded by Nathan Shumate: *Space Eldritch* (2012). The concept: simple—Lovecraft in Space. The execution: far more complex, as stories by D.J. Butler, myself, Nathan Shumate, David J. West, Carter Reid and Brad Torgersen, Robert J Defendi, and Howard Taylor explored the infinite possibilities of other dimensions, of aliens and alien worlds, of space-and-time travel in multiple forms, all wrapped in the impenetrable darkness of H.P. Lovecraft's inimical, loathly universe.

And this year, a third anthology: *Space Eldritch II: The Haunted Stars* (2013). New to the volume are Michaelbrent Collings, Larry Correia (who provided the introduction to the parent volume), Stephen J. Peck, Steven Diamond, and Eric James Stone; the remaining stories are by five contributors from the first volume, myself included. Again, there are no limits—physical, spiritual, psychological—to the darkness of the imagined universes, to the terrors and horrors that, through fiction (and though fictive) help define what it is to be human.

Earlier this year, my son Michaelbrent Collings, began his most ambitious project. A multi-volume zombie-apocalypse-human-survival epic…set in southwestern Idaho. *The Colony: Genesis, The Colony: Renegades,* and *The Colony: Descent* draw from the western landscape—

from the anomalous mixture of city and wide-open spaces—to speculate on what might happen if, within a matter of minutes, the vast proportion of the human race transformed into zombies with powers of mutation and intercommunication, and others not yet disclosed. How would the remaining fraction survive, and what would be important enough to them to *want* to survive? As with his earlier horror novels—especially *Strangers* (2013), *Darkbound* (2013), and *The Haunted* (2012)—he has no fears of darkness, even darknesses where other horror writers might first hesitate.

And finally, a personal note. I have published two works that became Bram Stoker Award® Finalists for 2012: *Writing Darkness,* a collection of essays on the nature of horror, the nature of writing, and the intersections between them; and *A Verse to Horror: An Abecedary of Monsters and the Monstrous,* which deals alphabetically with monsters in folklore, literature, and film...with one limerick allowed per monster.

In addition, I have published eight novels: two sf (*Wordsmith* and *Singer of Lies*), four overtly horror (*The House Beyond the Hill, The Slab, Shadow Valley,* and *Static!*), and two mysteries (*Devil's Plague* and *Serpent's Tooth*). All eight are "genre fiction"; not one of them is, I think, cursed by sunny optimism. There is darkness in every story. And I have published over eight hundred books, chapbooks, chapters, essays and articles, and reviews, the vast majority dealing with horror. Two of my volumes of poetry are explicitly horror-oriented, particularly *In the Void: Poems of Science Fiction, Myth and Fantasy, and Horror.*

Now to the point behind all of the facts, figures, and blatant name-dropping.

What do all of these writers share?

For one, they share a love of and devotion to genre fiction, specifically sf, fantasy, *and* horror. Not all write in each genre; certainly not all are quite comfortable being called "horror writers." But in the search for truth—even the truths underlying the universe and all of creation—they find the ideal outlet in an "escapist" form of fiction that allows them to rise above the grittiness of day-to-day tedium and enter far more into the realms of darkness—again, physical, emotional, spiritual, psychological—where we scramble toward "height and light." And none would deny the implicit greatness of the scrambling.

For another, they all have deep roots in a single geographic location: they are Westerners. Almost all either live or have lived in Utah, Arizona, or Idaho. Many come from families who settled those regions and, as the saying goes, "made the desert blossom as the rose." My great-grandfather was carried across the plains in his mother's arms while his father and the remaining children pushed a handcart. They settled southern Utah—that landscape, with its painted cliffs and neat valley farms, is as much my homeplace as any of the cities I've lived in. Simply by being part, to whatever degree, of the land, I share its history, its struggles, and its successes. So, in their own ways, do most of these writers.

For yet another, they mostly share a single religious heritage. Not all are Mormons, but most of those who are not have chosen to live within LDS environments, which gives them glimpses into the intensity of family and community. Those who are Mormon understand a point that Orson Scott Card articulated a number of years ago. In "On Sycamore Hill," he talks about the genesis of two stories in *The Folk of the Fringe*, a collection set in the landscape of a post-apocalyptic Utah. One evening, when the rest of the workshop group had left for dinner, he remained behind, at first thinking that he wanted to work on his stories. Gradually, however, he realized that, as a Mormon, he was not truly one of the group:

> ...this wasn't my community. These guys were Americans, not Mormons; those of us who grew up in Mormon society and remain intensely involved are only nominally members of the American community. We can fake it, but we're always speaking a foreign language....

From this comes a fourth, crucial point. Most of the writers listed above, whether Mormon or not, whether directly from the West or not, can understand the sense of being *isolated*...by vistas and landscapes, by religious beliefs and commitments, by shared historical heritages that set them apart...and by their choice to work within a genre that emphasizes, that embraces, that makes essential *isolation*. Horror by its nature begins in aloneness—whether in an old, creaking house, or in an ancient forest redolent with secrets and fear, or in the farthest reaches of space. And out of that aloneness, it struggles to create some kind of community, to establish ties with fellow humans, or, when that is impossible, with fellow aliens.

To return to the beginning of this essay: the most important points about Orson Scott Card and *Ender's Game* that Oppenheimer misses are *not* that Card writes genre fiction or that he is a member of a religion that has a peculiar and peculiarly optimistic outlook, as important as those might be.

What he misses is that Card and all of these other writers—*genre* writers, *western* writers, *Mormon* writers, progeny of pioneers of varying sorts—all of them have *chosen* horror in one way or another as a unique, for them ideal way of, as has already been said, scrambling "toward height and light."

And the struggle can be sublime.

Chapter 48

Some Thoughts on Writing as Therapy

A poem is a poem.[5]

It is not an act of social commentary.

It is not a paean to political propaganda.

It is not a form of therapy—physical, mental, or spiritual.

A poem is a *poem*—an exercise in verbal art and expression.

That having been said, let me now invoke the historical prerogative of all poets (and all artists) and contradict myself: a poem is not *exclusively* social commentary, or political plea, or mode of therapy. Not exclusively.

Because one of the glories of poetry—perhaps of every art—is that by virtue of setting aside as immediate goals such mundane matters as politics or social agendas or even leaky roof-shingles at the height of *El Niño* weather, a poem *as poem* potentially incorporates and transcends lesser concerns and, in doing so, elevates them into the stuff of art.

Thus *a poem is a poem*, which may (but does not have to) function as a vessel of therapy for writers...and often, with equal value, for readers.

A few years ago, I might have denied even such a vague accommodation of poetry to therapy. I might have (rather snobbishly, I admit) acquiesced so far as to allow that some of the lesser forms of poetry—confessional verse, for example, or naïve narratives couched in rhyme and meter—could *perhaps* serve the purpose of healing. More

---

[5] This essay was written in the late 1980s, at a time when health problems became increasingly debilitating and before I began expressly writing horror fiction. At the time, I could concentrate on a short verse; anything else was beyond my capabilities. It does not directly address horror, but the points made are indeed relevant. Simply translate *poem* as *story*.

elevated verse—and certainly *Poetry*—could not...nor should it be asked to.

Since then, to my relief (and, unfortunately, to my desperation), I think that I have grown in maturity as well as in years, in compassion as well as in criticism, and in experience as well as in arrogance. I have seen deeply embedded in great poetry a frequent fear, an anguish, possibly even a terror that the simple act of writing a poem—the immensely *courageous* act of writing a poem—has helped defeat. And more importantly, I have felt the workings of poetry in my own conscious and unconscious reactions to pain, distress, and fear.

The past decade or so has brought a number of changes into my life, not the least being my having passed the half-century mark (which, while not the trauma it might have been a hundred years ago, when the average life expectancy was barely more than that, is nonetheless at least momentarily unnerving). Before that crisis surfaced, however, several other key events had already triggered serious difficulties—physical, mental, and spiritual.

When my father died, not suddenly but still unexpectedly, after several years of increasing debilitation, his death took me so much by surprise that for almost a year afterward, I could not write anything, let alone focus on creating poetry. Then, in rapid succession, I lost sufficient hearing to require hearing aids in both ears; I developed constant tinnitus (multiple-toned ringing, banging, whistling, creaking, etc.) in both ears; I was diagnosed as having high blood pressure, then high cholesterol, and most recently, diabetes; and, not the least in terms of lasting effects requiring some kind of internal (and external) therapy, I realized a year ago that I have probably been suffering from severe clinical depression for at least thirty-five of my fifty years—with the past year being among the most intensely frightening and psychically painful ever.

None of these problems, of course, will prove fatal—at least, not directly. Hearing aids enable me to amplify student voices sufficiently that I don't have to read lips, although I will probably never truly hear the full subtleties of the pipe organ I play for church each Sunday. The ringing...well, the doctors generally just say "Learn to live with it" and move on to more complicated problems; to some extent, I am learning to live with it, or around it, if not to ignore it. The diabetes has proven, paradoxically, the easiest problem to confront; given a choice between injecting myself twice a day with long, thin needles, and eating regularly and wisely, I decided on the latter—six months and minus-forty-five pounds later, I no longer require additional medication for that problem, at least.

But the depression.... And the depression when my ears ring wildly; when I can't hear when my children talk to me, even though they almost yell; when the various medications for the physical problems have fatigued me until I can barely stand it—when the depression hits *then*, life becomes...shall we say "interesting."

All right—so I have proven that I can prattle on and on about my troubles. Most of us could do that as well as I, and many with infinitely more justification. But the point of the prattling (as much as a point exists at all) remains quite simple: Poetry has kept me sane, progressing out of darkness, and—I am convinced—alive.

I have never actively contemplated suicide, certainly not to the point that I've gone window-shopping at K-Mart for a cheap gun, or at OSH Hardware for a hank of rope, test weight at least two hundred pounds. Instead, I found myself thinking, just before falling asleep, how nice it would be just not to wake up. In addition, I lost concentration. I barely functioned as a teacher. I became short-tempered as a father and no doubt irritating as hell as a husband.

But, I discovered, in spite of all of these pressures, and much to my intense surprise, I *could still write poetry*.

About a year after my father's death, at the beginning of my own slide into illness and depression, I realized that I had never seriously confronted, in writing, the fact of death...his, mine, or anyone's. I had written a number of darkish poems—in fact, the bulk of my poetry, prose, and criticism to that time had been horror and dark fantasy—but I had never *faced* death.

A few rough drafts convinced me that I couldn't.

At least I couldn't as Michael Collings, husband, father, son, teacher, musician, poet.

So I invented Warren.

Warren (whose name, not coincidentally, refers to the twisting, dark den-passages of some frightened, subterranean creature) became my analog. Our lives touched at key points. I had lost a father; he had lost a father. I had become inarticulate; he had never been able to speak about grief and loss. Together we explored his life, beginning from moments we shared, then diverging.

And a miraculous thing happened.

As I—Michael Collings—worked on understanding Warren's life, as I struggled to give his emotions form and expression, to focus and direct them, to bring some of them under the control of metaphor, rhyme, and meter—as I worked with Warren, I could see sense emerging in my own life. The act of writing words made the emotions lurking behind those words less horrifying. The act of emerging from strict biography into fiction and poetry made frightening moments in my own life easier to think about, to handle, to accept. With the "Warren Poems," in fact, I faced for the first time events that I had not thought about for nearly forty years, and, through organizing, structuring, and interpreting them, set many of them to rest.

The series concluded about a year after it began, with a poem self-consciously titled, "Warren Says Farewell to His Father's Ghost." Since then, Warren has remained silent. I owe him a vast debt of gratitude, but in all honesty, I do not really *miss* him. (Lest anyone worry about my mental stability at this point, I always *knew* that Warren was imaginary, of course, but the fiction let me say things I could not say in my own voice.)

Through Warren, I learned that I could speak for myself, through myself.

As my physical and mental problems increased in the months and years following the last Warren poem, I learned to appreciate more fully the uses of poetry in dealing with pain, fear, stress. Out of major problems came opportunities for exploring new directions. Hearing problems suggested poems dealing with sound, music, rhythm. Depressive episodes led to poems that explored up-states and down. Health concerns resulted in poetry that examined physical relationships past and present and the relationship between physical and spiritual, physical and emotional, physical and artistic.

But more than these relatively superficial forms of "therapy," poetry provided some specific means to combat an array of difficulties:

ORGANIZATION:

Poetry by its nature requires an act of organizing; depression by its nature encourages chaos. When we approach a poem, we are flooded by possibilities: diction, sounds, rhythms, line lengths, stanza forms, etc. And when the poem takes as its subject our own lives—particularly those lives as defined by grief, pain, and fear—the options become uncountable. Shall I tell about that precise moment? Is it really necessary for me to remember that other one specifically enough to incorporate it? Does this image really define the way I felt, or would that one perhaps be better? The very act of compressing reality into a *form*—a fourteen-line sonnet, a seventeen-syllable haiku, a sequence of free-verse lines, a seven-thousand-line Miltonic epic—in and of itself combats one of the most critical components of illness and depression: inability to concentrate, to focus, to decide.

DISCIPLINE:

Similarly, all poetry disciplines, even as it is disciplined. In the most fundamental sense, there are those forms that require "discipline": rhyme, metrical rhythms, sound patterns, syntactical patterns for arranging words. When we speak, we often just struggle to get words out, to say "what we mean"; when we write poetry, we *shape* the possibilities of language into art. Regardless of whether the final poem is as intricately complex as a sonnet or a villanelle, or as superficially arbitrary as breath-unit free verse, the act of poetry requires an act of discipline. And discipline in one area frequently spills over into another. By writing, I prepare myself, no matter how marginally, for the greater conflicts of living with illness, with frustration, with depression.

CONTROL:

People suffering from depression often desperately need to *control*—or, perhaps better put, to maintain the *illusion* of control. And certainly major consequences of any continuing, debilitating illness, whether physical or mental, is the persistent, insistent, never-to-be-denied sense that we can no longer control significant portions of our lives. Poetry provides a means by which we can regain the sense of control, foster the illusion that we do still have final say over some things. When we decide which word, which line, which image, which metaphor truly belongs in the center of our poem—or even which poem to write, and when—we exercise our need to form and shape the world around us, in ways that contribute to health and well-being.

UNDERSTANDING:

The art of writing leads to greater understanding—of ourselves, our world, our fellow-sufferers, our conditions. Perhaps the poetry has led to deeper research about the difficulties we face. Research in turn can generate understanding, and understanding can generate compassion, ways of coping, sympathy and empathy, and greatness of spirit and soul. When we read any great poem, we often lose sight of the supposed "subject" of the poem. When I re-read *Paradise Lost*, for example, I usually don't worry too much about whether or not Adam and Eve will again eat the Forbidden Fruit. Instead, I become transfixed by the vision of blind Milton struggling to understand his world, a world in which God might still act but now in increasingly mysterious and difficult ways. When I write poetry, the same process recurs, more intensely, closer to my core. I lose sight of the particular image, or thought, or metaphor that I began exploring, and discover more completely the truths beneath what I thought I was saying. Poems about deafness or tinnitus frequently transmute into meditations about love and loneliness, or about family and friendship—important things, enduring things.

DIRECTION:

From understanding comes a sense of new direction. I may begin with the idea that I am going to write about my father's death, or my deafness, or the persistent clangor inside my head. With time, I realize that I have become more interested in larger issues that transcend the initial stimulus. Nearly five years after writing my first tinnitus poem—a gush of anger and frustration and fear that struggled merely to define what it is like to live with such a condition—I suddenly realized that I had written several dozen poems about it, some maudlin and melodramatic, to be sure, but some more focused, more external than I would ever have thought possible. And suddenly the poems presented more than just an opportunity for me to talk about my own private problems; they became a means by which I could try to communicate with others like me, or with others who suffer physical problems that affect their lives. They became, in fact, a small chapbook of intensely personal, public poems called *Faint Echoes of a Feather Kissing Snow: Tinnitus Poems*.

AUDIENCE:

At this point, the poems have become more than just therapeutic without losing their concentrated therapeutic value. As I worked through the drafts of the tinnitus poems, for example, I found myself forced to step away from them, to remove myself from the intimacy of psychological and physical pain they implied, and to examine them. I organized, formed, focused, disciplined, and controlled—and at the end of that process, I had something I could willingly share with an audience other than myself. These may be my pains, I think (hope?) the poems asserted, *but they are not* me. *These are my pains, but I can overcome them by transforming them into the raw material of art. These are my pains, but they are not mine alone, either to suffer or to bear, because I share my pain with any others who read these poems and find understanding, solace, definition, or hope.*

FREEDOM:

In the end, these poems, and others like them, set me free. Free from self-involvement, since in order to create them, I had to step out of myself, at least for the duration of writing. Free from self-pity, since the act of writing poetry implies universality, which equally implies the co-humanity of each and all of us. Free from the pain of the moment, because the art of writing becomes so intense that fear, grief, longing are subsumed beneath stronger, more positive emotions: creativity, joy in language, awareness of the intricate world around us.

And thus, although a poem is a poem, it can (and perhaps should) also partake of therapy—an administration designed to improve or ameliorate. We improve ourselves by writing and by reading; we improve our readers by writing; we improve our world by caring enough about it to enter into our pains, and there to endure them, to transform them, and, ultimately, to surmount them.

Thirty Years Later....

Since I wrote the first portion of this essay a number of things have changed.

My hearing loss progressed to the point that even with hearing aids I could no longer understand my students...a serious debility when teaching creative writing classes in which students presented poems and stories orally. In late 2005, my college granted me a disability retirement that allowed my wife and me to move to Idaho where my hearing gradually continues to separate me from most social occasions.

The tinnitus increased, although understanding its cause and its effects and the reasons why a cure has not and probably will not soon be discovered has helped me cope to some extent. Recently, an audiologist actually tested the extent of the tinnitus—for the first time since the ringing began—and on the basis of that test placed me in the top five percent of tinnitus sufferers. He offered little besides confirming that what I was hearing was severe and real and stressful.

My diabetes has progressed to the point that I am now intimately familiar with that thin needle—four times a day. And now my blood sugars have reached the point that probably some additional treatments will be required.

And....

And thanks to the late Robert Reginald, John Betancourt, and several other editors and publishers, I have found an additional outlet and a new form of therapy: writing, and writing about, horror.

Everything in the earlier portion of this essay still holds true. Although the quantity of poetry I write has dropped off in lieu of stories and novels, the essence of writing remains true. And, perhaps as an indication of how effective writing darkness has been as therapy, my last concerted effort at verse was...comic. *Averse to Horror: An Abecedary of Monsters and the Monstrous* (2012) not only made the final list for the Bram Stoker Awards®, it allowed me to look at darkness itself from a new—and I think more healthy—perspective. It pulls from memory every monster I've encountered and, by imprisoning them within limericks (perhaps the most rollicking of verse forms) tamed them.

Prose fiction has also become a major way of asserting myself over my difficulties. Each novel—either written or completely revised during my retirement—has in some way addressed darkness and, particularly in *The House Beyond the Hill,* transformed it into light.

And non-fiction, such as this volume, gives me the opportunity to view horror—and fear and terror and all of its various permutations—objectively. Seeing how and why it functions in other people's writing helps me understand my own stories, and the impetuses behind them.

The consequences of these experiences? The understanding that I much underrated writing as therapy and discovery in the initial version of this essay. Were I writing it today, I would probably begin:

A story—whether told in prose or verse—is a story.
It is not an act of social commentary.
It is not a paean to political propaganda.
It is not a form of therapy—physical, mental, or spiritual.
A story is a *story*—an exercise in verbal art and expression.
And, as needed, it may be *all* of the above.

Chapter 49

Writing Horror—What Do I Get Out of It?

Some time ago, I received the proof copy for a collection of essays on writing, emphasizing horror, *Writing Darkness*, which eventually became the core of the current collection.

Most of the essays were stimulated by my work with JournalStone Publishing. Since affiliating with them, I've judged novel competitions, read short fiction, read novels for possible publication, written an introduction to a fine novel by a powerful new writer, edited novels and short stories, and—perhaps most important—written a series of short articles about writing for the JournalStone website.

In the process of doing all this, a number of things happened.

First, I wrote enough articles to trigger *Writing Darkness*...the impetus for that book came from those articles.

Second, I had the opportunity to look at horror from multiple directions: as a writer, as a reader, as a critic/reviewer, as an editor. I could see rough-cut stories and stories after their final polish. And more importantly, I could see what kept otherwise good stories from reaching their full potential and what could be done to help them along.

Third, I had multiple opportunities to think about horror—what it is, how it works, why it is popular, how it has evolved.

Fourth, I had the chance to merge those considerations with more practical ones: why does *this* sentence structure enhance a sense of horror while *that* one does not? How does punctuation, word order, word choice, sentence length impact horror?

And fifth, I was able to sit down and consider a hitherto unasked question: **What do I get out of writing it?** That is, other than the frequent strange looks that come my way when I admit to doing so.

Here are several answers:

I MAKE A LITTLE MONEY:

I am fortunate in that my life does not depend upon my writing. It never has. For thirty years my primary vocation was teaching, with writing an adjunct. University-level teaching requires publication, even when the publications are not always appreciated by colleagues. So I published. But not for a university audience. Most of my books on Stephen King, Orson Scott Card, and others had as their target audiences late high school and early college readers, young folks who might be excited to realize that literary criticism could justly be applied to science fiction, fantasy, and horror; and who might be equally excited to see their favorite genres treated with the same respect that is granted 'mainstream' writers.

In large measure, I think I succeeded. I have had a number of students contact me at school to request interviews, ask questions about comments made in one of my books or articles, even ask permission to use me as a source in a researched paper. Each time, I felt a certain level of gratification.

What I did not see, however—and did not *expect* to see—was a tidal wave of money heading my way. One of the early King studies, Starmont's original *Stephen King as Richard Bachman*, did earn around $5,000 the first year; but that was a stark exception, unmatched until my horror novel, *The Slab*, spent six months or so as a Wildside bestseller.

Since my own novels have appeared, I've seen an uptick in the number of people actually buying my books. Still nothing to shout about but enough to meet our increasing needs in my retirement.

So to that extent, horror has been good to me.

I MEET FASCINATING PEOPLE:

I am inherently an intensely—perhaps pathologically—shy person...have been for as long as I can remember. I don't make friends easily, feel intimidated by everyone around me when I'm in groups, can't imagine why anyone might be interested in getting to know me. These feelings have intensified over the past twenty years, since my triple-threat—deafness, tinnitus, and clinical depression—has to some degree taken over my life.

I don't attend social functions and haven't understood a word at church for the past decade (I attend; play the prelude; play the hymns as my wife conducts them and gives me signals about volume, tone, etc.;

play the postlude; then leave, often without speaking to anyone). My sole outlet is the conferences I attend each year. One is explicitly an SF/F symposium, another is a bit more open to horror...and twice now I've been invited as a Guest to World Horror Con.

That hasn't made me any less shy, but by sitting on panels (thanks to all who have so graciously interpreted audience questions and comments that I couldn't hear), I am 'forced' to meet new people. And that has been a life-saver, both figuratively and literally.

I'm not a techie, so my contacts with sf are perhaps the least strong; my interest in fantasy is primarily academic, Tolkien and Lewis specifically, so I often don't have a great deal in common with Fantasy writers.

But horror....

Now, that is something I can empathize with. I can talk blood and gore, pain and suffering, monsters and the monstrous along with the best of them (I hope) and enter into conversations I would never otherwise have had. Many of the points made in *Writing Darkness* stem from panels and presentations over the years; and many of the examples quoted and analyzed are from works by writers I would never have imagined getting to know. Through their books, whether I read for pleasure, to review, or to discuss; through their presence online and in emails; through their responses and encouragement, I feel more part of a community than I ever did while teaching.

And for that I am grateful.

I WRITE WHAT I WANT—WHAT INTERESTS ME:

During the few years, I have published:

- *Writing Darkness*, a book on writing horror, primarily drawn from *Collings Notes;*
- three novels—*Static!*, *Shadow Valley*, and *Serpent's Tooth;*
- four short stories—"Space *Opera*," "Space *Opera* II," "In the Haunting Darkness," and "Accommodation";
- *A Verse to Horror: An Abecedary of Monsters and the Monstrous*, a book of horror-limericks;
- *HAI-(And Assorted Other)-KU*, a book of primarily non-horror haiku, although there is a section of "HorrorKu";
- a 2-volume bibliography of my works;
- *Lines from Collings Hill*, an edition of my grandmother's poetry;
- *Deep Music*, a collection of LDS-oriented musical readings;

- *Perspectives*, an edition of some 350 reviews;
- *The Filamental Emblems*, a book of poem-and-crocheted-pattern combinations that try to communicate the same feeling or thought;
- *BlueRose*, a collection of half a dozen previously published chapbooks;
- *The Gummi Bear Omnibus*, a tongue-in-cheek annotated 'scholarly' edition of poems by my son and daughter detailing the rise and fall of the intergalactic Gummi Bear Empires.

Now, what do these have in common?

Just one thing. Me.

Not all are horror—two of the novels are cozy mysteries—but there is a sense of darkness in each book I've written/compiled. They reflect my imagination. Horror, in that sense, is not restrictive. It is not a matter of technological advance, or of the plausible improbable, but of emotion. Anything can carry a touch of the horrific.

Be that as it may, horror for me is often less a generic specification than an approach. I can have characters in one of the mysteries, *Devil's Plague*, walk along a forest trail in the middle of the night. They are simply going to the scene of a crime. There is no suggestion of anything supernatural about the death or the location. It is dark, yes, but they have strong flashlights, and two of the three have hiked the trail many times before.

The situation reminded me of a midnight hike when I worked at a Scout Camp over fifty years ago, and that similarity urged me to emphasize the spookiness, the aloneness, and impending sense of possible fear that I recall from that hurried hike. We had had a medical emergency at a distant lake, and one of the scouts needed to be taken back to the base camp. It wasn't life-threatening, but having just hiked to the lake that afternoon, not having eaten anything since breakfast (that is another story), being roused from almost-sleep, then force-marching down-mountain to the accompaniment of a moaning boy and constantly shifting shadows...well, I simply had to make one of my characters feel the same creepiness, eeriness, uncertainty.

And there it was, a moment of horror in a straight-forward mystery novel.

Or another, shorter moment: sitting outside on a bright spring afternoon, writing haiku about the tulips, then noticing that at the core of each—no matter the colors of the petals, red, pink, yellow, white—there was a hidden darkness, a deep blue-black spot in the center. And thinking, "what if?"

Another moment of horror…and several HorrorKu.

For me, horror is infinitely malleable. It can become obsessive and direct the movement of an entire novel; it can be momentary and bring little more than a tint of darkness to a story or poem.

As curious as it might sound, I owe horror a great deal. Beginning with my first essays on Stephen King's writings thirty years ago, it has been a recurring leitmotif in my life, making the internal more understandable and the external more bearable.

Many thanks.

Chapter 50

The Persistence of Darkness

Some time ago[6], the Humanities Division at my university sponsored an Arts Festival to commemorate the opening of the new Cultural Arts Center. Colleagues from the division—English, History, and Philosophy departments—were to present papers relating to their current research.

I was a bit taken aback when my division chair asked me to present one. He knew that my research centered primarily on horror—and on Stephen King in particular; and I knew that many in the division looked upon my activities as an aberration of an unsettled mind. One colleague, for example, noticed a King novel among the books one of his advisees was holding during a meeting in his office. He took the opportunity to explain to the poor benighted child that such books were not appropriate on a college campus and certainly not welcome in his office. The student—to my enormous gratification—calmly explained that the text

---

[6] This essay was presented as the Academic Guest of Honor Address at the World Horror Convention, Salt Lake City UT, March 26-30, 2008 and was reprinted in *Toward Other Worlds: Perspectives on John Milton, C.S. Lewis, Stephen King, Orson Scott Card, and Others* (Wildside, 2010). Portions were earlier presented during the Arts Festival, Seaver College, Pepperdine University, on November 19, 1991, as part of the opening celebration for the Cultural Arts Festival. A much shorter version appeared as the introduction to George Beahm's biography of Stephen King: "Introduction: The Persistence of Darkness—Shadows Behind the Life Behind the Story" in *The Stephen King Story: A Literary Profile* (Kansas City: Andrews & McMeel, 1991).

was required reading for one of his classes (mine, to be precise) and that even if it weren't, he would be reading it anyway.

Another colleague, whose attitudes toward any sub-literary forms, including science fiction, fantasy, and horror, were less than enthusiastic, took great pains to explain to the rank, tenure, and promotion committee the extent to which she felt I was wasting my time and the university's money in such trivial pursuits. She even objected to the fact that my early Starmont House King studies were printed in courier font— obviously the work of amateurs among the great unwashed. She made her point. Over my thirty years at the university, her attitude and similar attitudes among others, cost me several promotions.

Given his constant support for my work, however, I shouldn't have been surprised when the division chair extended the invitation, but I was. And a bit trepidatious, since I knew that the audience would include not only fellow professors but faculty from across the University; administrators, including most probably the president himself; wealthy potential contributors from nearby Malibu; and members of the board of regents...not a few of whom easily fit the category of conservative little old "blue-haired" ladies.

After some soul-searching, I decided, "Well, what have I got to lose?"

So I opened my presentation with the simple statement: "William Shakespeare was the Stephen King of his day."

I swear you could hear neck bones snap as heads jerked up. I tried not to look at those colleagues from the English program whom I knew had no senses of humor; but I did notice a mischievous twinkle in the division chair's eye.

I recall that experience because it has influenced my approach to most of my work since. I continued to write about Stephen King...and Orson Scott Card, Dean Koontz, Robert McCammon, Piers Anthony, Brian Aldiss, and pretty much anyone else who caught my interest. My subsequent division chairs, all three of them, continued steadfastly to support the directions of my research. And those persistent colleagues continued to try to block promotions or advancement...rather successfully, I'm afraid, and that in face of the fact that I had pretty much out-published the entire division combined. And the conclusions expressed in that presentation about the role and nature of horror continued to color everything I taught and wrote, whether it related directly to science fiction, fantasy and horror, or to Edmund Spenser, John Milton, and the Renaissance epic.

For that reason, I would like to recall, restate, and expand upon a couple of those points. And, as then, instead of trying to be theoretically cutting-edge or to 'deconstruct' the genre until it becomes clear that I really hate horror but figure I can get publication credits by writing about it, I would like to make some suggestions about the continuity of horror—both the monsters and the motifs—in literary history.

But first, a plot synopsis:

> *A handful of people have gathered in a building in the center of a small, isolated community. Inside, they have found safety...or at least the illusion of safety. Outside, there is only darkness, and fear, and death. Daylight is dying. With the night will come the monster. The people huddle close for warmth, for comfort. They know that by the time the sun dawns again, some, or most—or all—of them may be dead.*

Is this an outline of a horror novel? Koontz's *Strangers*, perhaps, or *Phantoms*? Or better yet, King's early novella, *The Mist*? Those would be good guesses. They seem logical. To a degree even probable.

But this summary doesn't actually speak to any of these. The story I had in mind was written a few years before King assumed the mantle, willingly or not, of "King of Horror," or before King, Koontz, McCammon, or the others began writing...or, for that matter, were even born. This story goes back somewhere between 1200 and 1400 years.

I'm speaking of *Beowulf,* the earliest and greatest of the surviving Germanic epics that helped to form our literary heritage. It is the exciting story (as long as you can read it in a good translation) of a small group of people forced to confront terror and horror. The building is the golden mead-hall, Heorot (upon which J.R.R. Tolkien modeled Edoras in *The Lord of the Rings*). The cluster of people are the warriors—the *comitatus*—of the Germanic king Hrothgar. And the monster is Grendel. The monster has visited the great mead-hall before, at night, and each time he has left a trail of blood and death. The poem survives in a single manuscript from the tenth century, preserved, probably not because it was obviously a masterpiece of early English writing, but because it was *about a monster*. Hastily written, it was bound with four other texts, including stories of adventures, wonders...and *monsters*.

It is intriguing and instructive, I think, to notice how closely *Beowulf* and, say, *The Mist,* represent departures from a similar narrative point. Both focus on small groups, the core of a culture that defines characters dually as individuals and as parts of their community. Both groups are isolated by the physical darkness of the landscape and the internal darkness of their fears. Individuals in both must work together for communal strength, protection, and survival—but their gathering does not work. In spite of everything, they must emerge and confront head-on the monsters...the darkness, and the fear, and the specter of death.

There are differences, of course. In *Beowulf*, we quickly learn that the poet has found a hero, a single warrior with the courage and prowess to combat monsters. Grendel has devoured thirty of King Hrothgar's retainers:

> Straightway he seized a sleeping warrior
> for the first, and tore him fiercely asunder,
> the bone-frame bit, drank blood in streams,
> swallowed him piecemeal: swiftly thus
> the lifeless corse was clear devoured,
> even feet and hands.... (XI)

The hero Beowulf, symmetrically enough, is endowed with the strength of thirty men. In the fury of single combat with Grendel, he rips the monster's arm from its body and nails the bloody trophy to the wall above the mead-hall door:

> For him [Grendel] the keen-souled kinsman of Hygelac
> held in hand; hateful alive
> was each to other. The outlaw dire
> took mortal hurt; a mighty wound
> showed on his shoulder, and sinews cracked,
> and the bone-frame burst. To Beowulf now
> the glory was given, and Grendel thence
> death-sick his den in the dark moor sought.... (XII)

In *The Mist*, events do not proceed quite as smoothly. There is no single hero, no outlander suddenly arrived to kill the beast and rescue the community. In a technologically oriented world such as ours, individual heroism is generally not encouraged; nor does King insult his readers' intelligence by importing one—not even from the distant, almost mythic shores of Geatland (Sweden). There are individual battles fought against the monsters that inhabit the mist, to be sure, but King's vision allows no simple ending. His characters are stripped of everything until all that remains is the courage of a few to face the darkness directly and to attempt to discover the extent of the mist...and the monsters.

And then the next wave of monsters strikes, in *Beowulf* as well as in *The Mist*. Even Beowulf, the impervious hero, ultimately suffers defeat in battle with the Firedrake. All that he has accomplished—the deaths of Grendel and Grendel's mother; the consolidation of his kingdom; his fifty years of faultless rule, summarized in a single phrase, "he was a good king"—all is called into doubt as his body burns and the forces of darkness gather once again. In *The Mist*, the time frame has been condensed from fifty years to hours and days but the effect is the same. Humanity may raise buildings, construct moral and civil codes, and create a veneer of civility, but in the face of the darkness most of that counts for little. The implications of such stories, ancient and contemporary, are consistent with a pervasive theme in Western literature, captured by both the *Beowulf*-poet and modern horror writers: 'Here there be monsters,' here in the darkness of the human soul, and here in the darkness of the worlds we imagine.

Nor did this concern with explicit horror die out with the passing of the culture that generated the *Beowulf*-poet. Throughout the middle ages, writers—and by implication—audiences appreciated the creation and re-creation of horror. One enormously popular form, the "metrical tragedy," incorporated tales of the "fall of great men" in rhymed verse that reveled not only in horrific details but in a particularly graphic—and thus, presumably, more spiritually elevating—death. According to scholars, such tales did not simply conclude with a death scene but expanded far beyond to a wholesale death, often prefigured by earlier slaughter. The results were frequent reproduction of the medieval image of the *Dance of Death*.

Beyond the more-than-coincidental fact that King borrowed a variation on the phrase for his own quasi-scholarly history of horror as genre, *Danse Macabre*, is the more salient fact that in many ways our world is also concerned with bringing some kind of moral value out of an increasing sense of the "essential horror of life." A society struggling under the weight of such disparate collective burdens as nuclear weaponry (with their threat of devastation even when used for peaceful means), disease, the implicit horrors of technology and its wildfire proliferation, and the constant threat of terrorism, might also search for illustrations of the idea—held in common with the *Beowulf*-poet—that after the short and bitter struggle comes a welcome death.

But enough of the middle ages.

Let's try another story.

Plot Summary:

A frightened man confronts a midnight apparition, a specter that by all logic cannot exist, but does. He speaks to it, he demands that it speak to him, and it reveals tales of darkness and fear and death. It grants him visions of murder, blood, revenge, and—again—death.

Does this describe King's *The Dark Half?* Or a segment of *It?* Koontz's *Phantom?* McCammon's *Stinger?* Perhaps. Certainly the synopsis could apply equally to a number of contemporary horror novels. But again, none of those was the story I had in mind. Instead, I was thinking of *Hamlet.* There, three times in the course of what is now almost universally hailed as the greatest tragedy in English literature (some would broaden that to include Western literature), we find...a ghost. A specter. A haunted shade whispering of murders past and murders yet to come.

By all accounts, the audiences of Shakespeare's day loved the play. They flocked to the Globe Theater to watch it, standing for the full four hours of its performance (unlike modern audiences, they were not subjected to editors and rewriters who know more about dramaturgy than the Bard himself). They might have stood in the rain to see it. They might have paid the equivalent of a week's wages for the privilege.

Why? Did they come to watch a performance of the greatest play by the greatest English playwright?

Hardly.

At the time of Shakespeare's death, a time when the death of a colleague might stimulate a dozen, scores, even hundreds of elegiac poems, not one poet or playwright so much as mentioned William Shakespeare's passing. In fact, until the middle of the eighteenth century—a century and a half after Shakespeare's death—there was remarkably little evidence of the "bardolotry" that has since colored our assessments of his works.

No, the Elizabethan playgoers were largely unimpressed with Shakespeare as an immortal literary figure. Instead, they went to the *Globe* to see a *drama*, and not coincidentally to see blood, and fear, and death...and a ghost. Samuel Johnson, writing over a century after Shakespeare's death about another of Shakespeare's initial theatrical successes, *Titus Andronicus*, urged that the play not be considered part of the Master's canon; it was too barbarous, to full of bloodletting to be palatable to any civilized audience. In fact, Johnson (and others since) argued, it was unlikely that the divine Shakespeare had any hand in its composition.

In spite of now being frequently excoriated as among Shakespeare's worst plays, to the point that many critics still struggle to demonstrate that Shakespeare only contributed part—or perhaps none—of the lines, *Titus Andronicus* was unusually and undeniably popular in its time. Based on tales preserved for over a thousand years in classical myth and specifically in Seneca's Latin revenge tragedies (one of the more popular genres of the Elizabethan period), the story was sensational and horrific even for the Elizabethans, full of graphic representations of blood and death. Many of the more objectionable episodes were eliminated in variants written by Shakespeare's contemporaries, but Shakespeare showed everything...with apparent glee.

Shakespeare's audience—not being 'modern playgoers' and lacking the foreknowledge that they were in the presence of a work by one of the premier dramatists of Western culture—found nothing absurd in the presentation of horrors. The blood-soaked episodes—not coincidentally—find close parallels in King's *The Stand* (1990 edition), with its extended passages of bloodletting in the face of global plague: ritual sacrifice; rape and mutilation; murder; and, as the highlight of the play, the on-stage removal of Titus Andronicus' hand, after which the character puns on multiple meanings of 'giving one's hand' as a symbol of loyalty. One of my undergraduate Shakespeare professors, in fact, lectured at length on that scene, noting that the actor portraying Titus Andronicus would often wear a bladder of pig's blood beneath his arm and, at the climactic moment, spray blood onto the footlings—those playgoers too poor to afford a seat in the galleries—surrounding the stage.

Many critics today argue that the play fails miserably although, in a society in which horror is an increasingly popular genre, the play is also increasingly accepted as having been written by Shakespeare. But Shakespeare's audiences apparently loved it.

Nor did his audience's responses differ substantively from the assessments of most of Shakespeare's contemporaries. Following Shakespeare's death, two acting companions of his, John Heminges and Henry Condell, put together a volume of his plays, the *First Folio*. The act of collecting plays was itself an anomaly during the period, since plays were considered ephemeral, certainly not 'literary' in the sense that poetry might be. As was the custom, the editors invited commendatory verses, of which only *one*—Ben Jonson's—suggested the status Shakespeare today enjoys:

Triumph, my Britain, thou hast one to show
   To whom all scenes of Europe homage owe.
He was not of an age, but for all time.

There is some evidence that Heminges and Condell were taking a calculated risk by publishing Shakespeare's works; unlike Ben Jonson, the first Poet Laureate and darling of the Royal Court, Shakespeare was common. He wrote, not for scholars and critics, but for his *audience*; he was a playhouse poet, writing sensational, unrealistic, often horrific, commercially successful but artistically flawed works, and would thus have been considered to some extent "academically incorrect."

Shakespeare's reputation during his lifetime apparently paralleled that of writers like King, Koontz, McCammon, and others: immensely popular with the masses but largely ignored or slighted by the critics and scholars. And there are good reasons for this. Jonson's avowed aim was to reform the English stage by restoring the virtues, values, and structures of classical drama; Shakespeare ignored such things entirely, concentrating instead on plays that elicited his desired responses from his audience. In Jonson's words (related by William Drummond of Hawthorndon, a Scots poet Jonson visited in 1619, three years after Shakespeare's death), "Shakespeare wanted [i.e., *lacked*] art." Whether by dramatizing ghostly visitations that lead to revenge and bloody death, or more directly by the on-stage removal of body parts, Shakespeare shows himself acquainted with the age-old techniques of fear, terror, and horror—including what King has described in his own works as the "gross out."

Now, let's examine yet a third story:

Plot Summary:

> *For a paltry price, a mysterious stranger offers the things dearest to a man's heart. The man accepts. For a while—a short while—he enjoys the pleasure his desire brings...but then the reckoning falls due, and he discovers that the thing he desired will ultimately cost him something even more precious: his soul.*

Again, the summary strikes a familiar tone, suggests King's *Needful Things*, for example, in which a mysterious stranger sets up shop in the small town of Castle Rock, where a steady stream of customers enter and leave one by one, each with a small parcel clutched under a protective arm, each with an oddly trance-like expression. As the narrative progresses, Mr. Gaunt, the proprietor of Needful Things, extracts from his customers fulfillment of the bargains struck, leading to an intensifying spiral of violence, viciousness, mayhem, and murder. At the end, the town itself explodes in a metaphorical eruption of the private emotions its inhabitants have been tempted to release. More than a little reminiscent of Mark Twain's "The Man Who Corrupted Hadleyburg," *Needful Things* becomes a powerful statement of horror's persistent analysis of the forces of light and dark as evil struggles to possess human souls.

Yet—perhaps no surprise at this point—King's *Needful Things* was not the title I had in mind when I wrote the plot summary.

Instead, I was considering another Elizabethan drama, nearly contemporaneous with Shakespeare's *Titus Andronicus*, and written by the leading pre-Shakespearean dramatist: Christopher Marlowe's *Dr. Faustus.*

To look for a moment at Shakespeare and Renaissance revenge tragedy demonstrates that King's *Needful Things* develops a close parallel. Each character is entrapped by the seduction he or she defines— Gaunt does little except provide them with an external, physical device by which they can explore and develop their own internal weaknesses, corruption, guilt, and obsessions. This pairing of action and morality echoes a similar pairing—coupled with frequent and violent death—that extends throughout the revenge play tradition: one commits an inhuman act, one must suffer an inhuman punishment.

This sense of judgment recurs throughout horror as genre. Human societies become corrupt, greedy, unfeeling, willing to pollute, destroy— and they are visited by appropriate monsters. On one of the narrowest levels, we see this in any number of horror novels and films when young people—too young to understand and consciously accept adult responsibility for their actions—engage in illicit sex...and die horribly as a result. Often during the act itself. A general social consensus (admittedly one more honored in the breach than in the keeping) has been ignored; justice is served...immediately.

Like *Faustus,* horror literature frequently anatomizes greed, avarice, vanity, lust for power, repaying a heedless humanity in a coin of our own choosing. McCammon's *Swan Song* makes this sense concrete as character after character emerges from a masklike growth that has covered their faces, to discover that they have altered physically. What they are truly like *inside* has become their *external* identity...and monsters are born.

Like *Faustus*, horror literature focuses on central fears of the society it anatomizes. *Faustus'* audience was concerned with matters of heaven and hell. Catholicism. Patriotism. Witchcraft. Damnation. And they took such concerns quite seriously.

In a rabid attack on the theater published in 1633, *Histriomastix*, William Prynne recounted a performance of *Dr. Faustus* at an inn-yard theater, in which a devil appeared onstage, much to the amazement and terror of actors and spectators. Not only did the onlookers think they saw an extra devil capering on the stage but they also fled the inn-yard *en masse* and refused to re-enter it for a year and a day.

We see different concerns confronting our society: the breakdown of home and family; the breakdown of educational institutions (King for one has always portrayed schools as places more dedicated to destruction than elevation); lack of ethics in politics, in government, in authorities; lack of central spiritual guidelines and a concomitant quest for spiritual truth—again, King provides a superb example of the latter in *Desperation*.

Marlowe's England—Shakespeare's England, the *Beowulf*-poet's Britain—were cultures experiencing turmoil similar to ours. They too experienced physical and spiritual threats, internal and external. They too confronted a future in which traditional standards and beliefs would be increasingly questioned, if not destroyed. They too stood on the threshold of a world in which everything they accepted would be challenged, in which their very conceptions of the universe itself would undergo radical alterations.

And they, like us, found a means of symbolizing, confronting, and adapting to that world: the images, emotions, and vicarious purgation of literary fear, terror, and horror.

About the Author

MICHAEL R. COLLINGS is a Professor Emeritus at Seaver College, Pepperdine University, where he directed the Creative Writing Program for over two decades; the Senior Publications Editor for JournalStone Publications; and a reviewer/columnist for *JournalStone.com*, *Hellnotes*, and *Dark Discoveries*.

He has published over 100 volumes of poetry, novels, short fiction, and scholarly studies of such contemporary writers as Stephen King, Orson Scott Card, Dean R. Koontz, and Piers Anthony. Recent works include *The Art and Craft of Poetry* (1996, 2009); *Toward Other Worlds: Perspectives on John Milton, C. S. Lewis, Stephen King, Orson Scott Card, and Others* (2010); *In Endless Morn of Light: Moral Agency in Milton's Universe* (2010); *In the Void: Poems of Science Fiction, Myth and Fantasy, and Horror* (2009); *Matrix: Growing Up West—Autobiographical Poems* (2010); *BlueRose and Other Chapbooks* (2012); *A Verse to Horrors—An Abecedary of Monsters and the Monstrous*; *HAI-(And Assorted Other)-KU* (2012); *Deep Music: A Collection of L.D.S. Musical Readings* (2012); and a Book of Mormon verse-epic, *The Nephiad* (1996, 2010).

His fiction, also published through Wildside, includes: *The House Beyond the Hill: A Novel of Fear* (2007); *Wordsmith, Volume One: The Thousand Eyes of Flame* (2009) and *Wordsmith, Volume Two: The Veil of Heaven* (2009); *Singer of Lies: A Science-Fantasy Novel* (2009); *Wer Means Man, and Other Tales of Wonder and Terror* (2010); *Three Tales of Omne: A Companion to* Wordsmith (2010); *Devil's Plague: A Mystery Novel* (2011); *Serpent's Tooth* (2011); *Static!: A Novel of Horror* (2011); *Shadow Valley*

(2011); and *The Slab* (2010), the story of a haunted tract house in Southern California...that consumes people.

Two of his books—the first edition of *Writing Darkness* and a collection of horror limericks, *A Verse to Horrors—An Abecedary of Monsters and the Monstrous*—were Finalists for the 2012 Horror Writers Association's Bram Stoker Awards® for Non-fiction and Poetry, respectively.

With his wife Judith, he has also published a unique cookbook, *Whole Wheat for Food Storage: Recipes for Unground Wheat,* a revision and expansions of their first joint project, *Whole Wheat Harvest* (1980).

He is now retired and lives in his native state of Idaho.